D1401730

CREATING
A MEMORY OF
CAUSAL RELATIONSHIPS

An Integration of Empirical and Explanation-Based Learning Methods

MICHAEL J. PAZZANI

University of California, Irvine

LEA LAWRENCE ERLBAUM ASSOCIATES, PUBLISHERS
1990 Hillsdale, New Jersey   Hove and London

Lawrence Erlbaum Associates, Inc., Publishers
365 Broadway
Hillsdale, New Jersey 07642

Library of Congress Cataloging-in-Publication Data

Pazzani, Michael John, 1958–
    Creating a memory of causal relationships : an integration of
empirical and explanation-based learning methods / Michael J.
Pazzani.
        p.   cm.
    Includes bibliographical references.
    ISBN 0-8058-0629-6.   -- ISBN 0-8058-0789-6 (pbk.)
    1. Artificial Intelligence. 2. Learning. 3. Memory. 4. OCCAM
(Computer program language) I. Title.
Q335.P378 1990
153. 1--dc20   90-34771
                                                   CIP

Printed in the United States of America
10 9 8 7 6 5 4 3 2 1

Table of Contents

ACKNOWLEDGEMENTS

First, I would like to thank Professor Michael Dyer, my thesis advisor for making my four years in the Artificial Intelligence Laboratory at UCLA intellectually rewarding. His thorough reading and critique of this dissertation and his insightful comments on memory and learning were greatly appreciated. In addition, Professor Dyer is largely responsible for creating an environment at UCLA conducive to creative research.

I also want to thank the other members of my committee. Professor Margot Flowers introduced me to the field of machine learning. It was in her class that I began research on integrated learning methods. Professor Jacques Vidal broadened my perspective on approaches to artificial intelligence.

One of the reasons that I enjoyed my work at UCLA is the excellent psychology department. I am indebted to the psychology members of my committee. Professor Mort Friedman deserves credit for providing the facilities for the psychology experiments that I ran and for many interesting discussions on psychology. I am thankful to Professor Keith Holyoak for comments on my research from the perspective of a psychologist who creates computational models. Professor Bernard Weiner first introduced me to a psychological perspective on causal analysis.

I am also grateful to the other members in the UCLA AI Lab. I will always appreciate their commentary on my research. In particular, I'd like to thank Sergio Alvarado, Stephanie August, Charlie Dolan, Ric Feifer, Mike Gasser, Seth Goldman, Jack Hodges, Dr. Erik Mueller, Valeriy Nenov, Alex Quilici, Walter Read, John Reeves, Ron Sumida, Scott Turner, and Dr. Uri Zernik. Seth deserves special credit for maintaining the machines in the AI Lab and together with John and Scott providing many interesting discussions on AI and professional wrestling.

My view of Artificial Intelligence was influenced by many others. Dr. Richard Cullingford first interested me in Artificial Intelligence at the University of Connecticut. Carl Engelman and Dr. Nort Fowler encouraged and supported my work on natural language processing at the Mitre Corporation. Dr. Michael Lebowitz provided some advice on learning and memory organization. Dr. Stephen Crocker started AI research at the Aerospace Corporation, which provided the equipment for much of my research. Carl Kesselman, Art Simoneau, and Rod McGuire made my time at Aerospace interesting. Much of this research was supported by a UCLA-RAND artificial intelligence fellowship.

I'd like to thank my new colleagues at the University of California, Irvine for their comments on this work. I particularly enjoyed trying to explain the work to Pat Langley, Dennis Kibler and Paul O'Rorke. I am also grateful to Glenn Silverstein, Wendy Sarrett, and Elenita Silverstein for commenting on a draft of this text. Extensions to OCCAM performed at UCI were supported in part by National Science Foundation grant IRI-8908260.

I also want to thank my parents and my Aunt Annette for supporting and encouraging my education.

I also wish to thank my children, Lynn and Karen, for a constant source of inspiration and amazement. Finally, I am eternally grateful to my wife, Christine, for never objecting when I decided to continue my education, for putting up with me during my productive, but antisocial periods, and for making life interesting while pursuing my research.

Chapter 1
Introduction

1.1. Predicting the Outcome of Events

Understanding what caused an event to occur enables the understander to predict, to plan for, to produce, to prevent, and to explain the occurrence of the event. Therefore, learning causal relationships is a crucial task in understanding and mastering the environment. An additional benefit of learning causal relationships is that future learning can be constrained by ignoring those possibilities that are inconsistent with existing causal knowledge.

In this book, I present an integrated theory of learning to predict and explain the outcome of events. This theory is implemented in a computer program called OCCAM. The theory integrates aspects of previous research in learning and memory (DeJong & Mooney, 1986; Kolodner, 1984; Lebowitz, 1980; Mitchell et al., 1986a; Schank, 1982) to model human learning in several different domains under a variety of circumstances. These domains include simple physical causes (e.g., breaking glass and inflating balloons), children's social interactions (e.g., coercion and agency), and complex planning situations (e.g., kidnapping and economic sanction incidents).

Many tasks require an understander to reason about causality. In the following sections, I consider the tasks of prediction, explanation, planning, and inference. For each task, I give examples of physical causality and social causality. In physical causality, a result occurs as a consequence of transmission of some sort of force. In contrast, transmission of forces does not play a major role in determining human behavior. Instead, human behavior is considered to be a consequence of intentions to achieve some goal. In spite of the differences between these domains, the same procedure is able to learn, store, and retrieve knowledge in each of the domains.

1.1.1. Prediction

Prediction is the task of determining the consequences of a future or a hypothetical event. For example, a political analyst at the Rand Corporation filled out a questionnaire to indicate the likely outcome of several hypothetical economic sanction incidents. Examples of some responses are given below:

Question: What would happen if the US refused to sell computers to South Korea unless South Korea stopped exporting automobiles to Canada?

Answer: S. Korea will probably buy computer equipment from some other country.

Question: What would happen if the US offered to sell coal to West Germany if West Germany agreed not to buy coal from South Africa?

Answer: W. Germany would agree since it wouldn't cost them a thing-- unless this move meant retaliation by S. Africa on W. Germany on some essential exports that W. Germany was highly dependent on.

Question: What would happen if the US threatened to cut off food aid to Ethiopia unless Ethiopia modernized its agricultural production?

Answer: Ethiopia would not agree. It would just ask for more help from the Eastern Bloc.

These economic sanction incidents are all examples of social causality. Countries, like people, have certain goals (e.g., survival and economic growth) and their actions are planned to pursue these goals. The ability to make predictions is dependent on an understanding of these goals.

In addition to social causality, I have looked at examples of utilizing knowledge of physical causality in prediction. For example, OCCAM learns to predict that a small child will be able to successfully inflate a balloon only after the balloon has been stretched.

1.1.2. Explanation

A prediction answers questions about *what* will happen under certain circumstances. Explanation, on the other hand, requires answering questions about *why* a cause results in an effect. The ability to explain is essential if a computer is to be trusted to make a prediction. If a computer (or a human) cannot articulate a convincing line of reasoning to justify a prediction, who would be willing to believe the prediction?

Typically, an explanation consists of a set of intermediate states that connect a cause and an effect. In physical causality, these intermediate states are states of the world. In social causality, the intermediate states are often mental states.

In addition to asking the political analyst at the Rand Corporation to make a prediction about hypothetical sanction incidents, I also requested an explanation to justify the prediction. An example explanation is given below:

Question: What would happen if the US refused to sell computers to South Korea unless South Korea stopped exporting automobiles to Canada?

Answer: S. Korea will probably buy computer equipment from some other country.

Question: Why?

Answer: If the US restricts S. Korea's supply of computers, they would be willing to pay a higher price for the computers and some other country would move in.

This explanation references several intermediate states: South Korea's goal of obtaining computers, South Korea's willingness to pay a higher price to obtain the computers, and some other country's goal of making a profit by selling computers to South Korea.

In the realm of physical causality, when OCCAM learns to predict that a small child will be able to successfully inflate a balloon after the balloon has been stretched, it also constructs a series of intermediate states: pulling on a balloon results in a state (i.e., the balloon is stretched out) that enables the child to make the balloon bigger by blowing air into the balloon.

1.1.3. Planning

One aspect of planning is to predict, prevent or prepare for anticipated events. If an outcome is not desirable, it may be possible to come up with a plan to change the outcome. For example, the United States stockpiles oil and strategic materials to mitigate the effects of an interruption in the supply of these materials. Similarly, South Africa has been stockpiling commodities that it imports to avoid economic hardship in the event that stricter economic sanctions are implemented and enforced.

Planning also requires the planner to reason about physical causality. Parents often give small children plastic cups to drink out of. Knowledge of physical causality (glass cups break when they are dropped; plastic cups are unbreakable; small children are likely to drop things) helps to prevent the undesirable consequences of giving a small child a glass cup. OCCAM is able to acquire knowledge of causality to support planning.

1.1.4. Inference

An important task in natural language understanding is inferring information that is not explicitly stated in a text. For example, consider the following story:

Kidnapping-1

John Doe, who was abducted on his way to school Monday morning, was released today after his father left $50,000 in a trash can in a men's room at the bus station.

This short story leaves many things unstated. For example, it does not state why the father put money in a trash can nor why John Doe was abducted or released. However, a typical adult reading this story has no difficulty answering these questions. General knowledge about kidnapping, including the motives of a kidnapper and the goals of a parent, must be used to infer the missing information.

Similarly, in the following story, knowledge of physical causality is necessary to infer a causal connection between the events:

Snowstorm-1

After two days of snow and rain, the roof of the old building collapsed, injuring two occupants sleeping in an upstairs bedroom.

In this story, the causal connection between the snow and the roof collapse is not explicitly stated. A temporal connection is given from which a typical adult reading this story can infer a causal connection. Similarly, there is no explicit mention of how the two occupants were injured, but a typical person reading this story can infer that part of the roof that collapsed must have fallen on the occupants.

1.1.5. Knowledge of causality facilitates future learning

Learning is one important task that can be aided by knowledge of causality. The learning of new causal knowledge can be facilitated by focusing on relationships which are consistent with existing knowledge. To illustrate, consider how one might learn that on cold winter days, roads that have been salted are less slippery than roads that have not been salted.

One way to acquire this knowledge is purely empirical. The slipperiness of roads on cold days would be noted under different conditions and eventually a regularity could be detected.

An alternative means of acquiring this knowledge is analytical. The fact that salted roads are less slippery is a direct consequence of two facts:

- Ice is slippery.

- Salt melts ice.

A learner who knows these two facts has a great advantage when it comes to learning that salted roads are less slippery. It is possible to deduce the effect of spreading salt on an icy road. Here, learning that salted roads are less slippery consists of simply storing the results of this deduction.

As OCCAM learns, it acquires knowledge that facilitates future learning.

For example, in physical causality OCCAM acquires the following knowledge:

- OCCAM is presented with examples of people attempting to open a refrigerator. Some people pull on the door and it opens; others pull on the door and it doesn't open. After many examples, it is able to determine that the age of the person pulling on the door (as opposed to the hair color or eye color, etc.) is a good predictor for determining whether the door will open. In addition to learning a specific fact (adults are strong enough to open a refrigerator), it also learns some general knowledge (adults are strong) that may be transferred to other problems.

- Once OCCAM has learned that adults are strong, it is presented with examples of people attempting to inflate balloons. Some people blow into the balloon and it is inflated; others blow into the balloon and it does not inflate. However, because it has already learned about strength (in the context of opening refrigerators), it requires fewer examples to determine that a balloon will be inflated when an adult blows into the balloon, but not when an infant blows into it. Because it has already learned about strength, it does not have to consider other hypotheses (e.g., persons with green eyes can inflate balloons, but people will blue eyes cannot) even though these hypotheses are consistent with the initial data.

In the area of social causality, OCCAM learns a number of facts that facilitate later learning:

- OCCAM is shown several examples of some persons assisting a child who gets hurt playing in a playground. From these examples, it induces that parents have a goal of preserving the health of their children.

- OCCAM is shown examples of people attempting to coerce another person. One is an example of a playground argument: "If you don't let me pitch, I'm going to take my ball and go home." OCCAM acquires general knowledge of coercion from examples such as this.

- Next, OCCAM is presented with an example of kidnapping. From this example, it specializes the coercion knowledge into kidnapping knowledge. In doing so, it combines some previously unrelated facts about coercion and parents' goals of preserving the health of their children to learn about why parents want to pay the ransom in kidnapping. The kidnapping knowledge that it acquires indicates that a good hostage in kidnapping is the child of a rich person.

- OCCAM is presented with examples of economic sanction incidents. General knowledge of coercion helps OCCAM learn when economic sanctions will achieve their desired goal. OCCAM is able to answer questions about hypothetical sanction incidents.

1.2. Learning to Predict the Outcome of Events

In the preceding section, I discussed several kinds of reasoning that a person or a computer can perform if they have knowledge of causality. How is that knowledge learned? This is the central question I try to answer in this book. Of course, to learn and use knowledge about causality, there are a number of other questions that must be answered. How is this knowledge represented? How is this knowledge stored in memory? How is this knowledge retrieved from memory? For answers to these questions, I borrow from other researchers in artificial intelligence and cognitive science. In this section, I sketch the general framework in which the theory of learning is embedded.

1.2.1. OCCAM

OCCAM is a computer program (implemented in LISP) that learns to predict and explain the outcome of events. OCCAM learns incrementally. Example events are presented to OCCAM one at a time and OCCAM adds the events to memory. When OCCAM adds an event to memory, any of a number of things may happen:

Storage: The event is stored in memory so that it may be retrieved later.

Generalization: The event may be generalized by removing some irrelevant details from the event. For example, by removing some of the details of a particular example of a person with blond hair who inflated a red balloon, a generalization can be created that describes the fact that when a person blows into a balloon, the balloon gets bigger.

Specialization: The event may initiate the specialization of existing general knowledge. For example, if the memory already contains general knowledge of coercion, adding an example economic sanction incident may start the process in which general coercion knowledge is specialized to economic sanction knowledge. Specialization adds additional information to existing knowledge. Economic sanctions can be viewed as a specialization of coercion where the threat is to refuse to sell a product to a country.

Revision: A new event added to memory may be inconsistent with existing general knowledge in memory. If this occurs, the existing general knowledge may be revised to accommodate the new event, the existing general knowledge may be abandoned altogether, or the new event may be remembered as an exception to general knowledge.

Figure 1-1 contains a block diagram of OCCAM. In a complete working system, the example events that serve as input to OCCAM would be in English. For example, newspaper stories of economic sanction incidents might serve as input. The first step in adding an event to memory is converting the example text from English to a representation of the meaning of the example. The information stored in human memory after reading a story is not the English language text of the story. Rather the meaning or the "gist" of a story is retained (Bartlett, 1932; Schank & Abelson, 1977). The process of converting text to a

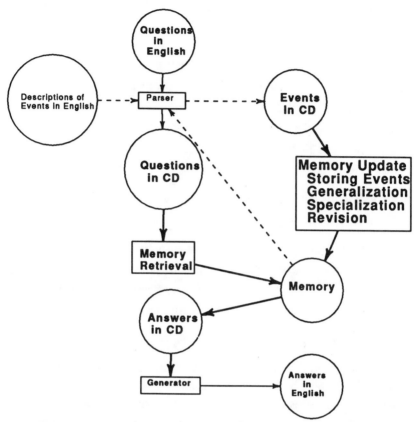

Figure 1-1:   Block diagram of OCCAM. The modules receiving
thorough treatment in this book are in bold.

meaning representation of the text is called conceptual analysis. In this book, I
will informally refer to it as parsing. OCCAM does not contain a parser to
process its input examples. Instead, Conceptual Dependency (CD) (Schank &
Abelson, 1977) is used to input the meaning of examples in OCCAM[1].

In order to demonstrate convincingly that OCCAM has indeed learned
something, it performs a question answering task. OCCAM answers questions

---

[1]The natural language descriptions of the events that OCCAM learns from are beyond the
capabilities of most natural language processing systems. The central issue discussed in this book is
learning. No effort was made to advance the state of the art in natural language understanding.

about the consequences of hypothetical actions.   This task involves both
prediction and explanation.   Figure 1-1 illustrates the following subprocesses of
question answering:

- Parsing questions into Conceptual Dependency: OCCAM converts
  questions about hypothetical economic sanction incidents from
  English into Conceptual Dependency. The restricted nature of the
  topic of the questions simplifies this task considerably. No claims
  are made about the generality or cognitive validity of the parsing
  process in OCCAM.

- Memory Retrieval: The memory constructed by OCCAM is searched
  to find the answers to queries.

- Generation: The answers retrieved from memory are represented in
  Conceptual Dependency. Generation is the process of converting
  the Conceptual Dependency representation of an answer to natural
  language. No claims of generality or fluency cf the generation
  process are made.

Those modules in Figure 1-1 which are in large bold letters received the
most thorough treatment in the theory of learning implemented in OCCAM. In
particular, the major focus of the research has been the acquisition of general
knowledge from examples. Other areas, such as memory retrieval, parsing and
question answering were developed to demonstrate that the general knowledge
that OCCAM learns can be put to use.

There is another way that OCCAM demonstrates its learning: OCCAM uses
the knowledge it has acquired to facilitate future learning. In situations where
OCCAM has already learned some relevant background knowledge, it is easier for
it to acquire new knowledge. The existing knowledge serves to constrain the
search for a new hypothesis. Therefore, when OCCAM has prior knowledge, it
requires fewer examples to learn.

1.2.2. Predicting the future

In this book, the central question I address is how can a person or computer learn to predict the consequences of a particular action? I discuss this question and related questions from a computational point of view in Chapter 2. However, it is still possible to explore this question in general terms. How can a person tell what aspects of a particular event will be repeated in future events? Pretend you've never heard about kidnapping before.   Now consider the following kidnapping story:

Kidnapping-2

John was abducted.   His father, a wealthy, fair skinned man, received a note that stated John would be killed unless he paid a $100,000 ransom.

What features from this particular story should one expect to see in future stories? Is it important that the hostage be named John? Is it important that a parent of the hostage is wealthy? Is it important that a parent of the hostage has fair skin?

One way to determine what features of previous experiences will be present in future examples is to correlate over a number of previous experiences. For example, consider another kidnapping story.

Kidnapping-3

Mary was abducted.   Her mother, a wealthy, fair skinned woman, received a note that stated Mary would be killed unless she paid a $100,000 ransom.

From Kidnapping-2 and Kidnapping-3 it is clear that the hostage does not have to be named John.   However, there are still a number of similarities between the two events. In both events, a parent of the hostage is wealthy and has fair skin.   Would a person given these two examples want to predict in future kidnappings that a parent of the hostage is wealthy and has fair skin?

Given any particular event, there will be certain aspects of the event which are similar to other events.   Some of the similarities will be coincidences.

Others will be *relevant* since they are consequences of some underlying physical or social cause. The distinction between relevant and coincidental similarities is important in learning the sort of knowledge required to make inferences. For example, if the only examples of kidnapping encountered are Kidnapping-2 and Kidnapping-3 and an intelligent person hears about another kidnapping, he might want to infer that the parent of the hostage is wealthy. On the other hand, he would not want to infer that the parent has fair skin. To avoid making erroneous inferences, a person must be able to tell which similarities are coincidental and which are relevant.

Of course, with more examples, the chances of a coincidental similarity are smaller. However, a person may not have enough data before he has to make a prediction. For example, there have been a number of economic sanction incidents in this century where the target country did not meet the demand but instead was able to find a supplier who would be willing to sell the product for a higher price. In all of these economic sanction incidents, there have been at least two similarities: the country which made the demand had a native language of English and the target country had a strong economy. Should sanctions against poor countries be expected to succeed? Should sanctions by countries which don't speak English be expected to succeed?

One way to avoid the problem of coincidentally similar features is to have an *a priori* set of features which are relevant. For example, it might be that wealth is always important and having fair skin never is. However, in general, the relevance of features is situation-dependent. For example, if OCCAM were learning about skin cancer, then fair skin would be a relevant feature.

In later chapters, I argue that the solution to the problem of determining the relevance of features involves using existing knowledge which explains why a feature was present in a particular set of examples. There is, of course, a good reason to believe that a kidnapper would select the child of a rich person as a hostage. On the other hand, there is no good reason to select the child of a fair skinned person as a hostage. The general rule is that the relevant features play a part in an explanation of why the event occurred.

1.3. Methodology

What am I trying to accomplish in this book? To develop a theory of human learning? To make computers learn? Both of these questions are worth studying in detail separately. However, in this book I address both questions together. In particular, I address the following questions about human learning from a computational point of view:

- Under what conditions do people infer a causal relationship?

- How does learning in small children differ from learning in adults?

- What sorts of information do people make use of when learning causal relationships?

- How can knowledge learned in one situation be applied to other situations?

There are several good reasons for developing a computer simulation of a cognitive process. First, a computer forces one to be precise. There is no such thing as a vague instruction for a computer. Quite often, when attempting to implement a computer model of a cognitive process, one finds that the process is more ambiguous than one had originally believed. It is often said that to truly understand something, you must teach it to someone. This is even more true when one attempts to instruct a computer, since it can't use common sense to interpret the instructions. In fact, often the task is to automate common sense. Second, in the process of implementing a computer model, one is often faced with several alternative ways of implementing a subtask. Sometimes a more thorough search of the psychology literature can suggest the correct alternative. If there is no answer in the literature, an experiment can be run to decide between the alternatives. Hence, the development of a computer model serves as a source of questions. Sometimes, following good scientific practice, the simplest alternative or the most parsimonous alternative can be selected and a hypothesis about human performance is generated. Finally, a computer model serves as a sufficiency proof. If there are any unforeseen consequences or inconsistencies in one's theory, these are rapidly detected in a computer simulation. The speed of a modern computer enables a researcher to test a theory on a greater number of examples as well as more complex examples than hand simulation of a theory. If the program behaves as expected, the program demonstrates that the theory upon which the program is based is sufficient to explain the cognitive process.

When attempting to build an intelligent machine, there are a number of good reasons for caring about human intelligence. First, for many tasks that require intelligence, people are the only existing "machines" with acceptable performance. Copying human methods may be the easiest or even the only way to make a computer perform these tasks. In addition, understanding how people approach certain problems, what information they use, what biases they have, often gives insight into efficient ways for computers to solve problems. For example, in Section 7.7, I criticize some prior theories of learning on two grounds. First, they do not explain human performance on some learning tasks. Second, they place unreasonable demands on the amount of time and space that a computer would need to solve some problems that people solve easily.

Research on OCCAM was originally begun to solve a particular problem in artificial intelligence. As progress is made on areas such as prediction, explanation, inference and planning, it is becoming apparent that these tasks require large amounts of knowledge. One way to get this knowledge in the computer is to have the computer learn this knowledge. However, existing theories of learning had a number of shortcomings. In particular, they did not recognize that the process of acquiring new knowledge can be facilitated by existing knowledge. The design of OCCAM was influenced by experiments in cognitive, social and developmental psychology that reveal what sort of information people make use of when learning to predict the outcome of events. During the development of OCCAM, I ran two experiments in collaboration with professor Mort Friedman of the Psychology Department at UCLA that also addressed this issue. In addition, wherever possible, the theory of learning proposed in this book is consistent with existing theories in cognitive psychology and artificial intelligence.

1.4. A Preview of OCCAM's Performance

In this book, I demonstrate how a learner can start with very little knowledge and become proficient in a particular area of expertise. As children, we start out with little knowledge of the world and, through experience, we acquire many facts about the physical and social aspects of our world. At first, the only possible learning mechanisms are empirical techniques which detect regularities between a number of examples. Later, the more knowledge-intensive learning techniques are necessary. As we acquire more and more facts about the world, we must organize this knowledge so that it is easy to recognize the situations in which each fact can be usefully applied. It is important to organize memory so that common interactions among existing knowledge can be found efficiently. Memory organization is important because there are many inferences that are warranted in a given situation, but few inferences will be useful in explaining the situation. Knowledge-intensive learning techniques create memory structures that summarize the interactions among existing knowledge and indicate the class of situations in which these interactions occur. An expert in a field such as economic sanctions is not proficient just because he knows a large number of disjoint facts about politics and economics. Rather, the expert has solved a number of problems using this knowledge and in the process has organized this knowledge so that it is easy to recognize the solutions of related cases.

OCCAM progresses from a system with very little world knowledge to a system with detailed knowledge about kidnapping and economic sanctions. At first, learning is slow (i.e., it requires many examples) because OCCAM must resort to data-intensive methods to acquire its initial knowledge. When OCCAM has acquired the relevant background knowledge for a domain, learning is easier (i.e., it requires fewer examples) as it organizes its memory by summarizing the interactions among this knowledge.

1.4.1. Learning about coercion

Economic sanctions and kidnapping are both specializations of coercion. OCCAM acquires a coercion schema that provides a general framework for understanding the goals and plans of the agents involved in coercion. This schema is acquired by empirical means, by noticing similarities between several plans for achieving a goal. The examples that OCCAM "observes" to learn about coercion include the following:

Playground-1

Mat and Sam are playing football. Sam tells Mat that if he doesn't allow Sam to kick the ball, Sam will take his ball and go home. Mat decides that he does not want to play with Sam, and that he will go buy a frisbee. Mat goes to the store, but finds that he does not have enough money to buy a frisbee.

Broccoli-1

Chris wants Karen to eat her broccoli. Chris tells Karen that if Karen eats her broccoli, then Chris will let Karen have some soda to drink. Otherwise, Chris will give Karen water. Karen decides to eat her broccoli and Chris gives Karen some soda.

Playground-2

Brian tells Ben that unless Ben gets off the swing and gives Brian a turn, Brian will hit Ben with a stick. Ben doesn't get off, so Brian hits him.

To learn about coercion, OCCAM must perform two tasks. First, it must create a cluster by grouping together similar incidents. In the coercion example, the cluster groups together those plans to achieve a goal which consist of an actor threatening another person. It is not important to OCCAM that these examples occur one after another in its input. For example, even if Play-Doh-1 and Refrigerator-1 are interspersed among the above examples, OCCAM will still create the same cluster.

Play-Doh-1

Lynn wants some Play Doh. She asks her father, Mike, to give her some, and he does.

Refrigerator-1

Karen wants to open the refrigerator. She pulls on the door, but it doesn't open.

Since these two events differ substantially from Playground-1, Broccoli-1, and Playground-2, OCCAM will not include them in the same cluster. Once OCCAM has decided to form a cluster, it creates a general description of the class of situations of the events in the cluster. The general description serves as a new schema that organizes future similar incidents. In the coercion example, this general description describes those plans to achieve a goal that consist of an actor telling a person that the actor will cause a goal failure for the person, unless the person achieves a goal for the actor. Chapter 3 describes the learning mechanism that creates schemata such as the coercion schema. Section 7.1 describes the acquisition of the coercion schema in more detail.

1.4.2. Learning background knowledge to understand kidnapping

By the same method that it creates a coercion schema, OCCAM also acquires a **delta-agency** schema, a plan to achieve a goal by asking another person for assistance (Schank & Abelson, 1977). Once **delta-agency** is learned, OCCAM must also understand the conditions under which the plan is likely to succeed. OCCAM has general strategies for learning and intelligently indexing in memory exceptions to general plans. For example, what should be done when Apple-1 is encountered?

Apple-1

Karen wants an apple.   She asks her mother Chris for one and Chris tells her that she doesn't have any apples.

In this case, OCCAM is able to come up with a hypothesis for why **delta-agency** fails. OCCAM constructs a possible explanation: in order for Chris to give an apple to Karen, she must possess an apple. OCCAM learns a general principle from this situation (see Section 4.7): in order to give someone an object, one must first possess the object. This general rule plays a role in understanding a kidnapping incident. In particular, it is important to demand a ransom from a wealthy person because a wealthy person will have the money the kidnapper wants.

OCCAM also learns a rule that it finds useful in explaining why a person would want to pay the ransom in kidnapping. From examples, such as the following, it learns a rule that indicates that members of the same family have a goal of protecting one another[2]:

Playground-3

Lynn is playing on the swing and she falls off and scuffs her knee. Her mother, Chris, gets a band-aid and puts it on her knee. Her neighbor, Tiffany, gets on the swing and rides it.

---

[2]OCCAM does not require that a relative help in every situation and a stranger not help in every situation to build such a rule (see Section 3.4).

Playground-4

*Lynn is playing on the monkey bars and she falls off and scuffs her
elbow. Tiffany's mother, Loreli, who is eating an ice cream near
the monkey bars does not help.*

Playground-5

*Karen falls off her bike and bruises her lip. Her sister, Lynn, gets
an ice cube to put on Karen's lip.*

1.4.3. Kidnapping

Once OCCAM has acquired a general framework for coercion, and learned
some rules that indicate how someone is able to pay a ransom and why someone
would want to, it is in a position to use analytic techniques to learn about
kidnapping. It is presented with the following example:

Kidnapping-4

*John, a 10-year-old child, was abducted on his way to church on
Sunday morning by a heroin addict. His father, Richard, a wealthy,
fair skinned man, received a phone call that evening.   The
kidnapper threatened that John would be killed unless Richard paid
a $100,000 ransom.   Monday at noon, Richard left the money in a
locker at the train station. Four hours later, his son was released in
a wooded area two miles from the train station.*

When it encounters Kidnapping-4, OCCAM infers that the kidnapper's goal
is to obtain money. This inference makes use of its knowledge of coercion (i.e.,
the goal is achieved by the demand). OCCAM next tries to explain why the
kidnapper's plan was successful. It determines that Richard was able to afford
the ransom because he was wealthy (by making use of the rule learned from
Apple-1). It determines that Richard wanted to pay the ransom because Richard
had a goal of preserving John's health (by making use of the rule learned from
Playground-3, Playground-4 and Playground-5). Because OCCAM can explain
how the plan succeeded, it can construct a general description of the class of
plans that will succeed for the same reason. This general description is a
kidnapping schema. The kidnapping schema indicates that a good hostage is the
relative of a wealthy person. Since the description of the hostage in OCCAM is
derived analytically rather than empirically, OCCAM only requires one example

to learn the kidnapping schema. Chapter 5 discusses this type of learning in more detail.

1.4.4. Some complications in learning kidnapping

In the above scenario, when OCCAM learns about kidnapping, all the examples are presented in just the right order. OCCAM learns some simple rules, and is provided with enough examples so that it learns the correct version of each rule. Then OCCAM is presented with a complex kidnapping event that can be understood in terms of its simple rules. If OCCAM does not have enough examples, its empirical component cannot decide among two (or more) equally likely hypotheses. It makes a random choice by favoring one hypothesis over another. Problems can arise when OCCAM "guesses" incorrectly. For example, after encountering just Playground-3 (repeated below) OCCAM learns an erroneous rule:

Playground-3

Lynn is playing on the swing and she falls off and scuffs her knee. Her mother, Chris, gets a band-aid and puts it on her knee. Her neighbor, Tiffany, gets on the swing and rides it.

The incorrect rule indicates that tall persons have a goal of protecting others. This rule is formed because there are several differences between Tiffany and Chris and OCCAM randomly selects the height as the significant difference. If OCCAM is now presented with a kidnapping example, it learns that in kidnapping, the ransom note should go to a tall, rich person. When OCCAM is presented with an example of a kidnapping that doesn't conform to this incorrect pattern, it must revise its kidnapping schema. For example, the following story would generate an expectation violation because the ransom is demanded of a short person:

Kidnapping-5

While filming a television show for the new season, Webster was interrupted with an important phone call. His mother was being held hostage and the kidnapper demanded $50,000. Webster had his chauffeur deliver the money immediately.

This expectation violation causes revision of OCCAM's existing kidnapping schema. OCCAM uses intelligent revision strategies that make it robust. The mechanism that OCCAM uses to revise schemata is described in Section 7.5.

1.4.5. Further specializations of kidnapping

OCCAM is able to further specialize its kidnapping schema. For example, OCCAM forms a specialization of kidnapping when it is presented with the following episode (Alix, 1978):

Kidnapping-6

In May 1933, Mary McElroy, twenty-five-year-old daughter of the city manager of Kansas City, Missouri was abducted.   The abductors demanded $60,000 for her safe return. They accepted a $30,000 ransom and released the hostage unharmed from a farm in Kansas where she had been held for twenty-nine hours.   The kidnappers were arrested by the FBI. The testimony of the victim was largely responsible for their conviction.   The kidnappers received a sentence of life in jail.

In this episode, the kidnappers' goal of preserving their freedom was thwarted when they received the punishment of life in jail.   To create a specialized kidnapping schema, OCCAM must identify the circumstances that led to this goal failure. OCCAM analytically determines that abducting the hostage results in the hostage seeing the kidnapper and enables the hostage to testify against the kidnapper. OCCAM generalizes this explanation and uncovers an inherent flaw in kidnapping: the hostage sees the kidnapper when he is abducted and can testify against the kidnapper. A new schema is created and indexed in memory under the kidnapping schema.   This new schema represents a specialized subclass of kidnappings and is created and indexed in memory under the more general kidnapping schema.   As more kidnapping examples are encountered, OCCAM forms a memory of kidnapping incidents indexed at varying levels of generality and specialization.

Another kidnapping episode results in a different specialization of kidnapping that avoids the problem of the previous incident (Moorehead, 1980):

Kidnapping-7

On June 2, 1920, Blakely Coughlin, the thirteen-month-old son of a wealthy Pennsylvania family vanished from his bedroom. A ladder was found abandoned near the window to the nursery. Several nights later, a letter arrived that instructed Mr. Coughlin to pay a $12,000 ransom.

When this kidnapping episode is added to memory, OCCAM constructs an explanation which indicates that the kidnapper selected this particular hostage as a plan to avoid the failure of the kidnapper's goal to preserve his freedom. OCCAM determines that this plan does not share the same flaw because infants cannot identify the kidnapper and testify in court. A specialized kidnapping schema is indexed under the kidnapping schema by the age of the hostage since this feature was needed to construct an explanation of why this particular class of hostage was chosen.

1.4.6. Robustness of OCCAM

OCCAM integrates a variety of mechanisms to construct general schema from specific instances, to revise incorrect schemata, to create explanations, and to specialize overly general schemata. As a result, OCCAM is a robust learning system that can use whatever knowledge it has acquired to facilitate future learning.

OCCAM learns most quickly and most accurately when the relevant domain knowledge is complete and correct. OCCAM can also learn quickly and accurately when there is little or no domain knowledge, if there are few irrelevant features in the training examples[3]. However, OCCAM can function as conditions diverge from either of these ideals.

With little domain knowledge and many irrelevant features, OCCAM's learning is slower, because it must eliminate irrelevant features initially through trial and error. OCCAM can take advantage of the knowledge acquired via the slow learning process, so that learning will speed up over time as OCCAM learns to form correct causal explanations for the domain. OCCAM also contains general mechanisms to detect when its domain knowledge is producing

---

[3]Section 4.6 discusses the relationship between the number of features and the number of examples required by OCCAM.

erroneous explanations, and to revise its initial hypotheses to more accurately account for further experiences.

1.4.7. Economic sanctions

In the kidnapping domain, OCCAM demonstrates how it takes advantage of knowledge acquired by empirical means to perform explanation-based learning. In the economic sanctions domain, OCCAM makes use of hand-coded knowledge of politics and economics in addition to the the general coercion knowledge that it learns. However, since OCCAM has received no training examples of purely economic events (e.g., the price of beef decreasing, when the supply of beef is high), OCCAM has not learned any purely economic rules. To demonstrate how OCCAM can most effectively specialize coercion to learn about economic sanctions, I bypassed OCCAM's empirical learning component and gave some strictly economic rules to OCCAM. These rules are stored in OCCAM's memory in the same manner as the rules that OCCAM learns (see Section 5.2.2). This is not very artificial, since most people acquire economic knowledge through formal teaching of economic principles.

Knowledge of economics and politics is not sufficient to make one an expert in the field of economic sanctions. Rather, the knowledge must be organized through experience so that the useful implications can be easily recognized. OCCAM constructs several specializations of coercion to recognize common patterns of economic sanction incidents. Once OCCAM has been presented with a number of cases, it can answer questions about hypothetical sanction incidents.

1.4.8. Learning from economic sanction incidents

OCCAM uses its knowledge of supply and demand to understand why the following sanction incident did not achieve the desired goal:

Economic-Sanction-1

In 1983, Australia refused to sell uranium to France, unless France ceased nuclear testing in the South Pacific. France paid a higher price to buy uranium from South Africa and continued nuclear testing.

From this example, OCCAM acquires a schema that indicates that if a country that exports a commodity tries to coerce a wealthy country that imports the commodity by refusing to sell them the commodity, then a response might be to buy the commodity at a higher price from another country.

OCCAM uses its knowledge of political goals to discover that there could a political (as opposed to an economic) motive when a country assists the target of a sanction incident. Economic-Sanction-3 is one such example:

Economic-Sanction-3

In 1961, the Soviet Union refused to sell grain to Albania if Albania did not rescind economic ties with China. Albania continued the ties with China, and China sold Albania wheat imported from Canada.

From this incident, OCCAM creates a specialized form of coercion which indicates that a sanction incident can fail when the source country has an adversary that can gain political influence by assisting the target.

When OCCAM has sufficient domain knowledge, it creates new schemata from just one example. When a new case fits the pattern of a known schemata, it is simply indexed under that schema. After acquiring new schemata from the two previous sanction incidents, OCCAM is presented with Economic-Sanction-2:

Economic-Sanction-2

In 1980, the US refused to sell grain to the Soviet Union unless the Soviet Union withdrew troops from Afghanistan. The Soviet Union paid a higher price to buy grain from Argentina and did not withdraw from Afghanistan.

Economic-Sanction-2 is indexed under the schema learned when OCCAM explained Economic-Sanction-1 in spite of the fact that it has more surface features in common with Economic-Sanction-3. The reason for this is that Economic-Sanction-2 shares the relevant features which were needed to explain the outcome of Economic-Sanction-1.

OCCAM also learns that, in some situations, sanctions can be effective. For example, the schema learned from Economic-Sanction-3 does not apply to Economic-Sanction-7:

Economic-Sanction-7

In 1983, South Africa threatened to block the import of goods into Lesotho (a small country completely surrounded by South Africa) if Lesotho did not expel members of the African National Congress. Twenty-two members of the African National Congress left within two weeks of the implementation of the blockade.

The reason that the schema acquired from the Soviet threat to Albania does not fit this pattern is South Africa does not have an adversary who would gain politically by helping Lesotho. From this example, OCCAM acquires another economic sanction schema that indicates when a country is of low strategic importance, poor economic health, and the actor does not have a wealthy adversary, then a threat to cut off imports will produce the desired effect.

Section 7.2 contains more details about the economic sanction incidents that OCCAM processes and the schemata it learns. Section 6.2 compares the performance of OCCAM as a knowledge-based system for predicting the effect of economic sanction incidents when it learns empirically to when it learns analytically.

1.4.9. Question answering

Although the central focus of this work is modeling learning and memory, OCCAM contains a simple natural language interface so that it may demonstrate its knowledge of economic sanctions by answering questions about hypothetical economic sanction incidents. It accepts questions in a very limited form of English, finds the meaning representation of the question, traverses memory to find a schema that applies to the situation, and generates an English response. Section 7.3 contains more details on question answering.

OCCAM answers simple hypothetical questions. The answers that OCCAM produces to these questions are similar to those produced by an expert in the field.

Question: What would happen if the US refused to sell computers to South Korea unless South Korea stopped exporting automobiles to Canada?

OCCAM: **The goal of the United States that South Korea not sell automobiles to Canada will fail and South Korea will agree to purchase computers from a country which exports computers.**

Question: What would happen if the US refused to release $100 million of Iranian assets unless Iranian agreed to reimburse the US $25 million for nationalized oil companies?

OCCAM: **The goal of the United States will succeed.**

Question: What would happen if the US threatened to cut off food aid to Ethiopia unless Ethiopia modernized its agricultural production?

OCCAM: **The goal of the United States will fail and Ethiopia will seek aid from an adversary of the United States.**

Question: What would happen if the US refused to sell guidance systems to Israel if Israel did not withdraw from Lebanon?

OCCAM: **The goal of the United States will fail and Israel would build guidance systems.**

Question: What would happen if the US threatened to cut off aid to Greece if Greece did not permit the US to expand military bases in Greece?

OCCAM: **The goal of the United States will fail and Greece will seek aid from an adversary of the United States.**

1.5. The Learning Task and the Performance Task

OCCAM receives as input descriptions of an observation, and creates schemata that can be used to predict and explain the outcomes of future observations. In this section, I elaborate on the representation of the input, the representation of the learned knowledge and the processes that make use of the learned knowledge. The remainder of the book describes the learning processes.

1.5.1. Input representation

The training data for the learning task in OCCAM are represented in Conceptual Dependency. Conceptual Dependency (CD) (Schank & Abelson, 1977) is a system for representing the meaning of events. The idea behind Conceptual Dependency is that meaning is represented in a canonical, language-free manner. Two sentences that have identical meaning, such as "John was kicked by Mary." and "Mary hit John with her foot." will have an identical CD representation. It is important for learning that the similarities between several events can be detected easily. For this reason, CD representations are used in OCCAM. In CD, "John was kicked by Mary." is more similar to "Mary hit John with her foot." than to "John was kissed by Mary." Grammatically, the reverse is true.

Each event is described by a set of attributes (e.g., actor, object, type, etc.). Conceptual Dependency also provides a small set of primitive actions that are needed to understand the examples in this book including the following[4]:

---

[4]CD is not dependent on a particular set of primitive actions. It is rather the methodology behind selecting primitives that is stressed: The meanings of two sentences with the same meaning (i.e., that denote the same event) should have the same representation. The set of CD primitives given here has proven useful in OCCAM as well as a number of other programs.

- ATRANS- the transfer of possession, ownership or control: *buy, give, sell, etc.*

- PTRANS- the transfer of physical location: *walk, run, fly, etc.*

- MTRANS- the transfer of information: *see, tell, hear, remember, etc.*

- PROPEL- the application of a force: *push, throw, kick, etc.*

- INGEST- taking an object into the body: *eat, smoke, drink, etc.*

- EXPEL- pushing an object out of the body: *spit, cry, etc.*

An example should help to illustrate the CD system of meaning representation. The sentence "John gave Mary a book." is represented as follows:

```
ACT type ATRANS
    actor HUMAN name JOHN
                gender MALE
                hair-color BROWN
                age ADULT
    object PHYS-OBJ type BOOK

    from HUMAN name JOHN
                gender MALE
                hair-color BROWN
                age ADULT
    to HUMAN name MARY
                gender FEMALE
                hair-color BLOND
                age ADULT
```

Attributes are indicated by lowercase letters in figures. The values of attributes, indicated by all capital letters, may be simple objects (e.g. ATRANS) or composite objects that have additional attributes (e.g., PHYS-OBJ type BOOK).

1.5.2. Relationships between events, states and goals

In the preceding section, the representation of individual events and states was presented. It is also important to be able to represent the relationship between a number of events and states. The following <u>causal links</u> are used to create clusters of events:

- RESULT- a physical event can result in a state.

- ENABLE- a state can enable a physical event to occur.

In addition to causal links, a set of intentional links have been proposed (Dyer, 1983) which specify the relationships between events, goals (i.e., wants or desires), and plans (means for accomplishing goals). The following is a subset of the intentional links which have proved useful in OCCAM:

- ACHIEVES- an event can result in the satisfaction of a goal.

- THWARTS- an event can cause the failure of a goal.

- MOTIVATES- an event can cause the creation of a goal.

- REALIZED- a plan can be realized by an event.

- INTENDS- a plan can be a means for accomplishing a goal.

Figure 1-2, shows the relationship between several events, goals and states. The event illustrated is Chris (the mother of Lynn) giving some Play-Doh to Lynn. This achieves Lynn's goal of possessing the Play-Doh and results in Lynn possessing the Play-Doh. (Presumedly Lynn possessing Play-Doh enables Lynn to play with the Play-Doh which achieves some higher level goal such as entertainment.)

Conceptual Dependency and intentional links serve an important role in OCCAM. They permit OCCAM to work with a language-free representation of the meaning of an event. To the learning module of OCCAM it does not matter how an event is stated in English. Alternative phrasings of Economic-Sanction-1 would have the same CD representation and would all be treated identically by OCCAM:

Economic-Sanction-1

In 1983, Australia refused to sell uranium to France, unless France ceased nuclear testing in the South Pacific. France paid a higher price to buy uranium from South Africa.

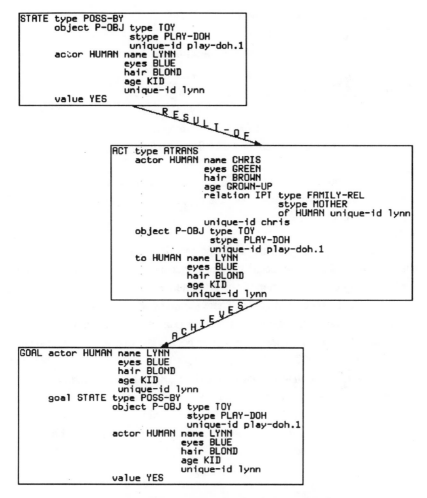

Figure 1-2: CD representation of Chris giving Play-Doh to Lynn
which achieves Lynn's goal of possessing some Play-Doh.

Economic-Sanction-1a

In 1983, Australia threatened to stop exporting uranium to France
if France continued testing atomic weapons in the South Pacific.
South Africa sold France the uranium at a premium.

Other descriptions of the situation would have similar representations. For
example, the representation of Economic-Sanction-1b would differ slightly from
that of Economic-Sanction-1 because the agent of the Australian government

who delivered the threat is specified.

Economic-Sanction-1b

In 1983, the Australian ambassador informed the French government that his country would not ship uranium to France until France abandoned its program of exploding nuclear weapons in the South Pacific. France searched for another supplier of uranium and signed a lucrative contact with South Africa.

Since examples in the real world are not in Conceptual Dependency, it is important that the assumptions about the capabilities of the interface to the real world be defined.

In some domains, such as economic sanctions and kidnapping, a natural language interface could read simple newspaper stories. The minimum capability required is to map English sentences into primitive Conceptual Dependency acts, states and goals. There are many important issues for natural language processing, such as word sense selection and pronominal reference that OCCAM simply ignores. These issues have been addressed in programs such as FRUMP (DeJong, 1977), IPP (Lebowitz, 1980) and BORIS (Dyer, 1983) that can perform tasks similar to that required by OCCAM. For example, OCCAM assumes that a natural language interface could parse a sentence such as "Australia refused to sell uranium to France, unless France ceased nuclear testing in the South Pacific." The output of the parsing process would be the CD representation for this sentence:

```
ACT type MTRANS
    actor AUSTRALIA
    to FRANCE
    object COND if ACT type EXPLODE
                     actor FRANCE
                     object WEAPONS type NUCLEAR
                     location SOUTH-PACIFIC
                     mode NEG
               then ACT type SELL
                        actor AUSTRALIA
                        to FRANCE
                        object COMMODITY type URANIUM
               else ACT type SELL
                        actor AUSTRALIA
                        to FRANCE
                        object COMMODITY type URANIUM
                        mode NEG
```

In addition, I am assuming that the lexicon of the parser would contain access to some long-term memory that has detailed information on various countries. In OCCAM, this information was derived from the World Almanac (Hoffman, 1986). Numerical information was hand converted into discrete symbolic categories. For example, the life expectancy for South Africa is 57 years. In OCCAM's representation, this is *FIFTIES*. The representation for South Africa is:

```
COUNTRY name SOUTH-AFRICA
        language ENGLISH AFRIKAANS
        location SOUTHERN-HEMISPHERE
        business-relationship US JAPAN FRANCE AUSTRALIA UK
        economic-health strong
        government PARLIAMENTARY
        life-expectancy *FIFTIES*
        ... ...
        imports COMMODITY type OIL ...
        exports COMMODITY type URANIUM ...
```

When OCCAM acquires the coercion schema, it also creates patterns to convert events represented in terms of CD primitive acts and goals into the high-level coerce representation. This capability is discussed in Section 3.3.5 together with the rationale for changing representations. The performance component of OCCAM does contain a parser that parses questions about the outcomes of hypothetical sanction incidents. The output of this parser is a CD goal and action representation of the question. During the memory search to find a schema to answer the question, the representation of the question is converted to the high-level representation. For example, the high-level representation of "Australia refused to sell uranium to France, unless France ceased nuclear testing in the South Pacific." is:

```
COERCE the-actor AUSTRALIA
        the-target FRANCE
        the-demand ACT type EXPLODE
                       actor =THE-TARGET
                       object WEAPONS type NUCLEAR
                       location SOUTH-PACIFIC
                       mode NEG
        the-threat ACT type SELL
                       actor =THE-ACTOR
                       to =THE-TARGET
                       object COMMODITY type URANIUM
                       mode NEG
        the-alternative ACT type SELL
                          actor =THE-ACTOR
                          to =THE-TARGET
                          object COMMODITY type URANIUM
```

The coerce representation contains several role names that are meaningful in English. For example, it refers to terms such as coerce, the-demand etc. When OCCAM creates a schema such as the coerce schema, it asks for a user to type names for these objects. In unattended mode, OCCAM generates its own names such as schema.007 and role.017 for these objects. The meaningful names serve to make OCCAM's output and intermediate states easier for a person to understand. However, coerce or schema.007 mean the same thing to OCCAM: a particular plan for achieving a goal in which entity-1 tells entity-2 that entity-1 will cause a goal failure for entity-2 unless entity-2 performs some act that achieves a goal for entity-1. Similarly, the-demand and role.017 both refer to the act that entity-1 wants entity-2 to perform to achieve the goal for entity-1. Structurally, the-demand can be found as the filler of the if role of the filler of the object role of an mtrans.

A natural language interface to OCCAM is not appropriate for domains in which OCCAM learns about physical causality. Certainly, young children do not (and can not) read newspaper accounts of events such as "A child dips a small yellow balloon in water, blows air into the balloon and the balloon is inflated." Instead, children simply observe the event. However, the ability to take a visual image of an event and convert it to a symbolic representation is beyond the capabilities of current vision systems. (See (Hanson & Riseman, 1978) for an overview of this field of research.)

The hypothetical machine vision interface to OCCAM must have a number of capabilities. It is not unreasonable to assume that people also have these capabilities. First, the vision system must be able to identify objects in a scene and associate attributes with the objects (e.g., small, yellow balloon or "child with blond hair and blue eyes"). The biggest assumption is that the vision system is able to parse temporal sequences of visual sensations into segments called events. For example, consider the following temporal sequence:

```
t1:  A small yellow balloon is on the table.  A glass of
     water is on the table.  A child with blond hair is
     next to the table.
t2:  The child's hand is on the balloon.
t3:  The balloon is in the child's hand.
t4:  The child's hand and balloon are above
     the glass of water.
t5:  The child is holding the balloon in water.
t6:  The child's hand and balloon are above
     the glass of water.
t7:  The balloon is in front of the child's mouth.
t8:  The tip of the balloon is in the child's mouth.
t9:  The child is inhaling.
t10: The child is exhaling.
t11: The balloon is larger.  The child is inhaling.
t12: The child is exhaling.
     The balloon is as large as the child's head.
t13: The balloon is larger than the child's head.
```

A person observing this temporal sequence would segment it into a number of events (Neisser, 1976). Memories and descriptions of this time sequence would be in terms of these events. From t2-t8 the balloon is being dipped in water and from t8-t13 the child is blowing air into the balloon. After t13, the balloon is inflated. The CD representation for these events is shown in Figure 1-3. It assumes that the person observing the event can identify the actor, object, and destination of the actions and notice which objects have changed state.

Once an event has been represented in CD, it is up to OCCAM to determine which actions and features of the actions are responsible for the state changes. OCCAM cannot learn if the input representation does not contain the proper relevant features. However, OCCAM can learn if irrelevant features are also included in the input representation. It is the role of learning to characterize which of the features in the input are relevant. A topic for future research is to

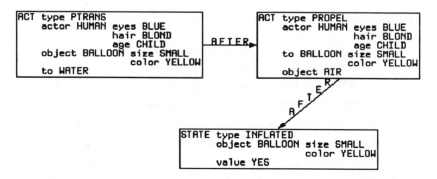

Figure 1-3:   **CD representation of "A child dips a small yellow balloon in   water, blows air into the balloon and the balloon is inflated.".**

direct an interface to the world to look for additional features when the input does not appear to have the necessary relevant features.

1.5.3. The representation of learned knowledge: Schemata

The output of the learning process is a hierarchy of schemata.

A schema is comprised of several components. These components include:

A generalized event-- A schema includes a template for recognizing instances of the schema. This template is a Conceptual Dependency pattern that is an abstract description of a class of events.

A sequence of events-- Typically, a schema can be decomposed into a small set of actions or scenes. For example, a schema that represents economic sanctions can be broken down into several simpler components that represent a threat, a demand and an outcome. An abstract description of these actions and their interaction is an integral part of the schema. The relationship between these events are specified by causal, temporal and intentional links. The generalized event of a schema indicates *what* the effect of a certain action is. The sequence of events indicates *how* the action brings about the effect.

Indices-- A schema may organize more specialized schemata and specific instances. These are indexed by features that elaborate on the generalized event of the schema. An index consists of a feature name (e.g., `actor`) and a feature value (e.g., `human`).

Support-- A schema also includes information about the source and the confidence in the schema. This information can include the justification for the schema (if the schema was created by generalizing an explanation) or the strength of the schema as represented by the number of successful and unsuccessful times a schema has made a prediction (if the schema was created by empirical methods).

1.5.4. The coercion schema

In this section, I use the coercion schema as an example to provide more details on the components of a schema. The generalized event of the coercion schema is shown in Figure 1-4. A generalized event consists of a Conceptual Dependency description of a class of events. The description consists of a head (e.g., `coerce`) and a number of roles (e.g., `goal`, `outcome`, `the-ask`, `the-demand`, `the-threat`, `the-actor`, `the-target`, etc.) In Figure 1-4 (and all figures in this book) roles names are printed in lowercase letters and heads are printed in capital letters. The generalized event of a schema contains restrictions on the entities which can fill the roles. Consider the role, `the-ask`, which is the act that the actor performs to get the target to achieve a goal for the actor in **coerce**. **the-ask** must be an **act** of type **mtrans**. The actor of **mtrans** must be the actor of the **coerce**[5]. The **to** of the **mtrans** is the target and the **object** of the **mtrans** is a CD representation of "If the target does the demand, the actor will do the alternative. Otherwise, the actor will do the threat".

```
COERCE goal GOAL outcome =OUTCOME
            plan =PLAN
            goal =GOAL-STATE
            actor =THE-ACTOR
    goal-state STATE actor =THE-BENE
    outcome GOAL-OUTCOME goal GOAL goal =GOAL-STATE
                                     actor =THE-ACTOR
                       actor =THE-ACTOR
    plan PLAN plan =THE-ASK
            actor =THE-ACTOR
    the-ask ACT type MTRANS
            actor =THE-ACTOR
            object COND if =THE-DEMAND
                       then =THE-ALTERNATIVE
                       else =THE-THREAT
                       to =THE-TARGET
    the-prep ACT actor =THE-ACTOR
    the-demand ACT actor =THE-TARGET
                  object =DEMAND-OBJ
    the-threat ACT actor =THE-ACTOR
                  object =THREAT-OBJ
                  to =THE-TARGET
    the-alternative ACT actor =THE-ACTOR
                  object =THE-ALT-OBJ
                  to =THE-TARGET
    the-sub-goal GOAL-CONFLICT actor =THE-TARGET
                  goal1 GOAL-OUTCOME-LINK goal-b GOAL actor =THE-TARGET
                                          goal-a GOAL actor =THE-TARGET
                  goal2 GOAL-OUTCOME-LINK goal-b GOAL actor =THE-TARGET
                                          goal-a GOAL actor =THE-TARGET
    the-sub-plan PLAN plan =THE-TARGET-RESPONSE
                  actor =THE-TARGET
    the-target-response ACT object =RESPONSE-OBJ
                  actor =THE-TARGET
    the-actor-response ACT actor =THE-ACTOR
    the-target-outcome GOAL-OUTCOME actor =THE-TARGET
```

Figure 1-4:   The generalized event for the coerce schema.

The generalized event of a schema indicates what the components of the schema are. The sequence of events indicates the relationships between these components. The sequence of events of **coerce** is illustrated in Figure 1-5.

The sequence of events can be instantiated by matching a particular instance of coercion against a pattern for the coercion. This pattern simply binds one variable for each role of the schema[6]. For example, the variable **?THE-ASK** is bound to the CD structure that fills **the-ask** role.

---

[5]The fact that the actor of **mtrans** must be the actor of the **coerce** is indicated by the notation **=THE-ACTOR** in all figures.

[6]Figure 3-23 on page 98 illustrates one such pattern.

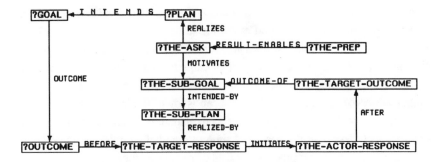

Figure 1-5:   The sequence of events for coerce.

The sequence of events specifies relationships between the entities described by the generalized event.   For example, **?THE-ASK** is an act that realizes the plan that achieves the actor's goal (**?GOAL**).   **?THE-ASK** motivates a subgoal for the actor.

The coercion schema plays an important part in this book.   The coercion schema is acquired via similarity-based learning in OCCAM by noticing regularities between several events[7] with the same type of plan for achieving a goal.   The plan is for an actor to ask a person (the target) to perform an action. The actor tells the target that if he does not perform the action, a threat (i.e., an act that causes a goal failure for the target) will be carried out.   Using explanation-based learning, OCCAM specializes the coercion schema to form a kidnapping schema (which has a more specialized threat of harming a family member of the target) and economic sanction schemata (which have threats such as the actor refusing to sell the target a commodity).   Section 7.1 discusses the acquisition of the coercion schema and provides more details on the roles and sequence of events of this schema.   Section 7.2 describes the specializations of coercion created by OCCAM to deal with economic sanction incidents.

1.5.5. The performance system

After learning, there are three reasoning tasks supported by the hierarchy of schemata.   First, the outcome of a future event can be predicted by recognizing a test example as an instance of an explanatory schemata.   Second, an explanation can be generated for why an outcome is predicted by recognizing a test example

---

[7]approximately 10

as an instance of an explanatory schemata and instantiating the causal chain of the schema. The first and second reasoning tasks are the performance tasks of OCCAM. Finally, an observed outcome can be explained by chaining together schemata. Note that occam does not attempt to chain schemata together to predict or explain the outcome of test cases. Rather, it only uses chaining to explain observed outcomes. It has been shown (DeJong, 1986) that the computational cost of chaining together an explanation for an observed outcome is considerably less than the cost of chaining to predict an unobserved outcome. Each step in the chaining process consists of recognizing that the antecedent of an existing rule applies and then instantiating the consequent of that rule. Explaining an observed outcome by chaining is not a performance task in OCCAM. However, it is an important step of some forms of learning.

1.5.6. Finding the most specific schema

Finding the most specific schema in memory that accounts for an example is a crucial initial step in both the learning and the performance tasks in OCCAM.

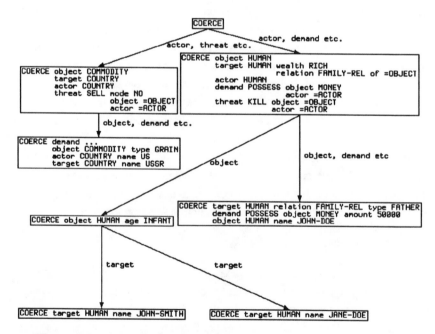

Figure 1-6: Organization of schemata in OCCAM's memory.

Since the most specific schema in memory provides the most detailed expectations and inferences, it is important that memory be organized and searched in a manner that allows the most specific schema to be found accurately and efficiently. For example, Figure 1-6 illustrates some schemata indexed under the **coercion** schema in OCCAM's memory. When an example of kidnapping is presented to OCCAM, the schemata in memory explain why certain actions occur. Let's assume that OCCAM encounters an example where an infant is kidnapped. Figure 1-7 illustrates the representation of one such example where David Jones, an infant with blond hair is kidnapped. If only the coercion schema were in memory, the explanation for abducting the infant would be "the **actor** wants the **target** to do something". If the kidnapping schema were also in memory (illustrated beneath and to the right of **coerce** in Figure 1-6) then the explanation would be "the **actor** wants the **target** to give him money because the **target** doesn't want the **actor** to kill the **object**." If there were a specialized schema for kidnapping infants in memory (illustrated beneath and to the left of the kidnapping schema in Figure 1-6), then the explanation for kidnapping the infant would be "the **actor** wants the **target** to give him money because the **target** doesn't want the **actor** to kill the **object** and the **actor** wants to avoid being convicted so he's kidnapping an infant since infants can't testify".

```
COERCE target HUMAN wealth RICH
                    name MOLLY-JONES
                    eyes BROWN
                    hair BROWN
                    relation FAMILY-REL of =OBJECT
                                        type GRANDMOTHER
       object HUMAN gender MALE
                    name DAVID-JONES
                    age INFANT
                    hair BLOND
       threat KILL object =OBJECT
                   actor =ACTOR
```

Figure 1-7: A kidnapping example.

The algorithm that OCCAM uses to search memory is illustrated in Figure 1-8. Memory search starts at the most general node in memory. There is one root node in memory. Indexed under this node are very general nodes for each type of schema (i.e., **plan**, **goal**, **coerce**, etc.). When finding the most specific schema for the kidnapping example in Figure 1-7, search would start at the **coerce** schema. Since there are no features of **coerce** that are contradicted by the example, the confidence in **coerce** is increased and the search recurses on the specializations of **coerce**. There are two specializations of **coerce**, but only one of them is indexed by a feature that is shared by the

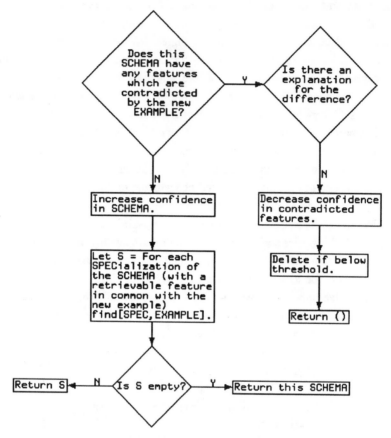

Figure 1-8: find[SCHEMA, EXAMPLE]: The procedure that OCCAM
uses to find the most specific schema in memory.

new example. The kidnapping schema is a specialization of **coerce** that has
the same **threat** as the new kidnapping example. Therefore, the search for the
most specific schema recurses again on the kidnapping schema. There is a
specialization of kidnapping in memory indexed by the **object** role that is
compatible with the new example. This is the kidnapping infants schema. Since
it has no specializations, it is returned as the most specific schema that accounts
for the example.

As memory is searched for schemata, the support for schemata that make
successful predictions is increased and the support for schemata that make
unsuccessful predictions is decreased. Chapter 3 elaborates on this topic further

and includes several examples. The important point to note is that this is an efficient process that is part of the normal update and traversal of memory (Lebowitz, 1982).

1.5.7. The learning task

There are three inputs to the learning system. The first input is a series of examples. The second input is the prior knowledge represented in the existing hierarchy of schemata. The third input is a representation of general knowledge of causality. The output of the learning system is an hierarchy of explanatory schemata. An important aspect of the learning task is that the hierarchy of schemata used by the learning system may be acquired by the learning system.

1.6. Organization of the Book

In the remainder of this book, I explore in depth the possible strategies for learning causal relationships. In Chapter 2, I describe the major problems that must be addressed in a theory of learning causal relationships. I argue that no single approach, either empirical or analytical, is adequate and propose that an integrated approach is required. Chapter 3 presents a broad overview of the theory advocated in this book and describes the architecture of OCCAM.

The remainder of the book discusses the approach to learning as implemented in OCCAM from a computational point of view. Chapter 4 describes the process of learning by detecting features common to a number of examples (similarity-based learning or empirical learning) and discusses its role in an integrated learning system. The primary role of similarity-based learning is to "bootstrap" a learning system by detecting regularities and postulating laws in unfamiliar domains. Chapter 5 argues that people possess a general theory of causality and demonstrates the advantage of making use of this theory in a machine learning system. In Chapter 6, I describe explanation-based learning (an analytical learning method) that utilizes existing knowledge to guide the learning process. Chapter 7 elaborates on the approach to integrating the three learning methods.

In Chapter 8, I present a number of examples of causal and social relationships learned by OCCAM. In this chapter, the primary benefit of a learning system that integrates empirical and analytical learning methods is apparent: OCCAM is unique among explanation-based learning systems in that it has the ability to acquire by empirical means the knowledge needed for explanation-based learning. Chapter 9 also demonstrates how the knowledge-base for a system that predicts the outcome of economic sanction incidents is learned by OCCAM. Finally, Chapter 9 compares OCCAM with a number of different approaches to learning and describes possible directions for future learning research. Each chapter concludes with a summary that describes the major points for the reader who is already familiar with the subject matter or uninterested in the details.

The book contains four appendices. Appendix A describes a micro-version of OCCAM. Appendix B is an annotated trace of OCCAM. In Appendix C, the Prolog code of a micro-micro-version OCCAM is described. Appendix D lists the causal rules used by OCCAM. The economic sanction incidents that serve as training and test data for OCCAM are listed in Appendix E.

Chapter 2
What OCCAM is up against

There are several problems that must be addressed in schema acquisition:

- Relevance of features

- The level of generality of schemata

- Integrating multiple sources of information

2.1. Relevance of Features

Determining which features of an example (or set of examples) should be incorporated in a schema is the central issue in schema acquisition. In Chapter 1, this problem was called deciding which features are relevant. For example, consider the following economic sanction incident:

Economic-Sanction-1

In 1983, Australia refused to sell uranium to France, unless France ceased nuclear testing in the South Pacific. France paid a higher price to buy uranium from South Africa.

A Conceptual Dependency representation of this incident is illustrated in Figure 2-1[8]. What lesson should be learned from Economic-Sanction-1? That economic sanctions never achieve their desired goal? This conclusion would be overly general. That economic sanctions never work against countries that export wine? This conclusion would be wrong. That economic sanctions won't work when Australia refuses to sell any country a commodity that is sold by South Africa. This is close to being true, but is probably too specific to apply to many future cases. The problem here is to identify which features of Australia,

---

[8]This representation is simplified considerably to conserve space.

```
COERCE actor COUNTRY name AUSTRALIA
                     imports COMMODITY type OIL
                     exports SET COMMODITY type WOOL
                             =OBJECT
                     government DEMOCRACY
                     location SOUTHERN-HEMISPHERE
                     language ENGLISH
          object COMMODITY type URANIUM
          target COUNTRY name FRANCE
                     imports SET =OBJECT
                                 COMMODITY type OIL
                     exports SET COMMODITY type WINE
                                 COMMODITY type WEAPONS
                     government DEMOCRACY
                     location NORTHERN-HEMISPHERE
                     language FRENCH
                     economic-health STRONG
          helper COUNTRY name SOUTH-AFRICA
                     imports COMMODITY type CARS
                     exports SET =OBJECT
                                 COMMODITY type DIAMOND
                     location SOUTHERN-HEMISPHERE
          demand ACT type EXPLODE
                     actor =TARGET
                     object WEAPONS type NUCLEAR
                     location SOUTHERN-HEMISPHERE
                     mode NEG
          threat ACT type SELL
                     actor =ACTOR
                     object =OBJECT
                     to =TARGET
                     mode NEG
          response ACT type SELL
                     actor =HELPER
                     object =OBJECT
                     price MONEY dollars 3000000
                                 value >MARKET
                     to =TARGET
          outcome FAILURE
```

Figure 2-1:   Simplified CD representation of Economic-Sanction-1.

South Africa, France, and uranium as well as the features of the demand (to stop nuclear testing in the South Pacific) and the threat (to not sell uranium) were necessary to explain why Australia did not achieve its goal. A reasonable generalization to make from Economic-Sanction-1 is that if a country tries to threaten a country with a strong economy by refusing to sell a commodity, then the threatened country will buy the product elsewhere. Figure 2-2 illustrates this generalization.

2.1.1. Prediction vs. explanation

There is a problem with the generalization as illustrated in Figure 2-2. It is useful for making a prediction about what might happen when an economic sanction incident meets this pattern. However, as illustrated in Figure 2-2, it does not contain the knowledge necessary to explain a predicted outcome. What is needed is a causal explanation that indicates the intermediate states that connect the event of one country (the actor) refusing to sell a product to another country (the target) with the event that a third country (the helper) sells the

```
COERCE actor COUNTRY exports =OBJECT
       object COMMODITY
       target COUNTRY imports =OBJECT
                      economic-health STRONG
       helper COUNTRY exports =OBJECT
       threat ACT type SELL
                   actor =ACTOR
                   object =OBJECT
                   to =TARGET
                   mode NEG
       response ACT type SELL
                    actor =HELPER
                    object =OBJECT
                    price MONEY value >MARKET
                    to =TARGET
       outcome FAILURE
```

Figure 2-2: **A schema that indicates that if a country tries to threaten a country with a strong economy by refusing to sell a commodity, then the threatened country will buy the product elsewhere.**

target the product. This explanation in the example would reference the theory of supply and demand to indicate that the target will be willing to pay a higher price for the product and another country who is interested in making a profit would sell the product to the target. The explanation that should be associated with the generalization in Figure 2-2 is illustrated in Figure 2-3[9].

What is to be gained by associating an explanation with a generalized event in a schema? The major benefit is that when such a schema exists, explanation of new episodes is a simple task. The generalized event indicates what features of a new example are necessary for the stored explanation to apply to that new example. When a new example contains the features of the generalized event, the explanation associated with the schema is applicable. As the memory evolves and more schemata are created, finding explanations for commonly encountered events is greatly simplified.

There are two differences between an expert in a field, such as economic sanctions, and an average adult. First, an expert has more knowledge of the underlying economic and political theories. Second, and perhaps more important, the expert has a large set of schemata that recognize general situations. The information in these schemata is easily accessed for making

---

[9]To conserve space in this introductory chapter, Figure 2-3 illustrates the explanation in English. Of course, the meaning of the explanation should be associated with the schema rather than an English form of the meaning. In OCCAM, the explanation is in Conceptual Dependency. The reader who wants to jump ahead to see the details will find them in Figure 5-9 on page 162.

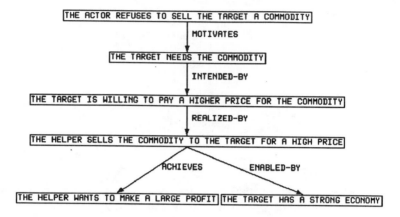

Figure 2-3: An explanation of why a country with a strong economy will be able to purchase a product from another supplier if the existing supply is cut off.

predictions or constructing explanations. A novice political science student may have the same political and economic knowledge. However, without the set of schemata built up over time by analyzing examples, a novice may miss an important implication of the existing knowledge. Although a novice may have a much harder time constructing an explanation for a new example, he may learn from his efforts. The next time a similar situation is encountered, the explanation process will be less complex, since the explanation needs to be found rather than constructed.

2.2. The Level of Generality of Schemata

When reading a story or participating in an activity there are two important questions an understander needs to answer. Why did things turn out the way they did? Why did the people do the thing they did? A memory of previous experiences can provide the answers to these questions in the form of predictions and inferences. Schemata describing previous experiences need to be represented at abstract levels, with unessential details removed.

There is a dilemma concerning the level of generality that should be represented in memory. A very abstract representation will apply to many future events. However, a more specific representation will provide more detailed predictions and inferences to facilitate the understanding process.

Consider the complexity of the inferences a person would need to make to understand Kidnapping-1 (repeated below) if there were an abstract schema describing coercion instead of a kidnapping schema in memory.   Neither Kidnapping-1 nor the coercion schema state that the kidnapper's goal is to possess money. Instead, the understander must infer this from other knowledge. For example, a person reading this story could infer that the kidnapper might threaten to harm John Doe unless his father helps the kidnapper achieve his goal. From this, and the fact that John is not harmed after his father puts the money in the trash can, a reader might infer that the kidnapper's goal is achieved by retrieving the money from the trash can.   Of course, when there is only a coercion schema, the search for an explanation must explore alternative explanations such as the kidnapper wanted John Doe's father to throw out money.

Kidnapping-1

John Doe who was abducted on his way to school Monday morning was released today after his father left $50,000 in a trash can in a men's room at the bus station.

In contrast, understanding Kidnapping-1 is much easier if a kidnapping schema has been learned. The task of explaining why the father puts money in a trash can is much easier: an understander can utilize an expectation from the kidnapping schema (that the father might pay a ransom to achieve his goal of preserving the health of his child) to interpret this otherwise unusual action. Similarly, identifying the kidnapper's goal is trivial since the goal of obtaining money is part of the kidnapping schema. The advantage that a kidnapping schema has over the coercion schema for understanding this story is that explanation is already associated with the kidnapping schema. In contrast, even if Kidnapping-1 is recognized as an instance of coercion, the explanation for the kidnapper's actions must be constructed from different information.

Although understanding kidnapping stories is much easier with a kidnapping schema, it is still possible to understand stories about kidnapping with a coercion schema. The coercion schema provides very general predictions while the kidnapping schema provides more specialized predictions.   For example, the coercion schema indicates that the threat could be any action; the kidnapping schema indicates that the threat will be to harm a relative of the person threatened. Kidnapping is called a *specialization* of coercion.[10]

A schema can be specialized by further specifying any of its features. For example, economic sanctions is a specialization of coercion where the threat is for one country to refuse to sell a product to another country. There is not always an English word for some specializations of coercion. For example, another specialization of coercion would represent those coercions that have failed because the target who is threatened does not mind if the actor performs the threat. This schema might be learned from childhood disputes such as "I won't be your friend, if you don't let me have the swing". If the child is smart enough to realize that no one needs this type of friend, a specialization of coercion can be formed. This schema would account for the following answer to a hypothetical situation presented to the political analyst at the Rand Corporation:

Question: What would happen if the US refused to sell rice to Japan if Japan did not reduce tariffs on imported fruits and vegetables.

Answer: Japan wouldn't do a thing since it does not want our rice.

It probably didn't take years of studying politics and economics for the political analyst to arrive at this conclusion. Instead, a little bit of common sense should be applied in this situation. This sort of common sense can be represented as a specialization of coercion that indicates that if an actor tries to threaten a target, and if execution of the threat will not lead to a goal failure for the target, then the goal of the actor to get the target to agree to the demand will fail.

One advantage that a general schema has over a more specific schema is that a general schema is applicable in a wider variety of situations. Consider, the following situations:

---

[10]The distinction between a specialization and a generalization is somewhat fuzzy. For example, the kidnapping schema is a specialization of the coercion schema. The kidnapping schema is also a generalization of several kidnapping incidents.

General-Hospital-1

Leo, the tall dark masseur at the Avalon Heath Spa, secretly filmed Amanda, a wealthy middle aged woman, while he seduced her. Then, he told Amanda that unless she paid him $10,000, he would show her husband the pictures of her being unfaithful.

Economic-Sanction-1

In 1983, Australia refused to sell uranium to France, unless France ceased nuclear testing in the South Pacific. France paid a higher price to buy uranium from South Africa.

Playground-1

John told the other kids at the playground that if they didn't let him pitch, he was going to take his ball and go home.

All of these examples can be understood as instances of coercion. The specialized kidnapping schema would be of little use for inferring the goals and plans of the participants of these examples. In fact, the kidnapping schema may provide the wrong inferences in many cases. For example, in kidnapping the anonymity of the kidnapper is important, while in blackmail (e.g., General-Hospital-1), it is not essential that the identity of the blackmailer be unknown to the victim. The more general coercion schema contains no information about the anonymity of the perpetrator. The coercion schema still provides a general framework for understanding General-Hospital-1. Of course, this story would be easier to understand if a specialization of the coercion schema for blackmail had been formed. Similarly, Economic-Sanction-1 and Playground-1 would be easier to understand if there were schemata for economic sanction incidents and playground arguments.

Very general schema such as coercion provide the opportunity for learning across domains. If the coercion schema were learned by a child from arguments with their parents and other children (e.g., Playground-1), it could provide a framework for understanding other types of coercion such as blackmail, kidnapping and economic sanctions. Through experience with these different types of coercion, specializations of the coercion for each of these areas will develop. These specializations of coercion simplify future understanding by providing more specific inferences and expectations. In Chapter 3, I describe the similarity-based learning component of OCCAM that can create very general schema such as coercion. In Section 7.1, I present an extended example in which OCCAM acquires a coercion schema. Chapter 5 discusses the explanation-based learning component of OCCAM. In Section 7.2, I show how OCCAM combines knowledge of coercion with knowledge of political and economic goals to create several economic sanction schemata. Section 7.5 shows how OCCAM uses EBL to create the kidnapping schema and Section 7.6 gives examples of OCCAM further specializing the kidnapping schema.

Since understanding is much easier using a specialized schema instead of a general one, a memory would need to contain a large number of specializations. Therefore, an important issue is the organization of memory such that the appropriate specialization can efficiently be found. The type of memory proposed by Schank (Schank, 1982) and implemented in IPP (Lebowitz, 1980) and CYRUS (Kolodner, 1984) provide a good framework for organizing memory so that the most specific schemata for a situation can be found efficiently. However, this theory of memory cannot provide a full account for schema acquisition, since as it has been implemented, it only makes use of correlational information when creating new schemata.

2.3. Combining Multiple Sources of Information

There are several sources of information that can be used in schema acquisition. These sources of information include:

- Inter-example relationships: Regularities among examples that reveal the conditions under which a cause produces an effect.

- Intra-example relationships: Temporal and spatial relationships between a potential cause and a potential effect that suggest a causal relationship. This type of information is called an intra-example relationship to stress the fact that the relationship is between components of a single example, rather than among several different examples.

- Prior causal and social theories: Prior knowledge that predicts and explains regularities in events. Note that this prior knowledge may be knowledge acquired by prior learning, or knowledge acquired through instruction (or in the case of the OCCAM, knowledge entered by a programmer). In some cases, this prior knowledge is a correlational among previous examples, which is stored as a schema and used to explain related events.

An important issue in this book is the integration of these three sources of information in a single theory of learning. Each source of information is applicable in certain situations, and has its own advantages and disadvantages. The approach I have taken to integrate these sources of information is to attempt to identify the situations in which people rely on each kind of information and to identify the situations in which each kind of information can be exploited for maximum benefit.

2.3.1. The use of correlation

Is it possible that people make use only of similarities and differences between events when acquiring new schemata? In this view, the features that are included in a schema are those features that are common to a number of examples. Of course, correlation alone cannot distinguish between those similarities that are coincidental and those that are relevant. For example, there are several similarities between Economic-Sanction-1 and Economic-Sanction-2.

Economic-Sanction-2

In 1980, the US refused to sell grain to the USSR unless the USSR withdrew troops from Afghanistan. The USSR paid a higher price to buy grain from Argentina.

Figure 2-4 contains a simplified Conceptual Dependency representation of Economic-Sanction-2. When the representation of Economic-Sanction-2 is placed on top of the representation of Economic-Sanction-1, then the areas of agreement between the two events are made obvious (see Figure 2-5).

Figure 2-6 illustrates more clearly all of the common features between the Economic-Sanction-1 and Economic-Sanction-2. The problem here is that there are too many similarities and there is no way to tell which of the common features are relevant and which are just coincidences. The ideal generalization would look like the one in Figure 2-2 and would only contain relevant information: the important features of the target country are that the target must

```
COERCE actor COUNTRY name AMERICA
                      imports COMMODITY type OIL
                      exports SET COMMODITY type WEAPONS
                                  =OBJECT
                      government DEMOCRACY
                      location NORTHERN-HEMISPHERE
                      language ENGLISH
          object COMMODITY type GRAIN
          target COUNTRY name USSR
                      imports SET =OBJECT
                                  COMMODITY type STEEL
                      exports SET COMMODITY type GAS
                                  COMMODITY type WEAPONS
                      government SOCIALIST-REPUBLIC
                      location NORTHERN-HEMISPHERE
                      language RUSSIAN
                      economic-health STRONG
          helper COUNTRY name ARGENTINA
                      imports COMMODITY type STEEL
                      exports SET =OBJECT
                                  COMMODITY type MEAT
                      location SOUTHERN-HEMISPHERE
          demand ACT type INVADE
                      actor =TARGET
                      object COUNTRY name AFGANISTAN
                      location NORTHERN-HEMISPHERE
                      mode NEG
          threat ACT type SELL
                      actor =ACTOR
                      object =OBJECT
                      to =TARGET
                      mode NEG
          response ACT type SELL
                      actor =HELPER
                      object =OBJECT
                      price MONEY dollars 17000000
                                  value >MARKET
                      to =TARGET
          outcome FAILURE
```

Figure 2-4: Simplified CD representation of Economic-Sanction-2.

import the commodity (so that the threat is meaningful) and that the economy of
the target is strong (so that they can afford to buy the product elsewhere at a
higher price). Taken literally, the schema in Figure 2-6 would indicate that
when an English-speaking democracy that imports oil threatens a country in the
Northern Hemisphere that has a strong economic health and exports weapons,
then the sanction will fail because a country in the Southern Hemisphere will
sell the product at a premium. Obviously, this generalization is not correct, nor
is it one that a rational adult would make from these data.

Although correlational information alone does not provide a complete
answer to the problem of generalizing schemata from examples, correlation can
serve several useful purposes:

- In an area where the learner has little or no existing knowledge,
  knowledge-intensive techniques such as EBL are not applicable.
  Basic facts can be acquired by correlational means. For example,

Figure 2-5: **An illustration of finding the common features of two events. When the representation of Economic-Sanction-2 from Figure 2-4 is placed on top of the representation of Economic-Sanction-1 from Figure 2-1, the common features become bolder and the differences are overwritten.**

few small children (or even adults) understand why glass objects break easily and plastic objects do not. This knowledge is acquired by experience alone instead of some underlying theory that indicates the strength of materials as a function of their composition.

• A schema formed by correlation can encode conventions or customs. Few people know or need to know the reason that rice is thrown at weddings or shoes are taken off at Japanese restaurants.

• A schema formed by correlation can propose a causal relationship for further study. Such a schema can describe those situations

```
COERCE actor  COUNTRY imports COMMODITY type OIL
                      exports =OBJECT
                      government DEMOCRACY
                      language ENGLISH
       object COMMODITY
       target COUNTRY imports =OBJECT
                      exports COMMODITY type WEAPONS
                      location NORTHERN-HEMISPHERE
                      economic-health STRONG
       helper COUNTRY exports =OBJECT
                      location SOUTHERN-HEMISPHERE
       demand ACT actor =TARGET
                  mode NEG
       threat ACT type SELL
                  actor =ACTOR
                  object =OBJECT
                  to =TARGET
                  mode NEG
       response ACT type SELL
                    actor =HELPER
                    object =OBJECT
                    price MONEY value >MARKET
                    to =TARGET
       outcome FAILURE
```

Figure 2-6: A possible schema formed by extracting all common features from Economic-Sanction-1 and Economic-Sanction-2.

where a coincidence is noted but there is no explanation. These coincidences might initiate and focus the search for new causal knowledge. For example, in medicine a correlational relationship (e.g., AIDS and homosexuality) may direct the investigation for a pathological explanation.

There is a major difference between a schema that encodes knowledge whose only support is the existence of several examples and a schema whose support also includes an underlying theory. There is no justification to believe that a similarity between past examples will be present in future examples. Therefore, schemata formed by correlation represent tentative generalizations that are always subject to further revision. For example, a person familiar with the fictious Canyon Killer will have formed a correlational schema predicting that his future victims will be blond cheerleaders just like his previous victims.

Canyon-Killer-1

The Canyon Killer who has murdered three blond cheerleaders in the past two months has struck again. This time, however, his victim was a 70-year-old retired mechanic.

In Canyon-Killer-1, the prediction that the Canyon Killer's victim would be a blond cheerleader is not accurate. The justification for believing that the Canyon killer's victim will be blond cheerleaders is simply that all previous victims were blond cheerleaders. When a victim who is not a blond cheerleader is encountered, the schemata must be corrected to account for this new example (Lebowitz, 1982). In contrast, the kidnapping schema should contain a justification for why the ransom would be paid: to protect a loved one. When a story such as Absurd-Kidnapping-1 violates this expectation it does not typically reduce the confidence in the kidnapping schema.

Absurd-Kidnapping-1

John Doe who was abducted on his way to school Monday morning was released today after the mailman on his block paid a $50,000 ransom.

Absurd-Kidnapping-1 is not totally understandable. Why did the mailman pay the ransom? Where did he get the money? The kidnapping schema cannot provide answers to these questions. However, because there was a justification for including the fact that a hostage has a rich parent in the kidnapping schema, the kidnapping schema is not abandoned when a story does not conform to the expectation. It is be possible to make the story conform to kidnapping schema by proposing that the mailman might secretly be John Doe's father or by postulating that the mailman is independently wealthy and just delivers mail for fun, or that the mailman is rich because he steals checks from the people on his route.

A primary difference then between a schema with a relationship supported by an underlying reason and a schema with a correlational relationship is what happens when new examples do not agree with the schema. The correlational schema is questioned when an example does not agree with schema. In contrast, when a new example contradicts a schema supported by an underlying theory, the example itself is questioned.

Only when the data withstand such questioning, or when the amount of data is overwhelming, is a schema supported by an underlying theory abandoned. This is an indication that the underlying theory is incorrect and needs revision to account for new empirical findings.

2.3.2. The use of prior knowledge

In addition to the data, a person or a computer can make use of existing knowledge to constrain the set of generalizations. Figures 2-6 and 2-2 indicate there can be several generalizations consistent with a set of examples. The set of generalizations consistent with a set of examples can be pruned by requiring that a generalization also be consistent with prior knowledge. Explanation-based learning is an approach to learning that makes use of underlying theories in the generalization process.

. The reason explanation-based learning is a useful learning strategy is that it is easier for a person (or a computer) to understand how a plan achieves a goal in a particular example than to come up with the plan himself. For example, on February 18, 1987, there was a unique robbery in Atlanta, Georgia. Most readers are probably familiar with robberies at automated teller machines. However, this robbery was somewhat different. Instead of holding up a customer and getting away with at most $200 (the maximum withdrawal at most automated teller machines), the thief had a plan to obtain more money. He tampered with the automated teller machine and notified the bank that it was out of order. The bank sent a repairman (who was a Vietnam veteran and a father of two children). When the repairman came, he held up the repairman who had access to the money inside the machine, and made off with over $20,000. Understanding why this plan worked is trivial for an average adult. It involves constructing an inference chain that relates several facts:

- A repairman will come if a machine owned by a large corporation is broken.

- A repairman has access to the inside of a machine.

- There is a large amount of money inside an automated teller machine.

- A person will usually do what you want if you threaten to kill him.

Each of these facts can be represented as a separate schema. These facts are combined to arrive at a novel type of robbery. It was not a trivial task for the robber to come up with this plan. However, once someone has thought of the plan, it is much easier to copy the plan. In fact, the FBI is worried that this type of robbery will be repeated in other parts of the country. Explanation-based learning techniques could be used to create an `attract-repairman-to-automated-teller-robbery` schema from just this one example. The fact that the repairman was a Vietnam veteran and a father of two are not needed to explain how the robbery worked and would not be included in the schema. In contrast, similarity-based methods would require several examples to rule these features out. If similarity-based methods were the only learning methods people had, then some copycat robbers would be finding ways to attract veterans or parents to automated tellers late at night.

Explanation-based learning creates schemata that can enable a very efficient inference process. Instead of repeating a long inference chain every time a commonly encountered situation is seen, the inference chain is saved as a schema. In addition, the schema contains a pattern to recognize the situation when a previous chain of reasoning applies. For some problems, it is important that a schema be created to avoid extremely complex inferences. One situation in which this occurs is when the motivation for a particular course of action is to avoid a potential goal failure. It is difficult, if not impossible, to determine why the action was decided upon without knowing about the potential failure. For example, OCCAM notices a similarity between several kidnappings whose victims are all infants with blond hair. However, it is not capable of finding an explanation for this similarity until it finds a kidnapping case in which there is a goal failure when the victim was not an infant. After the ransom was paid, the victim was able to give evidence that led to the arrest and conviction of the kidnapper (which is, of course, a goal failure for the kidnapper). With this new information, an explanation for the kidnapping of infants is found to be avoiding this goal failure since infants cannot give police evidence nor testify. Since the explanation does not refer to the infants hair color, this similarity is treated as a coincidence. Once a `kidnapping-infants` schema is created, it is simple to recognize new examples as instances of this schema.

2.3.3. Intra-example relationships

In addition to specific causal knowledge, people also have a general theory of causality that can assist the learning of new causal relations. Some relationships just "appear" to be causal in that the mechanism that translates the "causal force" from a cause to an effect is easily apparent. For example, during the Christmas of 1986 a new doll came on the market. When you dip this doll in water, its hair changes color. This fits a common pattern for a causal relationship. Something is done to the doll, and then the doll changes. On the other hand, some relationships do not look like causal relationships. For example, during the pre-game show of the Superbowl every year, the announcers bring up a pattern that has been noticed over time: every time an NFC football team wins, the stock market has a good year and when an AFC football team wins, the stock market has a bad year. This does not fit a common pattern for a causal relationship. If the New York Giants do something to the Denver Broncos, one might expect the Broncos to change, but not the stock market.

The importance of general theories of causality is apparent when there are several potential causes for an effect or several potential effects for a cause. For example, consider the following event sequence:

- First, two events occur at approximately the same time: a yellow taxi is seen driving on the street outside the kitchen window and a brown bird flies into the window pane.

- At the next instant, the window pane shatters.

- Shortly after that, a ladybug flies through the broken window pane.

General knowledge of causality can rule out the hypothesis that the window broke because the ladybug will fly through it since a cause must precede an effect. Although this may seem like a trivial piece of knowledge, existing machine learning systems (Lebowitz, 1986a; Salzberg, 1985) that predict the outcome of events don't make use of temporal information. Similarly, the taxi can be ruled out as a cause of the window breaking because the taxi is not acting on the window (in the same manner that the bird is). By ruling out the taxi and the ladybug as causes for the window breaking, the search space for the problem of determining what causes windows to break can be reduced. Of course, correlation is needed to determine that the color of the object that strikes the window is not important, but the weight and velocity of the object are. However, resources such as memory can be utilized more effectively if they are not also required to correlate the color and velocities of cars passing by.

General knowledge of causality can also help indicate which features of a particular example are relevant. Consider the situation of a television set turning on after a parent turns the knob. Is it important that the knob be turned with the right hand by someone wearing a white shirt? This situation fits a general causal pattern when an action is performed on an object (in this case the television) and the object changes. General knowledge of causality indicates that it is not important who performs the action or how the action is performed. Therefore, the features of the actor who turns the knob on the television are not relevant. OCCAM contains a learning mechanism that exploits intra-example relationships. I call this mechanism theory-driven learning (TDL) because learning is driven by a general theory of causality.

2.3.4. Integrating multiple sources of information

An important issue is discovering how these three different sources of information (correlational information, specific causal knowledge, and general theories of causality) can be integrated. Each source of information can perform a useful role in some situations. Knowledge of people's preferences or biases for using certain types of information can yield insights in the complexity of using each type of information. Section 7.7 reviews some relevant psychology experiments. An important issue to resolve is that a learning system should be able to take advantage of prior knowledge whenever possible, but be able to learn in the absence of prior knowledge. For example, theory-driven learning cannot learn about actions at a distance, such as the operation of a remote control for a garage door or television set. It is straightforward to use purely correlational techniques to detect this causal relationship. However, if a learning system relies solely on correlational techniques, its prior knowledge and prior learning will not facilitate future learning on other problems.

2.3.5. Integrated learning: An overview of OCCAM

In the next three chapters, the details on the the three learning methods used by OCCAM are presented. In order to understand how the learning methods interact, it is necessary to first present the general architecture used to integrate the methods. Here, two questions are answered:

- When does OCCAM need to extend or modify the memory of causal relationships?

- Under what conditions is each learning method used by OCCAM?

2.4. When to Learn

When should a new schema be created? In OCCAM, the driving force behind learning is the desire to gain an understanding of the environment. OCCAM attempts to create a new schema when its existing schemata do not adequately explain a new experience. When a new event is presented to OCCAM, it first searches its memory for the most specific schema that applies to the event. One of three things can happen:

- The most specific schema contains an expectation about what the outcome of the new event should be and this expectation matches the actual outcome. In this case, there is nothing to learn since there already is a schema that accounts for the event. The idea here is that when a novel situation is encountered, a lot of work must be done to understand the situation. Sometimes this work may be comparing and contrasting the new situation to previous similar situations to find a pattern or regularity. Sometimes, this work may be constructing an explanation by chaining together several existing pieces of knowledge. In either case, the results of this effort can be saved as a schema. In a familiar situation, understanding simply consists of recognizing a new event as an instance of an existing schema. For example, the first time (or first few times) a person encounters a new situation, such as renting a car or flying on an airplane, he has to reason why certain things are done and what order things are done in. After a few experiences, much of this reasoning is automatic (i.e., it is saved in a schema).

- The most specific schema does not make a prediction about the outcome of the event. In this case, a new schema may be created to account for the new event and to predict the outcome of future similar events. The creation of new schemata is the focus of this book. Section 2.4 contains an overview of schema creation in OCCAM.

- The most specific schema contains an expectation about what the outcome of the new event should be. However, the actual outcome of the event violates this expectation. In this case, one of four things may happen.

   1. An explanation can be constructed to indicate why this new event violates the expectation. In this case, a new schema is constructed that serves to explain future exceptions. For example, OCCAM encounters several examples of a child asking a parent for something and constructs a schema that indicates that a parent will give his or her child what the child asks for. Later, it encounters an exception when a parent doesn't give the child a kiwi fruit. However, when there is an explanation for the parent not giving the child the kiwi fruit (the parent doesn't have a kiwi fruit), a new schema is created that indicates that a parent will give a child what the child asks for unless the parent doesn't have it. Presumedly, other examples would create more exceptions, such as a parent won't give the child something that would hurt the child, or a parent won't give the child a snack too close to supper etc.

   2. If there are few exceptions to the schema (relative to the number of times the schema has made an accurate prediction) and no explanation can be found for this exception, the new event is simply remembered as an exception to the schema. The idea here is that it doesn't pay to abandon a well-established conclusion on the basis of a small number of exceptions. Minsky calls this strategy the **exception principle** (Minsky, 1986).

   3. If there are many exceptions to the schema and no explanation can be found for the exceptions and there is a

regularity to the exceptions, then a new schema is created to account for the exceptions. For example, a child might create a schema that indicates that glass things break when they are dropped. Later, a few examples of a glass object that has fallen onto the living room rug are encountered. Rather than abandoning the schema that glass objects break, an exception schema is created that indicates that glass objects that fall on rugs don't break. This is similar to finding an explanation for the exception with three important differences. First, since this is purely data-driven it is possible that the perceived regularity of the exceptions is just a coincidence. Second, there may be multiple ways of characterizing the set of exceptions. For example, all of the examples where a glass object falls on the living room rug can be characterized as glass objects falling on something soft or glass objects falling in a living room. Such an ambiguity may eventually be resolved with further examples such as a glass object falling on a rug in a bedroom. Finally, there is no explanation stored with the exception, such as a soft surface cushions the fall of the glass objects.

4. If there are many unexplained exceptions and there is no regularity to the exceptions, the most specific schema is abandoned since it is not making accurate predictions. In this case, after the schema is abandoned, future memory searches will return a more general schema that does not make the erroneous prediction.

How should several sources of knowledge be integrated into a single learning system? If general theories of causality are ignored for the moment, and attention is restricted to correlational information and prior causal knowledge, then there are four possibilities:

• Correlational information is used exclusively.

- Correlational information is preferred to prior causal knowledge.

- Prior causal knowledge is preferred to correlational information.

- Prior causal knowledge is used exclusively.

In Section 7.7, I review several psychology experiments that assess how correlational information is combined with prior causal knowledge. However, it is also possible to arrive at the same conclusion by considering the implications of each possibility.

If correlational information were used exclusively, then learning would never improve over time. Adults, in a new situation, would adapt as slowly as small children. The problem here is that no matter how much is already known, learning is not constrained by existing knowledge. There is no way to determine which similarities are relevant and which are coincidental. Another problem with relying solely on correlational information is the amount of memory and time required. For example, IPP keeps track of the predictability of individual features rather than combinations of features. Therefore, it can miss some causal relationships. This occurs when no one feature is predictive of another but a combination of features is. For example, in kidnapping when the ransom is demanded from a rich person who has a positive interpersonal relationship with the hostage, one could predict that the ransom would be paid. Of course, if the ransom were demanded from a poor relative or rich stranger, the prediction should not be made. The reason that IPP keeps track of the predictability of individual features rather than combinations is that even for a computer, there are a large number of combinations of features. If only conjunctive combinations (i.e., rich and relative) are considered, then if there are n features, there are 2^n. If a representation of a kidnapping story has 32 features (which seems like a very small number when you consider that the attributes of three people are part of the representation of a kidnapping story), then there are more than four billion combinations (4,294,967,296 to be exact). There is not enough memory in most computers to keep track of all these possibilities.

Relying on prior knowledge alone cannot fully account for learning because it does not explain where this prior knowledge comes from. At first, explanation-based learning may seem confusing. After all, isn't it just learning what is already known? For example, the schemata that OCCAM constructs encodes the same information that was in the several schemata that were combined to produce an explanation. Explanation-based learning produces generalizations that simplify understanding and prediction by storing the novel interactions between several schemata[11]. In this respect, the goals (but not the mechanism) of EBL are similar to those of knowledge compilation (Anderson, 1983) and chunking (Laird et al., 1984).

There has been one learning system constructed that prefers correlational information to existing knowledge. An extension to IPP called UNIMEM (Lebowitz, 1986a; Lebowitz, 1986b; Lebowitz, 1986c) uses this strategy. UNIMEM operates by applying explanation-based learning techniques to generalizations formed by empirical methods rather than explaining and learning from individual examples. UNIMEM first builds a generalization and identifies the predictive and non-predictive features. Then, it treats the predictive features as potential causes and the non-predictive features as potential results. Backward-chaining production rules representing domain knowledge are utilized to produce an explanation of how the predictive features cause the non-predictive features. If no explanation is found for a non-predictive feature it is considered a coincidence and dropped from the generalization. There are two possible reasons that a predictive feature might not be needed to explain non-predictive features: either it is irrelevant to the generalization (and should be dropped from the generalization) or the feature may in fact appear to be cause (i.e., predictive) due to a small number of examples but in fact be a result. To test the later case, UNIMEM tries to explain this potential result in terms of the verified predictive features.

The rationale behind using correlational techniques to discover potential causal relationships, which are then confirmed or denied by domain knowledge, is to control the explanation process. It could be expensive or impractical to use brute force techniques to produce an explanation. Since the predictive features are likely to be causes, UNIMEM's explanation process is more focused. However, UNIMEM is still limited to keeping track of the predictability of individual features rather than combinations of features since it must first form a generalization in the same manner that IPP did. The primary difference between IPP and UNIMEM then is that once UNIMEM builds a generalization, it checks with its existing theories to see if the generalization is consistent with the

---

[11]Dietterich calls this type of learning "symbol-level learning" (Dietterich, 1986) and distinguished it from "knowledge-level learning" in which the learner acquires addition knowledge so that more facts can be deduced (Newell, 1981).

existing theories.   The problem with this approach is that existing knowledge
doesn't guide or control data analysis, but merely censors the results of a data-
driven approach to learning.   It inherits many of the computational problems of
empirical learning techniques, but does solve the problem of determining which
similarities are relevant and which are coincidental.

The remaining alternative is the position I argue for in this book and the
strategy that I have implemented in OCCAM.   The strategy is to attempt to use
existing knowledge to perform EBL from novel examples.   If this fails,
empirical learning techniques are employed to try to create a schema by
searching for a regularity among several examples.   A schema once formed by
correlational means (or even by EBL) can then serve as an existing theory for
future learning.   Therefore, OCCAM prefers EBL utilizing existing knowledge to
empirical learning utilizing correlational information.   In Chapter 7.7, I review
some psychology experiments that demonstrate that people exhibit this same
preference.   However, even if one is not interested in modeling human learning,
there are good reasons to utilize this strategy:

- The demands on resources such as time and memory are minimized.
  Empirical techniques are only tried if EBL fails.   One might argue
  that producing an explanation also places demands on memory.
  However, seeking an explanation for why an event occurred is an
  integral part of understanding one's environment[12].   The only extra
  processing that I am proposing is to generalize and remember the
  explanation.

- Explanation-based learning can easily discover conjunctive
  combinations of features.   For example, explaining why a rich
  parent pays a ransom combines two separate facts: a wealthy person
  is able to pay a ransom, and a parent is willing to pay a ransom.
  Therefore, a good target for kidnapping is someone who is both a
  parent and a wealthy person.   The conjunction is created when these

---

[12]In fact, the affect that people report is a function of the perceived cause of an outcome (Weiner
et al., 1978) (Weiner, 1986).   For example, people typically feel guilty if they fail at a task because
of an internal controllable cause (e.g., not trying hard enough), and feel embarrassed when they fail
due to an internal, uncontrollable cause (e.g., not being tall enough).

two facts are combined. All other possible combinations of features need not be enumerated and considered as they would have to be in UNIMEM for it to learn a conjunctive relationship.

- The learning system will require fewer examples to produce accurate generalizations

In addition to similarity-based and explanation-based learning, OCCAM also utilizes theory-driven learning. How should theory-driven learning be integrated with specific world knowledge and correlational information in a single learning system? In OCCAM, I follow the general strategy that has proved useful in many AI systems of preferring the most specific knowledge (McDermott & Forgy, 1978). The utility of this strategy is best illustrated when a situation fits a general causal pattern that would suggest a causal mechanism which is not consistent with specific knowledge of mechanisms. For example, if someone died of cancer several seconds after the nuclear accident at Three Mile Island, specific knowledge of the time scale of death by cancer should rule out the accident as the cause of the cancer. However, theory-driven learning is preferred to pure empirical learning. The idea here is to allow what ever knowledge a person has (either specific or general) to constrain learning. It is in this manner that future learning can be facilitated by previous learning. Learning improves over time in OCCAM not because OCCAM learns to learn, but rather OCCAM acquires knowledge that constrains future learning.

Figure 2-7 indicates the top-level control structure of OCCAM. It describes the memory update process in OCCAM. Learning (i.e., creating a new schema through generalization or specialization) occurs when no existing schema can account for the outcome of an event.

First, EBL is attempted. If several existing schemata can be chained together to construct an explanation for an outcome that is unaccounted for, then a new schema is created by retaining those features of the example that were needed to produce the explanation. For example, given the knowledge that ice creams melts faster when it's hotter, melted ice cream is sticky, having sticky hands is undesirable, it's cooler in the shade, and trees produce shade, a schema could be created that indicates to avoid sticky hands when eating ice cream, it should be consumed under a tree[13]. The schemata created by explanation-based

---

[13]This example was prompted by a discussion with my daughter Karen when she was three years old.

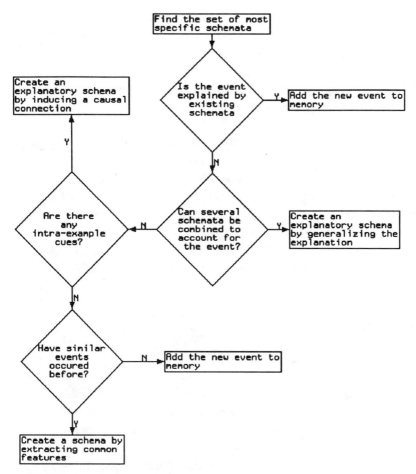

Figure 2-7:   **Top-level control of** OCCAM. **After finding that the most specific schema does not explain the outcome of an event, explanation-based learning is attempted, followed by theory-driven learning and, finally, by similarity-based learning.**

learning allow new situations to be recognized efficiently.

If existing schemata cannot be chained together to form an explanation, theory-driven learning is attempted.   Theory-driven learning operates by determining if a new event matches a known pattern for a causal mechanism. These patterns exploit *intra-example* relationships (i.e., relationships between potential causes and potential effect) to postulate a causal explanation for a temporal relationship. OCCAM contains approximately 20 causal patterns (see

Appendix D). The simplest pattern for a causal relationship indicates that if an action on a particular object immediately precedes a state change for that object, then the action results in the state change. Notice that this pattern requires that the object that the action is performed on be the same as the object that changes. This is an example of an intra-example relationship since there is a constraint between the cause and the effect.

Finally, if explanation-based and theory-driven learning are not successful, then empirical techniques are attempted. Empirical techniques are only applicable if there are a sufficient number of previous examples. If only one example of an event has been encountered, then OCCAM cannot find a regularity and simply remembers the event. When future examples are encountered, this event will be recalled and a regularity can be detected. The empirical techniques are like a safety net. Other techniques are more powerful and efficient, but if they fail, empirical techniques can detect regularities that may be present. The schemata created by empirical techniques allow additional events to be explained.

The theory implemented in OCCAM provides a general framework for learning how to make predictions in the physical and social environment. When there is little specific knowledge of the world, learning is driven mostly by the regularities in the data. It takes many examples for a small child (and OCCAM) to learn about coercion from examples of disputes with playmates and interactions with parents and siblings. Later, learning in familiar domains is mainly knowledge-driven, specializing and combining existing schemata. The knowledge used for EBL is the same knowledge it acquires through empirical learning techniques[14]. Once a child (or OCCAM) has acquired a general framework for coercion from playground arguments and other childhood experiences, learning about kidnapping and economic sanctions is simplified and someday the child may just grow up to work for the FBI or the Rand corporation. The data-intensive strategies provide the necessary background knowledge for later, knowledge-intensive learning.

---

[14]In people, much knowledge is acquired by teaching (formal or otherwise). In the machine learning literature, this has been called learning by being told (Winston, 1977). For example, the mechanism of transmission of common diseases are taught, rather than rediscovered by many individuals. In addition to knowledge acquired through SBL and TDL some of OCCAM's knowledge (e.g., the laws of supply and demand) are programmed in by hand.

An implication of the theory proposed in this book is that people and OCCAM have no real justification for their base-level beliefs. Simple causal laws may be supported only by the fact that they have worked well in the past. For example, one may not know <u>why</u> glass objects are fragile but only <u>that</u> glass objects are fragile. By "know why", I mean able to be inferred from other established facts and laws, perhaps knowledge of the molecular structure of glass and axioms that predict strength of materials from their molecular structure[15].

Although the base-level beliefs do not provide a sound foundation, acquisition of new knowledge can nonetheless build on this foundation. For example, if a person accepts as fact that glass objects are fragile, then this knowledge can be used to later learn that if one eats food from a glass container that has been dropped on the floor, a sliver of glass may cause a cut. The alternative to using "unjustified" knowledge such as glass objects are fragile to assist learning in this situation is to wait for more observations of eating food from fractured containers to arrive at the same conclusion. It seems fortunate that people do indeed form such base-level beliefs without logical justification. I am not attempting to answer a philosophical question of when one can be justified in predicting the future from past observations. Instead, I am proposing an answer to a psychological question of what information and processes people use when predicting the outcome of future events.

2.5. Summary

In this chapter, I presented the problems that I address in this volume. The central problem is the acquisition of explanatory schemata that predict the consequences of actions. There are three mechanisms for schema acquisition proposed.

1. Similarity-based learning creates new schemata by extracting features common to several examples. By making a prediction with such a schema, one is assuming that regularity detected in

---

[15]Even if one did know why glass objects are fragile, the problem that there is no real justification for the base-level beliefs exists. In this instance, the base-level beliefs are simply the axioms that predict strength of material from their composition. It is easy to see that this problem can regress infinitely. At some level, the only justification for a belief will be several observations, yet past observations of what has happened impose no logical restriction on what will happen in the future.

observed examples will hold in unobserved examples. This learning technique can propose absurd causal relationships (e.g., when Billy Martin is named to coach the New York Yankees, the stock market declines).

2. Theory-driven learning imposes additional constraints on cause and effect relationships by requiring that a proposed relationship conform to one of a number of common patterns of causal relationships.

3. Explanation-based learning produces schemata that encode novel interactions between existing schemata.

The central issue addressed in this book is the integration of these three learning techniques into a system that can exploit the most advantageous strategy to learn in familiar and unfamiliar domains.

OCCAM prefers to create new schema with explanation-based learning because this strategy does not require a large number of examples. If explanation-based learning is not appropriate because there is not enough knowledge to explain a surprising outcome, OCCAM attempts theory-driven learning, by focusing on those features of an event and its outcome that conform to common patterns of causal relationships. If all else fails, OCCAM attempts similarity-based learning to attempt to find some regularity in several examples. In any situation, OCCAM attempts to apply the most knowledge-intensive learning method that is applicable. In well-understood domains, learning is rapid because new schemata merely encode novel implications of existing knowledge. In unfamiliar domains, similarity-based and theory-driven learning, more data-intensive learning strategies, propose simple causal relationships that can serve as background knowledge for later explanation-based learning.

Chapter 3
Similarity-Based Learning in OCCAM

In this chapter, I illustrate the similarity-based learning process in OCCAM. Recall that this process is only attempted if there is no specific knowledge that would account for the outcome of an example and the example does not fit a known pattern for a causal relationship. In this case, the only type of learning that is applicable is similarity-based learning.

The first step in similarity-based learning is to detect a regularity between the outcome of a new event and the outcome of previously encountered similar events. Therefore, it is quite important to find clusters of events that share similar features. OCCAM is an unsupervised learning program that does not require a teacher to classify examples. Rather, OCCAM incrementally learns new concepts from examples as a natural consequence of constructing a memory that explains and predicts the outcome of new events. A teacher does not classify instances of concepts as positive or negative examples for OCCAM. Instead, the environment performs the classifications since OCCAM is designed to group together previous events with similar outcomes. Section 3.2 describes this process in more detail.

Once a set of events has been identified as a useful cluster, the second step is to construct a general description of the class of events. OCCAM takes a conservative approach to constructing this general description. The most specific description that is consistent with the examples is selected in a manner similar to Bruner's wholist strategy (Bruner et al., 1956). This strategy acknowledges that the initial concept description is bound to be wrong. By choosing the most specific consistent description, the revision process is simplified considerably. The only type of revision necessary is to delete parts of the concept description that do not describe later examples. The details of the incremental generalization process are described in Section 3.3.

Finally, when adding a new event to memory, the impact of this new example must be accessed. If the new event confirms a prediction of an existing schema, the support for that schema is increased. On the other hand, if the event contradicts a prediction of an existing schema, the support for that schema is decreased. The idea here is that the confirmation process should be able to tolerate some noise in the data. Sometimes, when a glass cup is dropped, it doesn't break. Section 3.4 describes this process in more detail.

3.1. Similarity-based learning and memory organization

A hierarchically organized memory of explanatory schemata has been proposed by some in artificial intelligence and cognitive psychology (Schank, 1982) as a model of human episodic memory. In this style of memory, a new experience is understood, missing attributes are inferred, and explanations are generated by finding the most specific schema in memory that accounts for the new experience. Here, we discuss IPP and CYRUS, two programs that organize memories of explanatory schemata.

3.1.1. IPP

IPP (Lebowitz, 1980) is a program that reads, remembers, and makes generalizations from newspaper stories about international terrorism. Its major contribution is on the role of a memory in understanding text. IPP starts with a set of MOPs (Schank, 1982) which describe general situations such as extortion. After adding examples of events to its memory, it creates more specialized MOPs (spec-MOPs). Spec-MOPs are created by noticing the common features of several examples. For example, after reading a number of newspaper stories, IPP created a generalization describing the fact that shootings in Italy often result in leg wounds. IPP would use this generalization to aid the understanding of future stories. For example, it could predict that there might be a leg wound when reading about a shooting in Italy. This prediction could enable the parser to select the proper sense of the word "calf" (i.e., "part of the leg" rather than "young cow").

Not all features of a generalization in IPP are treated equally. Some features are predictive; their presence allows IPP to infer the other features if they are not present. The predictive features are those that are unique (or nearly unique) to that generalization. The features that appear in many generalizations are non-predictive. IPP keeps track of the number of times a feature is included in generalizations. The idea is that the predictive features are likely to be causes of the non-predictive features. In the above example, the fact that the location of the shooting is Italy allows one to make the prediction that the shooting is in the legs. However, the fact that the shooting is in the legs does not allow one to make the prediction that the location of the shooting is Italy. The difference is that in all (or most) cases of shootings in Italy, the wound was in a leg. Therefore, the feature `country = Italy` is predictive of the feature `wound-location = leg`. However, IPP has seen a number of terrorist incidents in which shootings were in the leg and many of these were not in Italy. Therefore, the feature `wound-location = leg` is non-predictive.

3.1.2. CYRUS

CYRUS (Kolodner, 1984) implements a theory of long term memory. It records many experiences of former Secretary of State Cyrus Vance (e.g., diplomatic trips, negotiations etc.). It organizes events in memory and searches memory to recall events.   An important aspect of the theory of memory implemented in CYRUS is that recall is reconstructive. Rather than storing all information about each event in memory, CYRUS only stores the information that differs from the norm of that type of event. For example, when an experience such as a diplomatic trip to Israel is added to memory, such things as the landing of a plane are not recorded. However, CYRUS could still retrieve this information if requested by reconstructing it from the diplomatic trip MOP. In effect, if CYRUS were asked "Has Cyrus Vance ever landed in Israel?" it would search its memory to see if Cyrus Vance has ever had a diplomatic trip whose destination was Israel. If Vance did have a trip to Israel, CYRUS would reconstruct the fact that he must have landed in Israel.

There are several advantages to this sort of memory organization:

- Knowledge can be represented at various levels of generality.

- Retrieval   of   individual   events   (and   specializations)   is reconstructive. For example, the kidnapping episodes do not need to contain the knowledge that the demand is to pay a ransom. Instead, this information is encoded in the kidnapping schema and can be accessed when necessary.

- Individual events which are similar to each other are indexed under the same schema.   This facilitates building new schemata by extracting common features from a number of events since the entire memory need not be searched to find similar events.

• Predictions and expectations are made by traversing memory to find the most specific schema which accounts for a new event. In effect, the hierarchy of schemata serves as a discrimination net for finding explanations.

The major contribution of CYRUS is a process model of retrieval. CYRUS also addressed the issue of building new MOPs. When several events differ from a norm in the same manner, CYRUS creates a new MOP to organize those similar experiences by extracting common features from the events.

3.1.3. Empirical learning

Both CYRUS and IPP perform two learning tasks. First, these programs *aggregate* individual events into clusters (Fisher & Langley, 1985) by locating events that share similar features. In addition, these programs generalize clusters of events by extracting similar features from these events. Both IPP and CYRUS form the most specific conjunctive generalization that is consistent with the data.

A series of experiments in concept learning were described by Bruner, Goodnow and Austin (Bruner et al., 1956). The stimuli were a number of rectangular cards differing in various features such as number of objects on the card, shape of objects on the card, and color of the objects on the card. Each subject was presented examples one at a time and was asked to indicate whether the example was positive (i.e., an example of the concept to be learned) or negative (i.e., not an example of the concept to be learned). Then the subject was told the correct answer. This continued until the subject demonstrated that he had learned the concept by making no mistakes on a number of additional examples.

Bruner, Goodnow and Austin discovered that most of the subjects used one of two concept acquisition strategies. Approximately 65 percent of the subjects used the *wholist strategy* (see Figure 3-1).

The wholist strategy has several interesting properties. First, it is guaranteed to converge on the correct answer[16] by making the hypothesis more

---

[16]Provided that the correct answer can be expressed as a conjunction of features.

1. Take the set of all features of the first positive
   instance as the initial hypothesis.

2. As more examples are presented, revise the
   hypothesis according to the following table:

	Positive instance	Negative instance
Correct	Maintain the same hypothesis	Maintain the same hypothesis
Incorrect	Make the new hypothesis the set of features which the old hypothesis and the new example have in common	This cannot occur

Figure 3-1:   The wholist strategy for concept acquisition.

general when a positive instance is incorrectly judged to be a negative instance.
Second, it is impossible to incorrectly classify an example as negative since this
would imply a too general hypothesis[17]. Third, it is not necessary to remember
previous examples when revising the hypothesis.   The current hypothesis
"summarizes" the previous examples. Finally, the ultimate description of the
concept found when using this strategy is the most specific description that is
consistent with the data.   The approach to learning in IPP and CYRUS is
essentially the wholist strategy.

The second strategy that Bruner, Goodnow and Austin found was used by
about 35 percent of the subjects.   This strategy, called the *part-scanning
strategy*, is illustrated in Figure 3-2.

Subjects who use the part scanning strategy are in effect gambling. By not
including all features common to all examples, it is possible to quickly guess the
correct definition of the concept. The price paid for this gamble is a complex
revision if the hypothesis is incorrect[18]. The subject must remember all positive

---

[17]Berwick calls this property "the subset principle" (Berwick, 1986).

[18]It should be noted that if there is some *a priori* reason for including or ignoring certain features,
the gamble of the part-scanning strategy pays off, since fewer examples are needed to arrive at the
correct conclusion.

1. Take a subset of the features of the first positive
   instance as the initial hypothesis.

2. As more examples are presented, revise the
   hypothesis according to the following table:

	Positive instance	Negative instance
Correct	Maintain the same hypothesis	Maintain the same hypothesis
Incorrect	Revise hypothesis to make it consistent with past examples.	Revise hypothesis to make it consistent with past examples.

Figure 3-2:   The part-scanning strategy for concept acquisition.

instances, all negative instances, and all previous hypotheses to select a new, different hypothesis that correctly classifies all previous instances. Since there are significant demands on memory it is often the case that a subject utilizing part scanning will choose a hypothesis that is not consistent with all previous examples.

3.1.4. Empirical learning techniques

The approaches to learning proposed by Lebowitz, Koloder, and Bruner et al. all share a common theme. They utilize one source of information when creating a general description of a number of examples. This source of information is the data. Hence, these learning techniques are called empirical learning techniques. Often, these techniques operate by finding similarities among a number of examples and these techniques are also called similarity-based learning (SBL).

The task of learning an explanatory schema from experiences could be approached solely with empirical techniques. In particular, these approaches to learning concepts from examples all include techniques for finding the similarities between a number of examples and revising hypotheses that make wrong classifications or predictions. Empirical learning techniques are important for detecting regularities in data. However, one important ability is lacking: the ability to find an explanation for regularities in the data. Empirical learning techniques cannot distinguish between coincidental and relevant similarities.

Similarity-based learning in OCCAM was derived from IPP (Lebowitz, 1980). There are three major differences between IPP and SBL in OCCAM:

- In IPP, attribute values are atomic. In OCCAM, attribute values can be composite values that have their own attributes.

- OCCAM has a special type of attribute value called a role token. Recall that a role token indicates that the value of one attribute must be identical to an attribute of the activity. Role tokens allow a limited form of structured concepts to be generalized.

- In IPP, each training example consists of a single object. In OCCAM, a training example is an observation (i.e., a network of actions, activities and state changes connected by temporal and intentional links).

In the following sections, I present the similarity-based learning method of OCCAM and focus on the extensions to IPP necessary to acquire the more complex concepts that may serve as the background theory for EBL.

3.2. Aggregation

There are two major steps in finding a cluster of similar events to generalize when a new event is added to memory. The first step is to classify a new event by finding the most specific schemata that accounts for a new event. The second step is to find events that have features in common with the new event.

3.2.1. Classifying a new event

The memory organization in OCCAM classifies a new event according to the existing hierarchy of schemata. OCCAM starts with an initial hierarchy of schemata that represent the Conceptual Dependency actions, goals and states (see Figure 3-3). As new events are added to memory, the hierarchy is extended by creating specializations of the existing schema. The more specialized schemata are treated identically to the initial schemata.

Classifying a new event consists of finding the set of the most specific schemata in memory. The algorithm for traversing memory to find the most

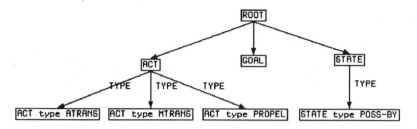

Figure 3-3:   Part of the initial hierarchy of schemata in OCCAM.

specific schemata is illustrated in Figure 1-8 on page 40. In general, there can be more than one schemata returned by memory traversal. For example, a new event, such as "Karen asking her mother to give her an apple", might have two most specific schemata: "The goals of Karen" and "Asking another person to achieve one's goal". Schank calls the latter schema **delta-agency** (Schank & Abelson, 1977). If more than one schema is returned when adding a new event to memory, the event is indexed under each schema. In addition, each schema may be further specialized by the learning mechanism described in this book. In practice, however, OCCAM typically finds only one most specific schema. This is a result of organizing memory with a single intent: to predict the outcome of events.

3.2.2. Finding similar events

Once a most specific schema has been found, retrievable events that have previously been indexed under that schema are examined to attempt to find a regularity between the new example and some prior examples. The set of events that OCCAM considers to be similar is a function of a number of things. First, all events that are indexed under a particular schema share some features in the first place. This is why they were indexed under the same schema. Only those features that elaborate on the generalized event for the most specific schema are considered (i.e., those features that are not included in the generalized event). Second, only those events that are *retrievable* can be included in the set of similar events. An event is retrievable if it has at least one feature that is compatible with the corresponding feature of the new event and there are not many[19] events that are indexed by this feature. The idea here is that features

---

[19]This is a parameter in OCCAM. The exact value is not crucial, but it should be a small integer. Currently, the value of this parameter is four.

that are unique or nearly unique are good retrieval cues (Kolodner, 1984). Finally, the set of similar events is also dependent on the number of features that a potential cluster of events has in common.

An example will help to make this process a little more concrete. Assume that the new event describes the situation where Karen asks her father, Mike, for a slice of pizza and her father gives it to her. The Conceptual Dependency representation of this situation is illustrated in Figure 3-4. For the remainder of this example, I will refer to this event as `pizza-1`. This example is simplified somewhat because it does not consider the intentional links that relate this goal to other plans and actions. In Section 3.3.4, the processing of intentional links is discussed. However, at this point, it is worth noting that the presence of intentional links does not affect the aggregation process. Rather than repeating all of the features of Karen, Mike, and the pizza in the representation of `pizza-1` in this figure, a short hand notation is used. The first time each concept is encountered a `unique-id` is given as one of the features. The remaining times that the same concept appears, the only feature listed is the `unique-id`. The `unique-id` is a means of noting when two concepts are identical. For example, if a glass cup is dropped on the floor, one might predict that particular glass cup (rather than any glass cup) will break. In this figure, `pizza.001` is used as the unique-id for the pizza, and `karen` is used as the unique-id for the actor.

In this example, assume the memory is as illustrated in Figure 3-5. In this case, the most specific schema for `pizza-1` is `goal`. Also, the following events are already in memory and they are indexed under `goal`.

1. `zoo-1`: Karen wants to go to the zoo. She asks Mike to take her to the zoo. Her goal succeeds. The CD representation of this event is in Figure 3-6.

2. `refrigerator-1`: Karen wants to open the refrigerator. She pulls on the door, but it doesn't open. The CD representation of this event is in Figure 3-7.

3. `play-doh-1`: Lynn wants some Play Doh. She asks Mike to give her some, and her goal succeeds. The CD representation of this event is in Figure 3-8.

```
GOAL actor HUMAN name KAREN
                age KID
                hair BLOND
                eyes BLUE
                unique-id karen
    goal STATE type POSS-BY
                actor HUMAN unique-id karen
                value YES
                object P-OBJ type FOOD
                            stype PIZZA
                            unique-id pizza.001
    plan ACT type MTRANS
                actor HUMAN unique-id karen
                to HUMAN name MIKE
                            relation IPT type FAMILY-REL
                                        stype FATHER
                                        of HUMAN unique-id karen

                        age GROWN-UP
                        hair BROWN
                        eyes GREEN
                        unique-id mike
            object ACT type ATRANS
                        actor HUMAN unique-id mike
                        object P-OBJ unique-id pizza.001
                        to HUMAN unique-id karen
    outcome GOAL-OUTCOME type SUCCESS
                        actor HUMAN unique-id karen
                        goal STATE type POSS-BY
                                    actor HUMAN unique-id karen
                                    value YES
                                    object P-OBJ unique-id pizza.001
```

Figure 3-4: pizza-1: Karen has a goal of possessing a slice of pizza. Her plan is to ask Mike for a slice of pizza. Her goal succeeds.

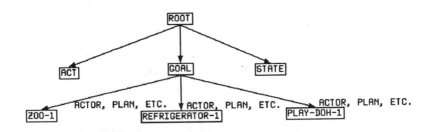

Figure 3-5: OCCAM's memory before pizza-1 is added. Three events are indexed under the goal schema.

The events in memory under goal are indexed by those features that elaborate on goal. Since goal has no features, there is an index for each feature of each event. For example, zoo-1 is indexed by the actor (Karen), the goal (be at the zoo), the plan (ask Mike to take Karen to the zoo), and the outcome (Karen's goal of being at the zoo succeeds).

What should the criteria be for finding a similar event? In UNIMEM, for

```
GOAL actor HUMAN name KAREN
                age KID
                hair BLOND
                eyes BLUE
                unique-id karen
        goal STATE type LOCATION
                actor HUMAN unique-id karen
                value YES
                object P-OBJ type LOCATION
                        stype ZOO
                        unique-id zoo.1
        plan ACT type MTRANS
                actor HUMAN unique-id karen
                to HUMAN name MIKE
                        relation IPT type FAMILY-REL
                                stype FATHER
                                of HUMAN unique-id karen
                        age GROWN-UP
                        hair BROWN
                        eyes GREEN
                        unique-id mike
                object ACT type PTRANS
                        actor HUMAN unique-id mike
                        object HUMAN unique-id karen
                        to P-OBJ type LOCATION
                                stype ZOO
                                unique-id zoo.1
        outcome GOAL-OUTCOME type SUCCESS
                actor HUMAN unique-id karen
                goal STATE type LOCATION
                        actor HUMAN unique-id karen
                        value YES
                        object P-OBJ unique-id zoo.1
```

Figure 3-6: zoo-1: Karen wants to go to the zoo. She asks Mike to take her to the zoo. Her goal succeeds.

```
GOAL actor HUMAN name KAREN
                age KID
                hair BLOND
                eyes BLUE
                unique-id karen
        goal STATE object P-OBJ type REFRIGERATOR
                                color WHITE
                                unique-id ref.001
                type OPEN
                value YES
        plan ACT type PROPEL
                actor HUMAN unique-id karen
                object COMPONENT type DOOR
                        of P-OBJ unique-id ref.001
        outcome GOAL-OUTCOME type FAILURE
                actor HUMAN unique-id karen
                goal STATE object P-OBJ unique-id ref.001
                        type OPEN
                        value YES
```

Figure 3-7: refrigerator-1: Karen wants to open the refrigerator. She pulls on the door, but it doesn't open.

an event to be considered similar, it must have a number of features that are exactly equal to the new event. Exact equality makes sense in UNIMEM because the features in UNIMEM are atomic. In contrast, in OCCAM, the values of features can be composite objects that have their own features. If exact equality were used in OCCAM, then zoo-1 and refrigerator-1 would be included in a cluster with pizza-1, since the actors of these events are

```
GOAL actor HUMAN name LYNN
                 age KID
                 hair BLOND
                 eyes BLUE
                 unique-id lynn
       goal STATE type POSS-BY
                 actor HUMAN unique-id lynn
                 value YES
                 object P-OBJ type TOY
                               stype PLAY-DOH
                               unique-id play-doh.1
       plan ACT type MTRANS
                 actor HUMAN unique-id lynn
                 to HUMAN name MIKE
                          relation IPT type FAMILY-REL
                                       stype FATHER
                                       of HUMAN unique-id lynn
                          age GROWN-UP
                          hair BROWN
                          eyes GREEN
                          unique-id mike
                 object ACT type ATRANS
                            actor HUMAN unique-id mike
                            object P-OBJ unique-id play-doh.1
                            to HUMAN unique-id lynn
       outcome GOAL-OUTCOME type SUCCESS
                            actor HUMAN unique-id lynn
                            goal STATE type POSS-BY
                                       actor HUMAN unique-id lynn
                                       value YES
                                       object P-OBJ unique-id play-doh.1
```

Figure 3-8: play-doh-1: Lynn wants some Play Doh.   She asks
Mike to give her some, and her goal succeeds.

identical. However, since these share only one feature, such a cluster would not
be useful.   The generalization built to describe this cluster would find all
common features of the goals of Karen.   Since the goals of Karen are varied
there are no features in common between these three events.   Intuitively, it
seems that zoo-1, play-doh-1 should be included in a cluster with
pizza-1 since they are all about asking someone to achieve a goal.   The
problem is that they differ according to the details of what the goal is and how it
can be achieved. The solution to this problem is to ignore these details.

In OCCAM, "ignoring the details" consists of looking for compatibility of
two events only to a certain level of detail.   This is implementing by first
constructing a skeleton of the new event by retaining more[20] levels of detail than
the generalized event of the most specific schema. A skeleton of pizza-1
with respect to the goal schema that includes one additional level of detail is
illustrated in Figure 3-9.   The skeleton with two levels of detail is shown in
Figure 3-10. This is the skeleton used in this example since this parameter was
set to 2. The amount of detail in the skeleton varies according to the contents of

[20]This is a parameter in OCCAM. The value used in this example is two.

memory. The skeleton does not simply retain two levels of detail from the new event. Instead, it retains two levels of detail more than the schema.

```
GOAL actor HUMAN
     goal STATE
     plan ACT
     outcome GOAL-OUTCOME
```

Figure 3-9:   A "skeleton" of `pizza-1` that retains one level of detail more than the `goal` schema.

```
GOAL actor HUMAN name KAREN
                 age KID
                 hair BLOND
                 eyes BLUE
                 unique-id karen
     goal STATE type POSS-BY
                actor HUMAN
                value YES
                object P-OBJ
     plan ACT type MTRANS
              actor HUMAN
              to HUMAN
              object ACT
     outcome GOAL-OUTCOME type SUCCESS
                          actor HUMAN
                          goal STATE
```

Figure 3-10:   A "skeleton" of `pizza-1` that retains two levels of details.

The aggregation process is illustrated in Figure 3-11. Once the skeleton of the new event with respect to the most specific schema has been created, the features of the skeleton are used as retrieval cues. Each feature of the skeleton is compared to the indices to attempt to retrieve similar events that share a number of features[21]. Each feature of the skeleton produces a cluster of events. The largest cluster (provided it is larger than three[22] events) is generalized to create a new schema by the process to be described in Section 3.3.

---

[21]The number of features that are compatible with the skeleton is a parameter of the OCCAM. Since the structures in OCCAM are bushy (i.e., that have few features, but each feature is complex), the value of the parameter should be very small. The value used in this example is two.

[22]This is another parameter of OCCAM. Its value should be smaller than the retrievability threshold so that OCCAM doesn't forget events before they are generalized.

```
Aggregate[Event, Schema]
     Skeleton ← CreateSkeleton[Event, Schema]
   Cluster ← ()
      for each F of Cdfeatures[Skeleton]
          Events ← RetreiveEvents[Schema, F]
          Events ← LargestSubset[F, Skeleton, Events]
          if length[Cluster] < length[Events]
              then Cluster ← Events
      add Event to Cluster
      if length[Cluster] ≥ MinClusterSize
         then return Cluster
         else return ()
```

Figure 3-11: Aggregate[Event, Schema]: The procedure that finds a set of similar events to generalize.

The procedure **RetrieveEvents** returns all of the events that are indexed under a schema by a compatible feature. Figure 3-12 illustrates this in more detail. The definition of **Compatible** is illustrated in Figure 3-13. Two concept descriptions are compatible if they are equal, or if for each feature that they have in common, the corresponding feature values are compatible. Finally, the procedure **LargestSubset** (Figure 3-14) finds largest subset of the retrieved events that have at least one other feature compatible with the new event. These procedures make use of the following primitive procedures:

CdHead[Cd]: returns the head of the CD structure. E.g., CdHead[(human name (john) gender (male))] is human.

CdFeatures[CD]: returns the set of features associated with a CD structure. Each feature is a pair of attributes and values.

FeatureName[Feature]: returns the name of a feature (e.g., actor).

FeatureValue[Feature]: returns a CD structure that is the attribute value.

Filler[Cd, FeatureName]: returns the value of the feature with FeatureName of Cd (or false if there is no feature or value).

MakeCD[Head, Features]: creates a new CD structure with the specified head and features.

MakeFeature[Name, Value]: creates a new feature with the specified feature name and feature value.

```
RetrieveEvents[Schema, Feature]
        Events ← ()
        Value ← FeatureValue[Feature]
        for each Index of Schema
            if Name[Index] = FeatureName[Feature]
               and Count[Index] < RetrievabilityThreshold
               and Compatible[Value[Index], Value]
               then add Event[Index] to Events.
        return Events
```

Figure 3-12: RetrieveEvents[Schema,   Feature]:   The
            procedure that retrieves events similar to Event
            indexed under Schema by Feature.

```
Compatible[Cd1, Cd2]
        if CdHead[Cd1] ≠ CdHead[Cd2]
           then return false
        Value ← true
        for each Feature in CdFeatures[Cd1] while Value
            Name ← FeatureName[Feature]
            Filler1 ← FeatureValue[Feature]
            Filler2 ← Filler[Cd2, Name]
            if Filler2
               then if not[Compatible[Filler1, Filler2]]
                       Value ← false
        return Value
```

Figure 3-13: Compatible[Cd1,   Cd2]:   The   procedure   that
            determines if two CD structures are compatible.

3.2.3. Finding similar events: An example

In order to create a schema using similarity-based methods, OCCAM must
find a number of previous events that share a number of features with a new
event. The previous section describes the process that finds a suitable cluster of
events for generalizing in OCCAM. To illustrate how this process finds a useful
cluster, I continue the example introduced in the previous section. Recall that
memory contains three events (zoo-1, refrigerator-1, and
play-doh-1) indexed under the goal schema when the new event,
pizza-1, is added to memory.

When pizza-1 is added to memory, goal is found to be the most
specific schema. The skeleton of pizza-1 that is illustrated in Figure 3-10 on

```
LargestSubset[Feature, Skeleton, Events]
     Cluster ← ()
        for each NewFeature of Skeleton
            TempCluster ← ()
            if NewFeature ≠ Feature
                then Cd ← FeatureValue[NewFeature]
                     Name ← FeatureName[NewFeature]
                     for each NewEvent in Events
                            F ← Filler[NewEvent, Name]
                            if F and Compatible[Cd, F]
                                then add NewEvent to TempCluster
                 if length[Cluster] < length[TempCluster]
                 then Cluster ← TempCluster
          return Cluster
```

Figure 3-14: LargestSubset[Feature, Skeleton, Events]:
The procedure that finds the largest subset of Events
that have at least two features in common that are
compatible with the corresponding features of
Skeleton.

page 83 is constructed. Each of the features of the skeleton is used by
Aggregate as a retrieval cue. RetrieveEvents finds the following sets of
events for each feature:

1. actor: {zoo-1 refrigerator-1}

2. goal: {play-doh-1}

3. plan: {zoo-1 play-doh-1}

4. outcome: {zoo-1 play-doh-1}

For each of these potential clusters, LargestSubset finds the largest
cluster of events that have at least one other feature in common that is
compatible with the skeleton. In the case that two clusters are of the same size,
one is selected arbitrarily. These clusters are:

1. actor: {zoo-1} (other compatible feature is plan)

2. goal: {play-doh-1} (other compatible feature is plan)

3. plan: {zoo-1 play-doh-1} (other compatible feature is
   outcome)

4. `outcome`: `{zoo-1 play-doh-1}` (other compatible feature is
   `plan`)

Finally, **Aggregate** selects the largest of these potential clusters as a cluster to be generalized and adds the new event to that cluster. If two clusters are of the same size, one is selected arbitrarily. In this example, the final cluster consists of `zoo-1`, `play-doh-1` and `pizza-1`. These three events represent those goals that succeeded and whose plan was to ask someone to perform an act (that achieves the goal). Once retrieved, these events are generalized to create a new schemata. In the next section, I describe OCCAM's generalization algorithm.

3.3. Constructing a General Description of a Cluster of Events

The strategy for SBL in OCCAM is to find all features that a cluster of events have in common. This is similar to the wholist strategy proposed by Bruner (Bruner et al., 1956). The primary difference is that Bruner's strategy is entirely incremental. It assumes the general description to be learned is initially the first positive example, and removes features from the general description that are not present in new positive examples. In contrast, the strategy implemented in OCCAM waits until a small number of examples are encountered and the general description is all features that these examples have in common. The reason for the difference is that OCCAM does not have a teacher to categorize examples for it. Rather, it waits until several events share a number of features, determines that these events should form a cluster, and creates a new schema by generalizing the events. The idea here is that a few initial events are formed into a new schema that will be further refined as more events are added to memory. Section 3.4 describes the refinement of schemata when additional episodes are encountered.

3.3.1. Finding common features

The approach that OCCAM takes to find all common features of a number of events is straightforward. First, all features in common between two arbitrarily selected events is found to create a general description. Next, the general description is updated by successively finding all features in common between it and the remaining event. The order in which the events are processed does not affect the final result.

The procedure that OCCAM uses to find all features in common between two events (or generalized events) is illustrated in Figure 3-15. This procedure ensures that the heads of two CD structures are identical. If the heads are identical, the procedure then recursively collects generalizations of all features that the two CD structures have in common.

```
MakeGeneralCd[E1, E2]
       if CdHead[E1] ≠ CdHead[E2]
          then return false
       Features ← ()
       for each Feature in CdFeatures[E1]
          Name ← FeatureName[Feature]
          Value1 ← FeatureValue[Feature]
          Value2 ←  Filler[E2, Name]
          if Value2
             then V ← MakeGeneralCd[Value1, Value2]
                  if V
                     then Feature2 ← MakeFeature[Name, V]
                          add Feature2 to Features
       return MakeCd[CdHead[E1], Features]
```

Figure 3-15: MakeGeneralCd[E1, E2]: The procedure that finds all features in common between two events.

3.3.2. Finding common features: An example

In this section, I continue the example of Section 3.2.3. The aggregation process has found a cluster of events (zoo-1, play-doh-1 and pizza-1) to be generalized. Figure 3-16 illustrates the result of finding all common features of these events. Note that to conserve space in the diagram, the first time a subconcept appears, a unique-id is given as one of the features and this notation is used for the subconcept when it is repeated. This generalization indicates that when a child with blue eyes and blond hair wants something and asks her father Mike who has brown hair and green eyes, the child's goal will succeed. Obviously, this generalization is not accurate, but it is a reasonable starting point. In Section 3.4.1, I describe how this generalization is refined by encountering more examples. Much of the generalization is too specific, such as the hair and eye color of the people involved, as well as the outcome.

3.3.3. Creating a new schema

Once a generalized event representation has been created, by the similarity-based means described in the previous section, or by theory-driven learning described in Chapter 4 or explanation-based learning described in Chapter 5, a

```
GOAL actor HUMAN age KID
                 hair BLOND
                 eyes BLUE
                 unique-id p.1
     goal STATE actor HUMAN unique-id p.1
                value YES
                object P-OBJ unique-id obj.1
     plan ACT type MTRANS
                actor HUMAN unique-id p.1
                to HUMAN name MIKE
                       relation IPT type FAMILY-REL
                                     stype FATHER
                                     of HUMAN unique-id p.1
                         age GROWN-UP
                         hair BROWN
                         eyes GREEN
                         unique-id p.2
                object ACT actor HUMAN unique-id p.2
     outcome GOAL-OUTCOME type SUCCESS
                actor HUMAN unique-id p.1
                goal STATE actor HUMAN unique-id p.1
                           value YES
                           object P-OBJ unique-id obj.1
```

Figure 3-16: **A generalized event formed by finding all the features in common between zoo-1, play-doh-1 and pizza-1.**

new schema is created. A new schema will contain the generalized event that serves as a template for recognizing new events as instances of the schema. The following steps are followed to index the new schema in memory so that it can be found by future memory searches.

1. Indices from each event in the cluster of similar events are removed from the most specific schema.

2. The new schema is indexed in memory under the most specific schema by those features that elaborate on the most specific schema.

3. The new event and each similar event are indexed by those features that elaborate on the new schema.

The impact of creating the new specialized goal schema on the organization of memory is shown in Figure 3-17. The event **refrigerator-1** and the specialized goal schema are indexed under **goal**. The events **zoo-1**, **play-doh-1** and **pizza-1** are indexed under the new schema. This organization allows the new schema to be located as the most specific schema when appropriate during future memory searches. In addition, the events indexed under the new schema can be found to specialize this schema even further. For example, if a new episode, such as Karen receiving an apple from

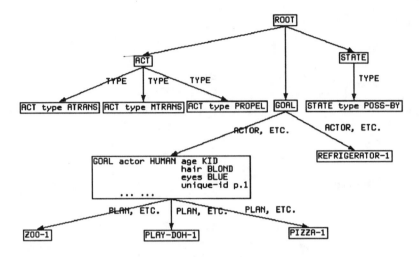

Figure 3-17: A picture of OCCAM's memory after the goal schema is specialized by extracting the common features of zoo-1, play-doh-1 and pizza-1.

Mike after she asks for it, is added to memory a new specialization will be created. This specialization will find the common features of play-doh-1, pizza-1 and the new event. These events elaborate on the goal feature, which is "to possess an object", and the plan feature which is "to ask for the object to be given" (see Figure 3-18).

3.3.4. Intentional links

In the discussion in the previous sections of aggregation and generalization, it was assumed that each input to OCCAM was a single Conceptual Dependency structure that was not related to any other structure. However, the actual input to OCCAM is a Conceptual Dependency structure that is related by intentional links to other Conceptual Dependency structures. In the examples in the previous sections, the input was a single goal. The relationship between play-doh-1 and other actions, plans, and goals is also represented. Figure 3-19 shows the network of related goals. To conserve space, the action, plans, and goals are given in English rather than CD[23].

The presence of intentional links does not alter the aggregation process nor

---

[23]Figure 1-2 on page 29 shows part of the CD representation of this example.

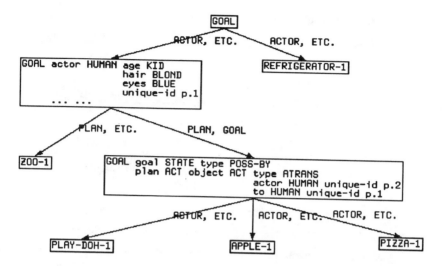

Figure 3-18: A schema that represents an actor's goal of possessing an object that is accomplished by asking someone to give the object to the actor. This schema is indexed under the specialization of the goal schema in Figure 3-17.

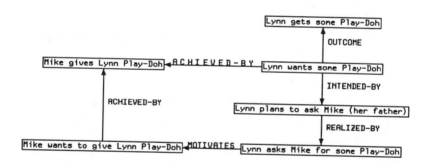

Figure 3-19: The relationship between play-doh-1 (i.e., Lynn wants some Play-Doh) and other actions, plans, and goals is represented by intentional links.

the creation of the generalized event. However, there are several complications that arise:

- One of the concepts from the network must be selected as the main concept. The memory search for the most specific schema utilizes just this main concept. Similarly, the search for similar episodes indexed under the most specific schema just utilizes the main concept. In OCCAM, since the input is in CD rather than English, the main concept is identified for OCCAM. However, there have been a number of natural language processing systems that locate the main concept of short stories (DeJong, 1977; Lehnert, 1982; Wilensky, 1982). The main concept in these systems is identified so that a reasonable summary of the story can be generated.

• In addition to extracting the common features of the main concepts, the common features of the concepts related to the main concept by identical intentional links are also found. It is in this manner, that not only is a goal generalized, but the means of accomplishing that goal are also generalized and linked to the generalized event of the main concept.

• When the network of generalized events connected together by intentional links is large, a **macro-schema** is created. In OCCAM, there are two types of schemata: simple schemata and macro-schemata.

A simple schema contains a generalized event that may be connected by means of intentional links to a small number of other generalized events. In addition, a simple schema also contains indices to other events and other schemata, as well as support information that indicates how the schema was created and how accurate the predictions of the schema have been. The schemata described in previous sections of this chapter and illustrated in Figures 3-17 and 3-18 are all simple schemata.

A macro-schema is a high-level knowledge structure that can be thought of as a shorthand notation for a useful network of concepts. The idea here is that instead of reasoning at the level of goals (e.g., obtaining an object), and actions (e.g., asking for an object), it is possible to reason at a higher level, treating the interactions between goals and actions as a single unit (e.g. `delta-agency`). A macro-schema contains a <u>sequence</u> <u>of</u> <u>events</u> as well as the components of a simple schema. When constructing a macro-schema the sequence of events is constructed from the network of generalized events connected by intentional links (by a process described in Section 3.3.5). The generalized event for a macro-schema summarizes the objects that play a role in the sequence of events. A script is an example of a macro-schema. For example, the restaurant script might have the following generalized event:

```
RESTAURANT customer HUMAN
           meal     FOOD
           ...
           payment MONEY
           waiter HUMAN
```

and a sequence of events that encode such information as the customer ordering the meal from the waiter and the customer eating the meal.

Figure 3-20 summarizes the algorithm that OCCAM follows to create a new schema with similarity-based learning methods. If there is a large enough cluster of similar events, a generalized event is created by extracting the common features of the similar events. The extraction of common features is then performed recursively on the related concepts by following the corresponding intentional links. If there are a number of related concepts[24] connected by intentional links, then a macro-schema is created.

The macro-schema serves as much more than a notational shorthand. There are several reasons for creating chunks of higher level knowledge:

* Storage economy-- Typically, there will be a sequence of events in a schema involving a number of different actors and objects. However, often the actors or objects of several different actions will be the same. By creating a macro-schema, the attributes of these entities need to be represented only once as attributes of the roles of the schemata.

---

[24]This is a parameter in OCCAM. Its value in the current version of OCCAM is four.

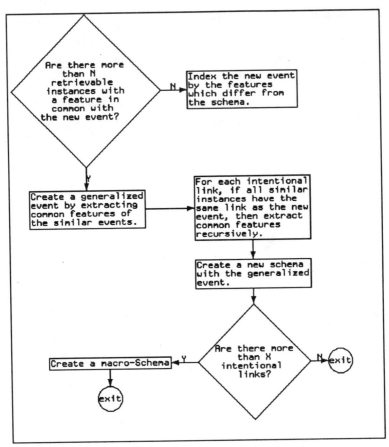

Figure 3-20:   Top-level overview of creating a schema with similarity-based learning in OCCAM.

- Ease of memory indexing-- New examples are indexed under the high level knowledge structure in memory rather than recording them with the primitive components. This simplifies recall and recognition of known schemata.

3.3.5. Creating a macro-schema: An example

The creation of a macro-schema is a relatively straightforward process. I will illustrate the process by continuing the example of Sections 3.2.3 and 3.3.2. In this example, the events zoo-1, pizza-1, and refrigerator-1 have been identified as a useful set to generalize. The following steps are followed to create a macro-schema:

1. A new simple schema is constructed. The generalized event of this schema is formed from the features common to the main concept of all the instances.

2. The intentional links of the main concept of each example are traversed. If each example has the same intentional link, a generalized event is constructed from the related concept. For example, the goal of `pizza-1` is achieved by Mike giving Karen pizza, the goal of `zoo-1` is achieved by Mike taking Karen to the zoo, and the goal of `play-doh-1` is achieved by Mike giving Lynn some Play-Doh. The common features of all of these actions is Mike doing something. The process of finding the common features continues recursively until all intentional links in common have been traversed. A network of generalized events is created. The results of this process are shown for the current example are shown in Figure 3-21.

3. A generalized event is created for the macro-schema. This is constructed by finding objects that play a role in the description of more than one event in the network of generalized events. These objects may be thought of as the roles of the schema. A unique name is given to each of the roles. In this example, there are three objects that are repeated. The actor of the main goal concept is called `the-actor`. The actor of the action that achieves the goal is called `the-helper`, and the object of the goal state is called `the-obj`[25]. A unique name is also selected for each of the events in the network of generalized events. These events may be thought of as the scenes of the schema. For example, in the current example, the main concept is called `the-goal`, the action that achieves the goal is called `the-sub-act`. A unique name is

---

[25] OCCAM operates in two modes. In unattended mode, OCCAM generates names for these roles (e.g., `ROLE-17`). In interactive mode, it asks the user to provide a meaningful name for the roles.

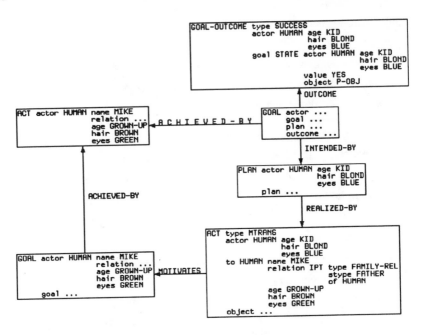

Figure 3-21: **The result of finding the common features of concepts connected by intentional links to the main concepts of zoo-1, refrigerator-1 and pizza-1.**

generated for the generalized event of the macro-schema. In the current example, the macro-schema is called **delta-agency**. The names of roles and the scenes become the feature names of the generalized event. The values of these features is constructed by replacing any occurrence of a role or a scene by a role token that represents that role. For example, instead of the actor of **the-sub-act** being a human named Mike with brown hair, the actor of **the-sub-act** is **the-helper**. It is in this manner that the creation of a macro-schema results in economical storage, since the attributes of the roles need not be repeated. Furthermore, it facilitates finding similarities among the scenes to specialize the macro-schema. Rather than noticing, say, a person with brown hair doing a particular action under certain circumstances for a person with blond hair, OCCAM can notice when **the-helper** does something for **the-actor**. Figure 3-22 illustrates the generalized event for the macro-schema for the current example. The notation =THE-ACTOR indicates a role token for the-actor.

```
DELTA-AGENCY the-outcome GOAL-OUTCOME type SUCCESS
                                       actor =THE-ACTOR
                                       goal STATE actor =THE-ACTOR
                                                  value YES
                                                  object =THE-OBJ
             the-sub-goal GOAL actor =THE-HELPER
                               goal ACT actor =THE-HELPER
             the-plan PLAN actor =THE-ACTOR
                           plan =THE-MTRANS
             the-sub-act ACT actor =THE-HELPER
             the-goal GOAL actor =THE-ACTOR
                           goal STATE actor =THE-ACTOR
                                      value YES
                                      object =THE-OBJ
                           plan =THE-MTRANS
                           outcome GOAL-OUTCOME type SUCCESS
                                                actor =THE-ACTOR
                                                goal STATE actor =THE-ACTOR
                                                           value YES
                                                           object =THE-OBJ
             the-mtrans ACT type MTRANS
                            actor =THE-ACTOR
                            to =THE-HELPER
                            object ACT actor =THE-HELPER
             the-helper HUMAN name MIKE
                              relation IPT type FAMILY-REL
                                           stype FATHER
                                           of =THE-ACTOR
                        age GROWN-UP
                        hair BROWN
                        eyes GREEN
             the-actor HUMAN age KID
                             hair BLOND
                             eyes BLUE
             the-obj P-OBJ
```

Figure 3-22: **The generalized event of a macro-schema. delta-agency represents a plan for achieving a goal by asking someone to perform an action that achieves the goal.**

4. The next two steps are performed to create the sequence of events. The general idea is that some reasoning can be done by treating the macro-schema as a black box. Typically, the macro-schema can predict what may occur. Other reasoning tasks require the black box to be opened up. The macro-schema can be decomposed into the sequence of events. The sequence of events indicates why a prediction can be made. The first step is to create a pattern that can be matched against an instance of the macro-schema to bind variables to the roles and scenes. This is accomplished by simply creating a variable for each feature of the generalized event. Figure 3-23 illustrates the pattern for delta-agency. In this figure, variables are preceded by a question mark.

```
DELTA-AGENCY the-goal ?V-17163
             the-mtrans ?THE-MTRANS
             the-helper ?THE-HELPER
             the-actor ?THE-ACTOR
             the-obj ?THE-OBJ
             the-sub-act ?THE-SUB-ACT
             the-plan ?THE-PLAN
             the-sub-goal ?THE-SUB-GOAL
             the-outcome ?THE-OUTCOME
```

Figure 3-23: This pattern can be matched against an instance of **delta-agency** binding the variables (which are preceded by a question mark).

5. The sequence of events is created by replacing each event in the network of generalized events created in step 2 with the corresponding variable created in step 4. An instance of a macro-schema can be decomposed into more primitive elements by matching the instance against a pattern that binds a number of variables. The sequence of events is then instantiated by replacing each variable by its bound value. The sequence of events for **delta-agency** is illustrated in Figure 3-24.

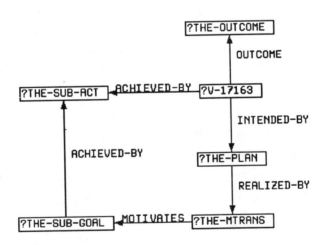

Figure 3-24: The sequence of events for **delta-agency**.

6. The final step is necessary to recognize new examples as instances of a macro-schema. What is needed is a means of transforming one representation into another. For example, **delta-agency** is

a particular configuration that represents the interaction between a goal and a means of accomplishing that goal (i.e., by asking). When a new example has the same configuration of goals, plans, and actions, it is recognized as an example of **delta-agency** and the representation is changed. This representation change is accomplished by matching the instance against a pattern in the old representation and instantiating a pattern in the new representation. The generalized event of the simple schema created in step 1 serves as a template for the old representation and the generalized event of the macro-schema serves as template for the new representation. Two patterns are created by replacing the corresponding components in the two representations by variables. Figure 3-25 illustrates the old pattern for **delta-agency** and Figure 3-26 displays the pattern for the new pattern. When a variable is followed by a CD structure in these figures (e.g., **?THE-MTRANS**), it indicates that the binding of the variable is permitted only if the component matches the CD structure (which may bind other variables). These two patterns are called representational transfers and are associated with the simple schema. The macro-schema is indexed from the root of memory (see Figure 3-27).

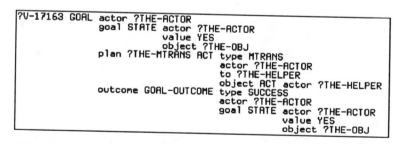

```
?V-17163 GOAL  actor ?THE-ACTOR
               goal STATE actor ?THE-ACTOR
                          value YES
                          object ?THE-OBJ
               plan ?THE-MTRANS ACT type MTRANS
                                     actor ?THE-ACTOR
                                     to ?THE-HELPER
                                     object ACT actor ?THE-HELPER
               outcome GOAL-OUTCOME type SUCCESS
                                    actor ?THE-ACTOR
                                    goal STATE actor ?THE-ACTOR
                                               value YES
                                               object ?THE-OBJ
```

Figure 3-25: The pattern for recognizing a particular configuration of goals and plans as an instance of **delta-agency**.

This algorithm is summarized in Figure 3-28. It creates a macro-schema as well as a means of recognizing new events as instances of the macro-schema. When searching memory for the most specific schema that accounts for a new

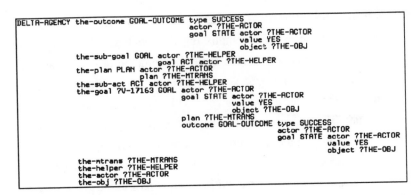

Figure 3-26: **The pattern for creating an instance of `delta-agency` once a configuration of goals and plans has been recognized as an instance of `delta-agency`.**

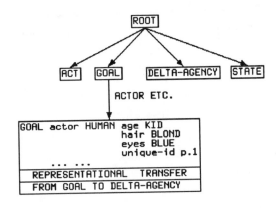

Figure 3-27: **The location of the `delta-agency` schema in memory. The simple schema indexed under `goal` contains a representational transfer pattern that recognizes `delta-agency`.**

episode, if a simple schema is encountered that has representational transfers, then the representation of the new episode is transformed to a higher-level representation. This is accomplished by matching the new episode against the pattern in the old representation. The pattern in the new representation is then instantiated and role tokens are inserted in the resulting new representation (as in step 3). Further memory search, as well as indexing and specialization, are done in the high-level representation.

```
CreateMacroSchema[NewEvent, Events, Schema]
1. Create simple schema
2. Generalize network of events connected by ilinks
3. Find objects that play multiple roles in the network
   Create a name for the macro-schema
   Create a role name for each event in network
   Create a role name for each repeated object
   Create role-fillers and insert role tokens
4. Create a pattern by making a variable for each new role
5. Create sequence of events by substituting variables
        in the network of generalized events
6. Create representational transfer
```

Figure 3-28:   A summary of the algorithm for creating a macro-schema.

3.4. Refining Schemata

There is a serious problem with making generalizations by comparing the similarities and differences among a small number of examples. The problem is even more severe if, as in OCCAM, the set of examples is small. The problem is that some of the generalizations are bound to be incorrect (Schank, 1982). Apparent regularities may, in fact, turn out to be mere coincidences. OCCAM contains a mechanism to deal with this problem. The approach implemented in OCCAM is similar to a technique developed by Lebowitz (Lebowitz, 1982). There are several differences, however, which I shall point out in the course of this discussion.

It is important to stress that generalizations are not required to be completely accurate. Instead, the generalizations in OCCAM describe what is usually true. For example, when a glass is dropped from about the height of a kitchen table onto a tile floor, it typically breaks. Although there are exceptions to this rule, it is true often enough that most parents do not give small children glass drinking cups.

Although generalizations are not required to be 100% accurate, it is desirable that they make correct predictions often enough to be useful. Therefore, it is important to evaluate a generalization when more data are available.

This evaluation process consists of a number of steps:

- Noticing when a generalization makes a correct prediction.

- Noticing when a generalization is contradicted by new data.

- Correcting an erroneous generalization.

As described in Figure 1-8 on page 40, the evaluation of a generalization is done as a natural part of the memory search for the most specific schema that accounts for a new example. OCCAM maintains two counters for each feature of a generalized event of a schema. These counters keep track of the number of times a particular feature is present or is contradicted when the schema is a candidate for the most specific schema[26]. From these two counters, it is easy to compute a ratio that indicates how accurate the generalized event is at predicting the value of each feature when it is applicable[27].

The rationale behind keeping track of the accuracy of each feature rather than an entire generalization is that a generalization that is making an erroneous prediction need not be discarded entirely. Instead, the generalization can be modified so that an erroneous prediction is not made in the future. For example, the **delta-agency** schema predicts that when a goal is achieved by asking a helper to perform an action, the helper will be a parent with brown hair named Mike. Obviously, this prediction is not accurate. Instead of abandoning the prediction entirely, it might be reasonable to predict that the helper has a positive interpersonal relationship with the actor.

When a new example contradicts a particular feature of a generalized event, and the accuracy of the generalized event in predicting that feature is lower than a certain ratio[28], then the generalized event is modified. In UNIMEM, the generalized event is modified by deleting the feature entirely. This makes sense in UNIMEM because the feature values are atomic. In contrast, in OCCAM the feature values can be composite objects that have their own features. Instead of deleting an erroneously predicted feature, the feature is generalized by retaining

---

[26]A schema is a candidate if its ancestor is a candidate, and the new example has a feature that is predictive of the schema (i.e., the feature is a unique or nearly unique index).

[27]UNIMEM maintains just one confidence that is incremented or decremented. The strategy implemented in OCCAM allows one to require a more accurate prediction when there is a large amount of data.

[28]This is a parameter in OCCAM. The current value of the parameter is 0.8.

those features that the predicted feature and the corresponding feature in the new example have in common. This revision process makes use of **MakeGeneralCd** (see Figure 3-15 on 88). For example, the predicted feature value may be "a parent with brown hair" and the new example may have the feature value "a sister with blond hair". In this case, the feature would be revised to "a relative". This revision step is similar to the manner that the concept is revised in Bruner's wholist strategy.

3.4.1. Refining a schema: An example

In this section, I continue the example of Sections 3.2.3, 3.3.2 and 3.3.5. In this example, **zoo-1**, **refrigerator-1** and **pizza-1** have been identified as similar events, a simple schema has been created that contains a representational transfer to the **delta-agency** schema. The **delta-agency** schema is extremely specific since it predicts that when a goal is achieved by asking a helper to perform an action, the helper will be a parent with brown hair named Mike. As new episodes are added to memory, this prediction will be refined. I will show how the simple schema and **delta-agency** are revised when the following events are encountered:

- **apple-1**: Karen wants an apple. She asks her mother Chris for one and Chris gives her one.

- **light-1**: Karen wants the light turned on in the bathroom. She asks her sister Lynn who turns on the light.

- **pizza-2**: Mike wants a slice of pizza. He asks his wife Chris to give him a slice and she does.

- **oil-1**: Chris wants some peanut oil. She asks her husband Mike who gets her some peanut oil from the store.

Adding some of these events to memory also creates some specialized versions of **delta-agency**. In this example, I will only concentrate on how **delta-agency** is refined. When **apple-1** is added to memory, the **goal** schema is encountered first. There are indices from the goal schema to a specialized goal schema from the **actor, outcome, plan,** and **goal** features (see Figure 3-17 on page 90). Since the specialized schema is the only schema indexed by the **actor** feature, and the **actor** of the **apple-1** (Karen) is compatible with the **actor** of the schema (a child with blue eyes and blond hair), the specialized schema is predicted to apply to this situation. However, the new event contradicts the **plan** of schema, since the **to** feature of the **plan** is predicted to be a father named Mike with brown hair and green eyes. Instead, it is a mother named Chris with brown hair and green eyes. The **plan** feature must be revised. The common features between the **plan** of the new instance, and the **plan** of the schema are found and replace the **plan** feature of the schema. Figure 3-29 illustrates the updated generalized event. A comparison to the old generalized event (Figure 3-16 on page 89) reveals that the only difference is that the **to** feature of the **plan** has been revised: the name is no longer required to be Mike, and the subtype of the interpersonal theme (**ipt**) is no longer required to be **father**[29]. In addition, since the revised schema contains a representational transfer to a macro-schema, these changes must be propagated to the macro-schema (**delta-agency**). The revised **delta-agency** schema is shown in Figure 3-30.

```
GOAL actor HUMAN age KID
                hair BLOND
                eyes BLUE
                unique-id p.1
     goal STATE actor HUMAN unique-id p.1
                value YES
                object P-OBJ unique-id obj.1
     plan ACT type MTRANS
                actor HUMAN unique-id p.1
                to HUMAN relation IPT type FAMILY-REL
                                       of HUMAN unique-id p.1
                        age GROWN-UP
                        hair BROWN
                        eyes GREEN
                        unique-id p.2
                object ACT actor HUMAN unique-id p.2
     outcome GOAL-OUTCOME type SUCCESS
                          actor HUMAN unique-id p.1
                          goal STATE actor HUMAN unique-id p.1
                                     value YES
                                     object P-OBJ unique-id obj.1
```

Figure 3-29: The revised generalized event after apple-1 has been added to memory.

When **light-1** is added to memory, the simple schema and the macro-schema need to be revised again. In this instance, **the-helper** is a small child with blond hair and blue eyes. The restriction that **the-helper** have brown hair and green eyes is removed. The changes to **delta-agency** are

---

[29]This change actually occurs for all instances of HUMAN with a unique-id equal to p.2 in the network of generalized events.

```
DELTA-AGENCY the-obj P-OBJ
             the-actor HUMAN eyes BLUE
                             hair BLOND
                             age KID
             the-helper HUMAN eyes GREEN
                              hair BROWN
                              age GROWN-UP
                              relation IPT of =THE-ACTOR
                                           type FAMILY-REL
             the-mtrans ACT object ACT actor =THE-HELPER
                            to =THE-HELPER
                            actor =THE-ACTOR
                            type MTRANS
             the-goal GOAL outcome GOAL-OUTCOME goal STATE object =THE-OBJ
                                                           value YES
                                                           actor =THE-ACTOR
                                                actor =THE-ACTOR
                                                type SUCCESS
                           plan =THE-MTRANS
                           goal STATE object =THE-OBJ
                                      value YES
                                      actor =THE-ACTOR
                           actor =THE-ACTOR
             the-sub-act ACT actor =THE-HELPER
             the-plan PLAN plan =THE-MTRANS
                           actor =THE-ACTOR
             the-sub-goal GOAL goal ACT actor =THE-HELPER
                               actor =THE-HELPER
             the-outcome GOAL-OUTCOME goal STATE object =THE-OBJ
                                                 value YES
                                                 actor =THE-ACTOR
                                      actor =THE-ACTOR
                                      type SUCCESS
```

Figure 3-30: The revised delta-agency schema. The only change is to the-helper feature.

shown in Figure 3-31. From this example OCCAM learns that a child can also be the-helper in this plan.

When pizza-2 is added to memory there is a new contradiction since the-actor is expected to be a child with blond hair and blue eyes. In this example, the-actor is an adult. However, the schema is not revised because this prediction has been accurate in five out of six cases. Instead, the confidence in this feature is lowered by incrementing the exception counter and remembering pizza-2 as an exception. Finally, when oil-1 is added to memory, OCCAM learns that delta-agency does not work just for children with blond hair and blue eyes. After the confidence in the-actor had been lowered by pizza-2, there is now enough evidence to revise the schema. The schema is revised once more to include this fact. Figure 3-32 shows the refined schema.

After these examples, the delta-agency schema is closer to being accurate. It contains the restriction that the-helper must be related to the-actor. This reflects the fact that a small child typically interacts with family members. Of course, there are many instances when a member of one's

```
DELTA-AGENCY the-obj P-OBJ
             the-actor HUMAN eyes BLUE
                             hair BLOND
                             age KID
             the-helper HUMAN relation IPT of =THE-ACTOR
                                           type FAMILY-REL
             the-ntrans ACT object ACT actor =THE-HELPER
                            to =THE-HELPER
                            actor =THE-ACTOR
                            type MTRANS
             the-goal GOAL outcome GOAL-OUTCOME goal STATE object =THE-OBJ
                                                           value YES
                                                           actor =THE-ACTOR
                                                actor =THE-ACTOR
                                                type SUCCESS
                           plan =THE-MTRANS
                           goal STATE object =THE-OBJ
                                      value YES
                                      actor =THE-ACTOR
                           actor =THE-ACTOR
             the-sub-act ACT actor =THE-HELPER
             the-plan PLAN plan =THE-MTRANS
                           actor =THE-ACTOR
             the-sub-goal GOAL goal ACT actor =THE-HELPER
                               actor =THE-HELPER
             the-outcome GOAL-OUTCOME goal STATE object =THE-OBJ
                                                 value YES
                                                 actor =THE-ACTOR
                                      actor =THE-ACTOR
                                      type SUCCESS
```

Figure 3-31: The revised delta-agency schema after apple-1 has
been added to memory.   the-helper feature is
changed again to remove the prediction that
the-helper have brown hair and green eyes.

```
DELTA-AGENCY the-obj P-OBJ
             the-actor HUMAN
             the-helper HUMAN relation IPT of =THE-ACTOR
                                           type FAMILY-REL
             the-ntrans ACT object ACT actor =THE-HELPER
                            to =THE-HELPER
                            actor =THE-ACTOR
                            type MTRANS
             the-goal GOAL outcome GOAL-OUTCOME goal STATE object =THE-OBJ
                                                           value YES
                                                           actor =THE-ACTOR
                                                actor =THE-ACTOR
                                                type SUCCESS
                           plan =THE-MTRANS
                           goal STATE object =THE-OBJ
                                      value YES
                                      actor =THE-ACTOR
                           actor =THE-ACTOR
             the-sub-act ACT actor =THE-HELPER
             the-plan PLAN plan =THE-MTRANS
                           actor =THE-ACTOR
             the-sub-goal GOAL goal ACT actor =THE-HELPER
                               actor =THE-HELPER
             the-outcome GOAL-OUTCOME goal STATE object =THE-OBJ
                                                 value YES
                                                 actor =THE-ACTOR
                                      actor =THE-ACTOR
                                      type SUCCESS
```

Figure 3-32: The delta-agency schema is refined to update
the-actor role when OCCAM encounters an example
that shows that this plan also works for adults.

family does not help to achieve a goal. In Section 4.7, I show how OCCAM deals with these. A major difference between OCCAM and UNIMEM is that OCCAM first tries to find an explanation for why a prediction does not hold before attempting the approach outlined in this chapter. There are many reasons that a parent might not give a child something: the parent might not have the desired object, or the parent might think the desired object will harm the child. If these explanations are available then these contradictions should not be treated as noise in the data. Rather, there is much that can be learned from these counterexamples.

3.5. Summary

In this chapter, I presented OCCAM's similarity-based learning algorithm. There are three essential components to SBL:

1. Aggregation-- Finding a group of similar events.

2. Generalization-- Describing a regularity among a number of events. In OCCAM's SBL algorithm, the generalization step is conservative in that it considers any similarity to be potentially relevant.

3. Evaluation-- Schemata formed by similarity-based learning may contain relationships that are purely coincidental. After a schema has been proposed, it is used to predict the outcome of future events. If it performs poorly at this task, the schema is revised. This revision process eliminates coincidental relationships that were present in the initial examples but did not hold for later examples.

Chapter 4
Theory-Driven Learning in OCCAM

In this chapter, I describe the theory-driven learning (TDL) process in OCCAM. A theory that relates potential causes and their effects can focus the attention of a learner so that a small number of examples are necessary to learn a causal relationship. Theory-driven learning lies somewhere between explanation-based and similarity-based learning. Like EBL, the goal of theory-driven learning is to improve upon SBL that requires a large number of examples to arrive at a correct hypothesis. However, like SBL, TDL does not share the principle shortcoming of EBL, since TDL learning mechanism can acquire new causal knowledge that is not a logical consequence of existing knowledge.

In OCCAM, when an unexpected event occurs, EBL is attempted first. If existing knowledge cannot explain the unexpected event, then EBL is not appropriate, and TDL is tried. Theory-driven learning determines if the event fits a known pattern for a causal relationship. If all else fails, SBL attempts to find a regularity between the new event and similar previous events.

This chapter starts by reviewing evidence from psychology experiments that demonstrate that people do indeed make use of a general theory of causality when learning new causal relationships. Next, I describe how such a theory can be represented for a computer, and demonstrate that TDL has the same benefits for a computer as it has for a person: attention is focused on a hypothesis that is consistent with the theory of causality. Hypotheses that are not consistent with the theory of causality need not be considered although these hypotheses may be consistent with the examples encountered so far. Therefore, TDL requires fewer examples than SBL to acquire causal relationships.

4.1. A Theory of Causality

In Chapter 3, I discussed the similarity-based learning process in OCCAM. In this chapter, I discuss how one can improve on SBL even when one does not have enough existing knowledge to produce the explanation required by EBL. Similarity-based learning exploits inter-example relationships; TDL exploits intra-example relationships.   Discovering a causal relationship with SBL consists of making an inductive leap[30]:

When an action is always followed by a state change, then the action causes the state change.

In contrast, theory-driven learning imposes additional constraints on causal relationships. One such constraint requires that the action operates on the object that changes state:

When an action on an object is always followed by a state change of the object, then the action causes the state change.

Theory-driven learning operates by taking advantage of the constraints (i.e., the intra-example relationships) between potential causes and potential effects to focus the search for a hypothesis. The intra-example relationships restrict TDL to those situations which are consistent with the theory of causality. OCCAM includes an SBL component to learn from data that are not consistent with the theory of causality. In doing so, I acknowledge that the theory of causality is incomplete.   Nonetheless, there are several advantages in using a theory of causality when applicable to guide learning to predict and explain. A theory of causality can:

1. Assist in determining the difference between a correlation and a causal relationship. Some correlations such as the relationship between the outcome of the presidential election and the World Series[31] just don't have the appearance of a causal relationship even though they are supported by several examples. On the other hand, some relationships have the appearance of a causal relationship because they conform to a common pattern of causal relationships.   For example, if an apricot is frozen and then defrosted, it will turn brown, mushy and unappetizing. A theory of

---

[30]In fact, this view also has two implicit assumptions about causality: that causes must precede effects and that changes of state require a cause.

[31]i.e., if an American League wins the World Series, a Republican is elected president and if a team from the National League wins, a Democrat is elected.

causality can distinguish between these two classes of relationships. It only took one example of an unappetizing apricot for me to conclude that this will happen in the future if I freeze an apricot. However, although the outcome of the World Series and presidential elections have been correlated in the past, I have no reason to believe that they will be correlated in the future. The difference is that freezing an apricot, followed by the apricot turning brown and mushy, is consistent with a causal theory while the relationship between the World Series and the presidential elections is not.

2. Determine the true cause in an ambiguous situation. For example, consider the following event sequence. First, two events occur at approximately the same time: a yellow taxi is seen driving on the street outside the kitchen window and a brown bird flies into the window pane. Next, the window pane shatters. By ruling out the taxi as a potential cause for the window breaking, the search space for the problem of determining what causes windows to break can be reduced. Of course, correlation is still needed to determine that the color of the object that strikes the window is not important, but the weight and velocity of the object are. However, resources such as memory can be utilized more effectively if they are not also required to correlate the color and velocities of cars passing by.

3. Select the relevant attributes. A theory of causality can focus attention on the relevant attributes. For example, if Chris breaks out in a rash after eating a peach in the kitchen, should she avoid eating peaches in the future or should she avoid eating in the kitchen? Specific knowledge (e.g., peaches can cause allergic reactions) could certainly rule out the location as a possible cause. However, a general theory of causality can favor the hypothesis that the peach is responsible for the rash, over the hypothesis that the kitchen is responsible, since the location of an action does not typically affect a causal relationships.

4. Constrain the set of potential hypothesis so that fewer examples

are necessary to arrive at the correct conclusion. For example, subjects required fewer examples to learn that a balloon could be inflated only after it has been dipped in water than to learn that a balloon could be inflated only after a child has snapped her fingers. A theory of causality suggests that some hypotheses are more likely than others.

An analogy can be drawn between OCCAM's use of intra-example relationships and STAHL's (Langley et al., 1986) heuristics that constrain the search for the components of a compound. For example, STAHL contains a heuristic that states that if a substance occurs in both sides of a chemical reaction, it does not enter into the reaction. It is conceivable that STAHL could still determine the components of compounds if it did not use this heuristic. However, the search space would be larger and more examples would be required to rule out alternatives. Similarly, in OCCAM, intra-example relationships reduce the search for potential causes.

It is necessary to make a distinction between a theory of causality and a theory of causation. By a theory of causality, I mean a set of general principles that lead one to believe that a particular action (or class of actions) has a necessary consequence. Section 4.1.1 enumerates several of these general principles. By a theory of causation, I mean specific inference rules that indicate the effects of particular actions. A theory of causation might also be called a domain theory (Mitchell et al., 1986a), or simply, causal knowledge. The objective of TDL is to construct a theory of causation given a theory of causality and a number of observations.

4.1.1. Constraints on causal relationships

There have been several studies investigating what relationships between an effect and a potential cause are required to attribute causality. These relationships include:

• Temporal order: Children as young as four require a potential cause to precede an effect (Shultz & Mendelson, 1975). Without such temporal information, one might conclude that eating food with artificial sweeteners causes one to be overweight (because people who eat diet foods tend to be overweight).

- Temporal contiguity: An effect must immediately follow a cause (Michotte, 1963). When all other factors are equal, people select a cause that is closest in time to an effect.

- Spatial contiguity: An effect must be in contact with (or near) a cause (Bullock, 1979). When all other factors are equal, people select a cause that is closest in space to an effect.

- Regularity: Since a cause must necessarily result in an effect, the cause and the effect must co-occur (Shultz & Mendelson, 1975). Note that causality does not demand a perfect correlation. However, it does imply that exceptions need to be explained by searching for other contributing causes or qualifying conditions.

- Mechanism: An important constraint on causal relationships is the existence of a mechanism that transmits a causal "force" to the effect. Mechanism appears to be the dominant constraint on causal relationships. When presented with potential causes that violate the other intra-example relationships, subjects prefer selecting a cause that obeys the mechanism constraint (Shultz, 1982). An understanding of the mechanism is also important in identifying whether a new situation that is slightly different will produce the same effect (Bullock et al., 1982).

In most simple examples of causal relationships, the above constraints agree and any one will suffice to identify a causal relationship (Anderson, 1987). The experimental finding that mechanism is preferred when contradictory information is present can be explained by the fact that knowledge of mechanism is specific causal knowledge which is preferred to more general knowledge of causality. In fact, spatial and temporal contiguity can be viewed as heuristics that reveal a simple mechanism in the absence of specific causal knowledge[32].

---

[32]Note that spatial and temporal contiguity are not useful for discovering hidden mechanisms, such as the remote control of television. OCCAM must rely solely on correlation to discover such hidden mechanisms.

4.2. The Role of General Theories of Causality

In this section, I present evidence that people possess a theory of causality that facilitates learning causal relationships when certain spatial and temporal relationships exist between a potential cause and a potential effect. These temporal and spatial relationships serve as cues that suggest causal relationships. Much work in discovering these cues has been done in developmental psychology. The rationale here is that young children do not have much specific knowledge of the world, but they appear to come equipped with a general theory of causality (Carey, 1984). Even adults have strong impressions of causality when these cues are present.

4.2.1. The effect of different tasks

A second experiment was run in collaboration with Professor Mort Friedman. In this experiment, we investigated a general relationship between the cause and the effect that facilitates learning.

The subjects in this experiment were 80 undergraduates fulfilling a requirement for an introductory psychology course. Each subject was shown a number of videotapes of a child picking up a balloon and then doing something (dipping the balloon in a glass of water, putting a necklace on, or snapping her fingers). In addition, on different tapes the balloons varied in size (small or large) and color (orange or yellow). Subjects were divided into "Inflate" and "Alpha" conditions. Subjects were shown a tape, asked to predict whether the child could inflate the balloon (or whether the tape was an alpha), and then informed of the correct answer. Trials continued until the subject was able to predict correctly on 6 tapes in a row. We recorded the number of the last trial on which the subject made an error. Subjects in each condition were subdivided into groups who had to predict based upon the action performed (either snapping her fingers or dipping the balloon in water).

We predicted that subjects in the "Inflate" condition would find it easier to learn that the child could only inflate a balloon which had been dipped in water than to learn that the child could only inflate a balloon after she snapped her fingers. The difference here is not due to any specific prior causal knowledge. Instead, knowledge about causal relationships in general is applicable. The sequence *dipping a balloon in water followed by blowing air into the balloon, followed by the balloon changing* fits a pattern for a causal relationship: an action on an object (dipping the balloon in water) results in a state change for the object, which enables a subsequent action (blowing into the balloon) to produce a state change. In contrast, snapping fingers before blowing into the balloon does not fit this general pattern. An important constraint is violated. For an action to cause an object to change state, the action has to operate on the object.

Of course, in the "Alpha" condition, general knowledge of causality should not facilitate or hinder learning. Therefore, we anticipated that it would take the same number of trails to identify the alpha tapes whether the child was snapping her fingers or dipping a balloon in water.

The results of this experiment confirmed our predictions. The results are significant at the .05 level ($F(3,76) = 8.88$):

- Subjects required less trials to learn to predict that a balloon which had been dipped in water could be inflated (3.5 trials) than to predict that a balloon could be inflated after the child snapped her fingers (7.6 trials). This finding indicates that general knowledge of existing causal relationships facilitates learning.

- Subjects required approximately the same number of trials to determine that a balloon being dipped in water is an alpha (5.7 trials) and to determine that the child snapping her fingers is an alpha (5.9 trials).

In this experiment, we have demonstrated that general theories of causality can facilitate learning to predict the outcome of an event. In particular, when there is a relationship between a cause and an effect that suggests a causal mechanism (e.g., a set of intermediate states), then fewer examples are required to identify a causal relationship. The results of this experiment indicate that the process of learning to predict the outcome of an event is not simply a matter of empirically associating two events that have occurred in succession.

4.2.2. Selecting a cause consistent with a general theory of causality

One way to demonstrate that general knowledge of causality can assist the learning of new causal relationships is to present subjects with a situation in which there are two possible causes if only covariation information is considered. For example, in one experiment (Shultz, 1982) children between the ages of two and thirteen were shown an ambiguous stimuli. Two tuning forks were simultaneously placed in front of an open box. One of the tuning forks was banged against a piece of rubber causing it to vibrate before being placed in front of the box. When a vibrating tuning fork is placed in front of the box, it resonates the air column in the box. The result of this experiment was that children as young as two tended to select the vibrating tuning fork as the cause of the sound produced by the box over the tuning fork that was not vibrating. Shultz proposed that children selected the vibrating tuning fork because it was transmitting energy. In later experiments, children even preferred the vibrating tuning fork over a nonvibrating tuning fork which was in direct contact with the box. This demonstrates that the transmission of energy has precedence over spatial proximity as a cue for a causal relationship (Shultz et al., 1986).

4.2.3. Knowledge of a causal mechanism

An understanding of the mechanism is also important in identifying whether a new situation which is slightly different will produce the same effect. For example, in one experiment (Bullock et al., 1982), children were shown an apparatus that consisted of a box containing a row of blocks. When a long orange rod was inserted in one end, the blocks fell down and pushed a rabbit out of the box. Next, they were shown different situations, such as a different color rod, or a short rod which could not reach the blocks, and asked to predict the outcome. Children as young as three were able to distinguish a modification which interfered with the mechanism from one which did not. This experiment suggests that even small children are not insensitive to a causal mechanism.

4.3. Representing a Theory of Causality

In OCCAM, a theory of causality is represented as a set of *generalization rules* that postulate explanations for similarities and differences between events[33]. The simplest generalization rule (*If an action on an object always precedes a state change for the object, then the action results in the state change*) is displayed in Figure 4-1.

Although the rule in Figure 4-1 appears to be very simple, it encodes many

---

[33]OCCAM contains approximately 20 generalization rules. Appendix D lists all the generalization rules.

```
(def-gen-rule
  ?state-1 = (state type ?stype          ;potential effect
                    value ?value
                    object ?object)
  after                                   ;temporal relation
  ?act-1 = (act type ?atype              ;potential cause
                 object ?object)
  ((?act-1 result ?state-1))              ;causal mechanism
)
```

Figure 4-1: An exceptionless generalization rule (variables are preceded by "?"):
            if an action on an object always precedes a state change for the object,
            then the action results in the state change. Comments that label the
            components of the generalization rule are preceded by ";".

assumptions about causal relationships that drastically reduce the search space. First, it encodes the intra-example constraint that the action must operate on the object whose state has changed. This would rule out a taxi driving past a window as a potential cause for the window breaking. Secondly, it indicates that the only important features of the action are the type of action (e.g., an application of force) and the object. The actor who performs the action, the time the action is performed and any instrument with which the action is performed are not considered relevant. For example, if a ball was kicked into a window pane and the window shattered, OCCAM would not consider the actor (or the actor's hair color) to be features of the potential cause. Finally, the generalization rule in Figure 4-1 also encodes a temporal constraint. Therefore, if a ladybug flies through the broken window after a ball has hit it, OCCAM would not produce the explanation that the window broke because [sic] the ladybug will fly through it.

The generalization rule in Figure 4-1 is called an exceptionless generalization rule because it applies when there are only positive examples. Other generalization rules focus on reasons that similar actions have different results. There can be two reasons that similar actions have different results:

1. A component of the action differs. For example, the action may be performed on a different object or have a different actor.

2. A prior action has changed the state of an object that enables the subsequent action to result in a state change.

For each of these reasons, OCCAM contains a class of generalization rules to explain the different results. For the first reason, the generalization rules are called <u>dispositional</u> generalization rules because they attribute a different result to differing dispositions[34] (i.e., properties) of actors or objects.   The generalization rules that account for the second reason that similar actions have different results are called <u>historical</u> generalization rules because they attribute a different result to different histories of the objects involved.

Figure 4-2 displays a protocol of a four-year-old child trying to figure out when she can inflate balloons and when she cannot. Each type of generalization rule is illustrated by this protocol.

1. Mike is blowing up a red balloon.
2. Lynn: "Let me blow it up."
3. Mike lets the air out of the balloon and hands it to Lynn.
4. Lynn blows up the red balloon.

5. Lynn picks up a green balloon and tries to inflate it.
6. Lynn cannot inflate the green balloon.
7. Lynn puts down the green balloon and looks around.
8. Lynn: "How come they only gave us one red one?"
9. Mike: "Why do you want a red one?"
10. Lynn: "I can blow up the red ones."

11. Mike picks up a green balloon and inflates it.
12. Mike lets the air out of the green balloon; hands it to Lynn.
13. Mike: "Try this one."
14. Lynn blows up the green balloon.
15. Lynn gives Mike an uninflated blue balloon.
16. Lynn: "Here, let's do this one."

Figure 4-2:   Protocol of Lynn (age 4) trying to blow up balloons.

Events 1 through 4 in Figure 4-2 can be accounted for by an application of an exceptionless generalization rule. It appears from these events that Lynn believes that she can inflate any balloon by blowing air into the balloon. In events 5 through 10, Lynn saw a counterexample to her initial hypothesis and had to come up with a hypothesis that accounts for a different result the second time she tried to inflate a balloon. The two balloons differed in color and her

---

[34]The use of the term "disposition" to refer to the potentials of actors and objects was derived from (Goodman, 1983). It should not be confused with it's more restricted usage in psychology.

hypothesis can be accounted for by a dispositional generalization rule that attributes the different result to the different color balloon. This hypothesis is contradicted by the next events (10 through 16) when she determines that the color of the balloon is not important. Instead, she attributes the difference in result to a different action that preceded her successfully inflating a balloon. This hypothesis can be accounted for by a historical generalization rule.

```
(def-gen-rule
  ?state-1 = (state type ?stype          ;potential effect
                    value ?value
                    object ?object)
  after                                   ;temporal relation
  ?act-1 = (act type ?atype               ;potential cause
                 object ?object)
  ((?act-1 result ?state-1))              ;causal mechanism
  (:difference ?act-1 actor)             ;difference note
)
```

Figure 4-3: A dispositional generalization rule: if similar actions performed on an object have different   results, and they are performed by different actors,   the differing features of the actor are responsible for the different result.

Dispositional and historical generalization rules focus on reasons that similar actions have different results. For example, OCCAM contains a dispositional generalization rule that blames the actor for different results of actions whose actors differ (see Figure 4-3). This rule would focus the search for an explanation on the different features of the actor. For example, there are many actions that adults can successfully perform but children cannot (e.g., a heavy object might move if an adult pushes it, but not a child). Of course, without prior knowledge, OCCAM must correlate features of the actor with outcomes over several examples to discover that age rather than hair color is relevant. Generalization rules in OCCAM are ordered by simplicity[35]. The dispositional rule in Figure 4-3 would only apply if the exceptionless rule in Figure 4-1 was not able to make accurate predictions without considering differences in the actor.

The final type of generalization rule attributes different results of similar actions to different histories of the objects involved. For example, one historical

---

[35]This is why I named the system OCCAM. The simplest generalization rule produces the simplest hypothesis.

rule (displayed in Figure 4-4) attributes the difference in a result to the existence of a state of an object that enables the result. This rule would reveal relationships such as removing the top from a bottle results in a state that enables the contents to come out if the bottle is overturned or that stretching a balloon results in a state that enables blowing air into the balloon to inflate the balloon. Recall that simpler generalization rules are tried before more complex ones. This rule would only apply if the effect is not adequately explained by simpler rules such as the ones in Figure 4-1 or Figure 4-3.

```
(def-gen-rule
  ?state-2 = (state type ?stype              ;potential effect
                value ?value
                object ?object)
    before                                   ;temporal relation
  ?act-2 =   (act type ?atype-2              ;potential cause
                object ?object)
    ((?act-2 result ?state-2)                ;causal mechanism
     (?act-1 result
                ?state-1 = (state object ?object))
     (?state-1 enables ?act-2))
    (:link ?act-2 before                     ;condition
           ?act-1 = (act type ?atype-1
                object ?object))
)
```

Figure 4-4: A historical generalization rule: if an initial action (?act-1) on an object is always present when a subsequent action (?act-2) precedes a state change (?state-2) for the object, then   ?act-1 results in a state (?state-1) that enables ?act-2 to result in the state change (?state-2).

The experiment discussed in Section 4.2.1 (when subjects found it easier to learn that a child could inflate a balloon after she had dipped it in water than to learn that the child could inflate a balloon after she snapped her fingers) demonstrates the necessity of the rule in Figure 4-4. In particular, the object of ?act-1 is the same as the object of ?act-2 when the balloon is dipped in water before blowing air into it. Therefore, the generalization rule in Figure 4-4 would apply and suggest that dipping the balloon in water results in some (unspecified) state that enables blowing into the balloon to make the balloon larger. In contrast, when the child could only inflate the balloon after she snaps her fingers the generalization rule in Figure 4-4 does not apply because the object of the two actions (snapping fingers and blowing air into the balloon) differ. In fact, OCCAM contains no generalization rules that match this situation and is forced to rely on empirical methods alone by comparing and contrasting features of positive and negative examples. As a consequence, it takes more examples for OCCAM to learn that snapping fingers is predictive of the balloon than to learn that dipping the balloon in water is predictive.

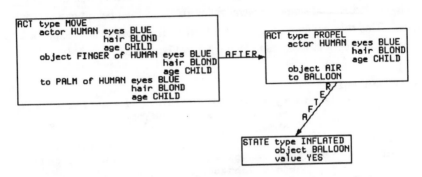

Figure 4-5: **A generalization created by empirical methods describing the situation when a balloon is inflated only after the child snaps her fingers.**

The rule in Figure 4-4 also illustrates an important capability of OCCAM. In addition to predicting the outcome of an action, OCCAM also constructs a causal mechanism that accounts for how the action brings about the outcome. Therefore, it should be able to predict the outcome of similar events by determining if they interfere with the postulated mechanism more accurately than approaches that rely entirely on similarities and differences between prior examples. Figure 4-5 illustrates the generalization that OCCAM constructs to describe the situation when a balloon is inflated after a child snaps her fingers. It is constructed entirely by empirical methods and contains temporal links but no causal links. In contrast, Figure 4-6 illustrates the generalization that OCCAM constructs to describe the situation when the child can inflate the balloon only after it has been dipped in water.

4.4. The Process of Theory-driven Learning

In OCCAM, a current best hypothesis (Mitchell, 1982) is formed by generalization rules that detect similarities and differences among the attributes of an observed event and recalled previous events. OCCAM selects a current best hypothesis rather than maintain a set of consistent hypotheses (Mitchell, 1982; Vere, 1975) for several reasons:

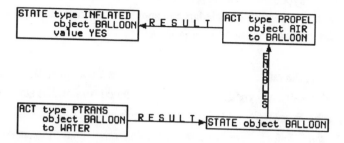

Figure 4-6:   A generalization containing a causal mechanism is created when a situation matches a known causal pattern. This generalization describes the situation when the child can inflate the balloon only after it has been dipped in water.

- The set of consistent hypotheses can be very large. For example, consider the following situation: Karen (a young girl with blond hair and blue eyes wearing a green sweater) pulls on the refrigerator door but it doesn't open. Mike (an adult male with brown hair and green eyes wearing a blue sweat shirt) pulls on the refrigerator door and it opens. There are six attributes with different values for Karen and Mike which can generate consistent hypotheses. (e.g., when a person with green eyes pulls on the refrigerator door, it opens.) In addition, these attributes may be combined conjunctively or disjunctively to form a large set of consistent hypotheses. Psychological evidence (Bower & Trabasso, 1968; Levine, 1967) indicates that only one or a small number of hypotheses are considered at one time. Thus generating a causal hypothesis is treated as searching the space of possible hypotheses.

- Before a sufficient number of examples have been encountered to rule out alternative consistent hypotheses, it may be necessary to predict the outcome of a new event. The current best hypothesis can serve as the source of this prediction.

When a new example falsifies the current best hypothesis, a new hypothesis is selected from the set of consistent hypotheses. In DALTON (Langley et al., 1986) and in RULEMOD (Buchanan & Mitchell, 1978), domain-specific heuristics select the new hypothesis. However, because theory-driven learning in OCCAM assumes no initial domain knowlédge, the approach advocated here differs from DALTON and RULEMOD in the following ways:

- Initially, the current best hypothesis is selected randomly from the set of consistent hypotheses[36] subject to the constraint that simpler hypotheses are selected first: single-attribute discriminations are selected before conjunctive combinations and disjunctive combinations (Schlimmer & Granger, 1986).

- Distinctions that have proven useful in the past influence the order in which causal hypotheses are generated. For example, after several examples, assume that the current hypothesis indicates that when adults pull on the refrigerator door, it opens. Later, when presented with examples of an adult with brown hair successfully inflating balloons, and a small child with blond hair unsuccessful at the same task, the age attribute would be preferred to the hair-color attribute. The hypothesis that when an adult blows into a balloon, it will inflate is considered before the hypothesis that when persons with brown hair blow into a balloon, it will inflate. As OCCAM learns about specific causal relationships, domain-specific heuristics (e.g., adults are strong) are also learned that guide the search for the current best hypothesis on new problems. Section 4.5 discusses this issue more thoroughly.

In RULEMOD, all previous examples are remembered so that the set of consistent hypotheses is always consistent with previous examples. In the ARCH program, no previous examples are saved so that the set of hypotheses may contain hypotheses that are not consistent with previous examples. OCCAM takes a compromise between these two extreme positions. In OCCAM, the exact number of previous events recalled from memory is dependent on the *retrievability* of each event as determined by the unique features of the events (Kolodner, 1984; Lebowitz, 1980; Pazzani, 1985). Typically, at least one

---

[36]OCCAM does not currently make use of cue salience information (Trabasso, 1963).

positive example and at least one negative example are recalled when selecting a new hypothesis.   In addition, the current example and the current incorrect hypothesis constrain the set of consistent hypotheses (Bower & Trabasso, 1968; Levine, 1966).

When a new event is added to memory, if there is no schema that accounts for the outcome of the event and the outcome cannot be explained by combining existing knowledge, TDL is attempted.   The process of TDL consists of the following steps:

1. Finding the most specific schemata and retrieving similar events (i.e., events that share at least one retrievable feature.)   These events may also include the generalized events of more specialized schema associated with a most specific schema.

2. Creating two sets of events, those with the same outcome as the new event (this set also includes the new event) and those with different outcomes.

3. If there are no events with a different outcome, the exceptionless generalization rules are tried.   If there are events with different outcomes, dispositional generalization rules are tried and if no dispositional generalization rules apply, then historical generalization rules apply.

4. To apply a generalization rule, first a generalized event is created by finding all features common to the set of events with the same outcome (see Section 3.3.1 on page 87). In the case that the set of events with the same outcome only contains the new event, the generalized event is the new event. Next, the generalized event is matched against the potential cause and potential effect of the generalization rule.   Applying generalization rules to generalized events ensures that the causal relationship obeys the regularity constraint.   Various generalization rules explicitly encode the temporal, spatial, and mechanistic constraints.   The remaining processing is dependent on the type of generalization rule:

- Exceptionless: A new schema is created. The generalized event of the new schema is constructed by replacing the variables in the causal mechanism by the corresponding components with all features removed in the generalized event[37]. For example, if a pattern is (performing an action on a component of an object):

```
ACT type ?atype
    object COMPONENT type ?ctype
                    of ?object
```

and the generalized event constructed from the set of events with the same outcome is (a blond female pulling on the door of a large white refrigerator):

```
ACT type PROPEL
    actor PERSON hair BLOND
                 gender FEMALE
    object COMPONENT type DOOR
                    of REFRIGERATOR
                                color WHITE
                                size LARGE
```

then the generalized event of the new schema is (pulling on the door of a refrigerator):

```
ACT type PROPEL
    object COMPONENT type DOOR
                    of REFRIGERATOR
```

- Dispositional: The difference note of the generalization rule (see Figure 4-3) indicates that a feature of the potential cause might be responsible for the different result. For example, the difference note of the generalization rule in Figure 4-3 indicates that a feature of the actor of the cause may be responsible. Any of the features of the actor which occur in the generalized event is a potential candidate. Those candidate features that are also present in an event with a

---

[37]This removing of features is a means of implementing generalization to the most specific class of the object.

different outcome are eliminated from consideration. (If there are no candidate features, then the generalization rule does not apply.) One feature is selected from the remaining candidates and hypothesized to be responsible for the different outcome (i.e., the causal relationship only holds when that feature is present). Section 4.5 describes this selection process in more detail. The generalized event for a new schema is created in a manner identical to the exceptionless generalization rules except that the generalized event also contains the feature hypothesized to be responsible for the different outcome.

- Historical: The condition of the generalization rule indicates that the causal relationship is conditionally dependent on some previous action (see Figure 4-4). The condition contains a temporal or intentional link that indicates how to find this action. This search is made for each event with the same outcome the retrieved actions are generalized by extracting common features and the resulting generalized action is matched against the pattern in the condition. If the match (or the generalization) is unsuccessful, the generalization rule does not apply. Otherwise, a new schema is created and the generalized event for the schema is created in a manner identical to the exceptionless generalization rule. Typically, the causal mechanism of a historical generalization rule is more complex than that of an exceptionless generalization rule.

The generalized event for a schema is perfectly suited for recognizing if a new example is an instance of that schema. However, it is not ideal for constructing an explanation by chaining several schemata together since the generalized event does not contain any variables. To address this issue, a "rule" format of the generalized event is also constructed. Any variable that appears more than once in the causal mechanism of a generalization rule is not instantiated in the rule format of the generalized event. This ensures that an object that appears in the cause is identical to the object that appears in the effect, rather than just compatible. For example, when a glass cup is dropped, one would expect that cup to break rather than a different glass cup. In Section 4.4.2, I illustrate the rule format of a generalized event.

4.4.1. Evaluation of schemata created by theory-driven learning

Typically, with TDL a schema is initially created from a small number of experiences. Such a schema is subject to revision when more examples are observed. The evaluation of these schema is accomplished in a manner similar to that of schemata formed with SBL (see Section 3.4). Generalizations are not required to be 100% accurate. A schema constructed by TDL contains a counter that is incremented during memory search when a successful prediction is made, and another counter that is incremented when an incorrect prediction is made. When the ratio of these counters is lower than a certain value[38], then the schema is eliminated. The correction step differs from the correction of schema created by similarity-based learning. In SBL, as implemented in OCCAM, there is a conservative incremental strategy for refining a hypothesis. In contrast, in TDL, OCCAM is gambling that its hypothesis is indeed correct. If this is the case, then less effort (in terms of hypotheses considered and examples processed) is required to arrive at the correct hypothesis. However, a price must be paid if the hypothesis is incorrect, since a new hypothesis cannot be easily constructed from the incorrect hypothesis. Instead, OCCAM must try other features of the example or other generalization rules to come up with a new hypotheses. The experimental evidence from psychology indicates that this gamble is worth taking (see Section 4.2.1), since learning is facilitated when a relationship is consistent with a theory of causality and is hindered when it is not. In addition, Section 4.6 compares the performance of OCCAM using TDL and OCCAM using SBL. The results indicate that fewer examples are required to find a correct hypothesis with TDL.

4.4.2. Theory-driven learning: An example

In this section, I illustrate the process of theory-driven learning with an example. The input to OCCAM is the Conceptual Dependency representation of the situations described in Figure 4-7. The data correspond to the experiment in which the child could only inflate a balloon after it has been dipped in water (see Section 4.2.1). The representation of the first example is illustrated in Figure 4-8.

When presented with the first example (the child inflating a small yellow

---

[38]This is a parameter in OCCAM. The current value of the parameter is 0.8.

1. The child dips a small yellow balloon in water, blows air into the balloon and the balloon is inflated.

2. The child snaps her fingers, blows air into a large yellow balloon and the balloon is not inflated.

3. The child puts on a necklace, blows air into a large orange balloon and the balloon is not inflated.

4. The child dips a large yellow balloon in water, blows air into the balloon and the balloon is inflated.

Figure 4-7:   Input to OCCAM describing the situation when the child can only inflate a balloon after it has been dipped in water.

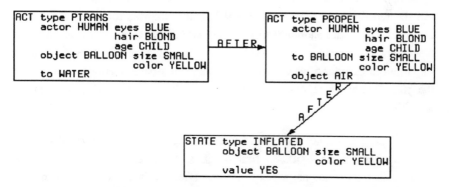

Figure 4-8:   CD representation for "the child dips a small yellow balloon in water, blows air into the balloon and the balloon is inflated."

balloon after dipping it in water), the situation matches a generalization rule similar to the one in Figure 4-1[39]. OCCAM constructs a generalization that indicates that blowing air into a balloon results in the balloon being inflated. This changes the temporal link "after" to a causal link "result" (see Figure 4-9).

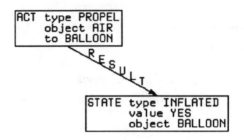

Figure 4-9: A generalization that indicates that blowing air into a balloon results in the balloon being inflated.

In addition to the generalized event, the schema created also contains a rule format of the generalized event that can be used for constructing plans or explanations.   The rule format contains a variable where the **balloon** is located in the generalized event since the balloon that is inflated must be the same balloon that has air blown into it. Figure 4-10 contains the rule format. For the remainder of this example, I will ignore the rule format of a schema. However, the reader should keep in mind that this is being constructed when a new schema is created. The rule format of a generalized event will be quite important in Chapter 5 which discusses explanation-based learning (which uses the rule format of schemata created by similarity-based and theory-driven learning).

The next example is the child not inflating a large yellow balloon after snapping her fingers. OCCAM first discards its current hypothesis, since it predicts that all balloons will be inflated after air is blown into them. A generalization rule suggests a difference in the size attribute of the balloons is responsible for the difference in the result: small balloons can be inflated and large balloons cannot (see Figure 4-11). (A number of subjects in the experiment reported afterwards that they entertained this hypothesis.)

---

[39]The generalization rule differs slightly because in Conceptual Dependency, the destination of an action can also change as a consequence of the action. In the representation of "blowing air into a balloon", the type of action is a PROPEL, the object is "air" and the destination is "balloon".

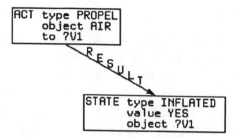

Figure 4-10: A rule format of the generalization that indicates that blowing air into a balloon results in the balloon being inflated. Variables are preceded by "?".

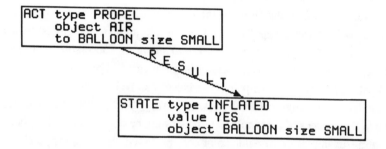

Figure 4-11: A generalization that indicates that blowing air into a small balloon results in the balloon being inflated.

A third example is consistent with the current hypothesis (the child not inflating a large orange balloon after putting a necklace on), so OCCAM retains its current hypothesis.

The next example (the child inflating a large yellow balloon after dipping it in water) does not agree with the prediction of the current hypothesis. It is discarded. A generalization rule similar to the one in Figure 4-4 suggests that the action before blowing air into the balloon (dipping the balloon in water) results in a state that enables blowing air into the balloon to inflate the balloon. The generalization that describes this situation is illustrated in Figure 4-6 on 121.

4.5. Dispositions

Recall that a dispositional generalization rule indicates that a certain class of actors or objects is required for a causal relationship to hold. However, a generalization rule does not indicate what particular class of actors or objects is required. OCCAM must come up with a current best hypothesis from the set of hypotheses that are consistent with the observed data. For example, when Karen cannot open the refrigerator but Mike can, a generalization rule indicates that some feature of the actor is responsible. But is it the hair color, eye color, age, or shoe size? In the absence of any knowledge, OCCAM must simply guess. In this section, I describe how OCCAM can do better than guessing, by learning what sort of hypotheses have been successful in the past.

How can prior learning facilitate the selection of the current best hypothesis from a set of consistent hypotheses? One simple approach might be to keep track of the features that have entered into previous successful hypotheses. However, this can lead the system astray in some cases. For example, consider a child eating pieces of a pineapple. The pieces can be different shapes (square or triangular) or different colors (yellow or white). Eventually, the hypothesis that the yellow pieces of pineapple taste better may be considered and supported by several examples. Should color be preferred in future hypotheses? Unfortunately, preferring color indiscriminately would hinder rather than facilitate learning in many situations. Consider the earlier example of the refrigerator opening after Mike pulls on the door, but not opening after Karen pulls on the door. If color were preferred, the best hypothesis might be that when a person with a blue shirt pulls on the door, the refrigerator will open. The problem with this simple approach is that the context in which a preference is made is ignored.

The approach that I take in OCCAM differs from the above simple approach in two ways:

1. Features that have entered into previous successful hypotheses are preferred in more restricted situations. These situations are determined by the type of the cause in the generalization rule and the type of the generalization rule. For example, after inducing that the refrigerator door will open after an adult pulls on it, the preference for age applies only to the actor of this type of the

action (propel, an application of a force) and to the same type of generalization rules (i.e., those which attribute a difference in a result to a difference in the actor).

2. The features that have entered into previous successful hypotheses are used to create **dispositions**. These dispositions represent capacities or potentials. For example, after OCCAM induces that the refrigerator door will open when an adult pulls on it, a dispositional attribute (which might be called "strength") is created. In this case, the dispositional attribute refers to the tendency for an application of force by a particular actor to result in a state change.

Learning dispositions that select a hypothesis from the set of consistent hypotheses can be broken into two subproblems. First, one must determine the class of situations to which the disposition applies. This is not learned by OCCAM. Instead OCCAM assumes that the class of situations is defined by the type of action and by the feature that the generalization rule indicates is responsible for the different outcome[40] Second, one must learn what features indicate that an actor or object possesses a disposition. OCCAM learns this when it postulates that different features are responsible for different outcomes. Dispositional attributes are created and used in the following manner:

1. A dispositional generalization rule has found two sets of similar actions with different outcomes. This dispositional generalization rule indicates that a difference in one of the roles of the action (e.g., the actor) may be responsible.

2. OCCAM looks for differences between the two specified roles of the two sets of actions. For example, an action may have one outcome

---

[40]A topic for future research is learning this class from examples. In practice, associating the disposition with the CD action has worked fairly well. However, there are some examples not accounted for by this simple strategy. For example, the "color" of food is an indicator of the "taste" of the food: yellow pineapple is sweeter than white. However, if OCCAM were to associate a "sweet" disposition with **ingest**, the CD primitive of verbs such as "eat" or "taste", it would also apply to other forms of **ingest** such as "smell" or "inject". The solution to this problem is to learn the class of situation in which each disposition applies rather than to assume it is at the same level of generality as the CD primitive actions.

when the actor is an adult with brown hair and a different outcome when the actor is an infant with blond hair. Each difference (e.g., age or hair color) is a candidate hypothesis that is consistent with the data. If there are no differences, then the dispositional generalization rule does not apply to this situation and other more complex generalization rules are tried.

3. OCCAM sees if there exist any dispositions that apply in this situation. For example, if the type of action is a propel, then OCCAM might have already learned a "strength" disposition that indicates that the actor's age can be responsible for the different outcome. If this disposition is consistent with the data, then a hypothesis is selected that indicates that "strength" and, therefore, "age" determined the outcome of the action. In addition, when a disposition suggests a hypothesis, the confidence in that disposition is increased. On the other hand, if the disposition should apply to the situation, but is not consistent with the data, the confidence in the disposition is decreased. If the confidence falls below a threshold, the disposition is deleted.

4. If there are no dispositions that apply, OCCAM creates one. This is accomplished by selecting one feature at random from the set of differing features. The user is asked to give this new disposition a name (or OCCAM generates an internal name such as disp.43) for this disposition. The differing feature becomes the feature that indicates the class of objects that have this disposition. The disposition is associated with the generalization rule indexed by the type of action. The disposition can be used to select future hypotheses as in the previous step. However, if it is not successful at this task (i.e., it proposes hypotheses that are not consistent with the data), then it will be abandoned and a different feature that is consistent with the data will be selected.

Dispositional attributes serve several purposes:

- Dispositions serve as intermediate conclusions (Fu & Buchanan, 1985).   Like Fu and Buchanan's intermediate concepts, dispositional attributes often correspond to named concepts in our domain (see Figure 4-12). If further information is found out about a dispositional attribute, it applies to all future and past examples. For example, in OCCAM, age is initially associated with strength. If other features are found that are indicators of strength (e.g., size of arms), they enter into future predictions.

Role	Action	Feature	Disposition
actor	propel	age	strength
object	ingest	composition	poisonous
actor	move	age	dexterity
actor	mbuild	species	intelligence
actor	mbuild	age	intelligence
object	propel	material	fragility

Figure 4-12:   Dispositional attributes: the role and the action determine the class of situations in which the dispositional attribute is applicable.   The feature indicates what sort of objects possess that disposition.   The name of the disposition is not used and has no special meaning to the program.

- Distributional attributes can be viewed as parent predicates (Goodman, 1983). In this manner, distributional attributes facilitate learning new causal theories. When learning that a refrigerator will open after an adult pulls on the door, two hypotheses are created:

  1. Adults are strong enough to open a refrigerator door.

  2. Adults are strong.

This second more general hypothesis facilitates learning in new domains.   For example, this hypothesis can be specialized to indicate that adults are strong enough to inflate balloons. Note that

OCCAM does not start with dispositional attributes such as "strength". Instead, dispositional attributes are learned to account for differences in capabilities (for actors) or tendencies (for objects). These dispositional attributes serve as <u>domain-specific</u> <u>knowledge</u> that guide the search for causal hypotheses.

- More support is given to hypotheses that are formed by making use of existing dispositional attributes. In this manner, prior learning also assists selecting among multiple hypotheses. For example, once OCCAM learns about strength, it encounters an example when an adult with brown hair can inflate a yellow balloon, and a child with blond hair cannot inflate a blue balloon. Clearly, the fact that adults are strong can rule out the hair color, or any other attribute that may correlate (e.g., height) as a reasonable hypothesis for the different results. However, there is also a generalization rule that indicates that a feature of the object could be responsible (e.g., the color of a balloon.) Two competing hypotheses are compared. Since there is no dispositional attribute for the color of the object of an application of force, the hypothesis that age (and strength) are responsible is postulated before the hypothesis that balloon color is responsible.

There are several issues that arise when using dispositional attributes to facilitate the search for causal hypotheses:

- When are dispositional attributes created? Dispositional attributes are created to account for a difference in the result of two (or more) actions[41].

- How is the creation of a new dispositional attribute for each new example avoided? The reuse of existing dispositional attributes is

---

[41]Figure 4-11 on page 129 was created by not using the module in OCCAM that creates dispositional attributes. The generalization in Figure 4-11 indicates that if a balloon is small it can be inflated. With dispositions activated, the generalization would indicate that if a balloon is "disp-17" then it can be inflated, and small balloons are "disp-17".

preferred to the creation of new ones.

4.5.1. Dispositions: An example

In this section, I demonstrate how learning dispositional attributes facilitates learning new causal theories. The example that I consider is the refrigerator opening after Mike pulls on the door, but not opening after Karen pulls on the door. In this case there are two events in memory. A simplified representation of Mike opening the refrigerator is illustrated in Figure 4-13.

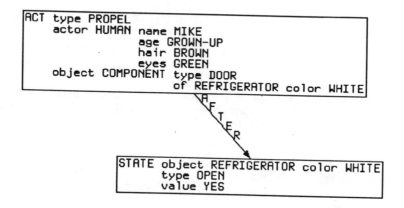

```
ACT  type PROPEL
     actor HUMAN  name MIKE
                  age GROWN-UP
                  hair BROWN
                  eyes GREEN
     object COMPONENT  type DOOR
                       of REFRIGERATOR  color WHITE
                          A
                           F
                            T
                             E
                              R

     STATE object REFRIGERATOR color WHITE
           type OPEN
           value YES
```

Figure 4-13: Simplified Conceptual Dependency representation of "Mike opening the refrigerator."

The generalization rule in Figure 4-3 suggests that a difference in the actor accounts for the different results when Mike or Karen pulls on the door. Since there are not yet any applicable dispositional attributes, OCCAM randomly selects one attribute of the actor that is different in Karen and Mike: eye color. OCCAM creates a new dispositional attribute[42] (disp-1) that represents the tendency for an application of a force by a person with green eyes to result in a state change. The current best hypothesis is that persons with green eyes are disp-1 enough to open a refrigerator. Figure 4-14 illustrates the schema that is built to indicate that when a person who is disp-1 enough to open a refrigerator pulls on the refrigerator door, the refrigerator door will open. Figure

---

[42]This tendency doesn't have a name in English, so I'll have to refer to it by OCCAM's name: disp-1.

4-15, contains the dispositional attribute created that indicates that persons with green eyes are **disp-1** enough to open a refrigerator.

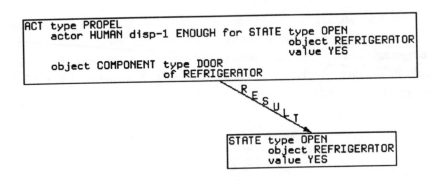

Figure 4-14: **A schema that indicates that when a person who is disp-1 enough to open a refrigerator pulls on the refrigerator door, the refrigerator door will open.**

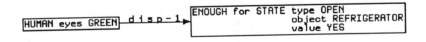

Figure 4-15: **A dispositional attribute: persons with green eyes are disp-1 enough to open a refrigerator.**

Next, OCCAM is presented with a counterexample of a small child with green eyes and blond hair who cannot open the refrigerator. This contradicts a prediction made by the current hypothesis. Since very little confidence had been built up for the current hypothesis, it is abandoned, and a new current best hypothesis must be generated. There are at least two possible hypotheses: persons with brown hair can open refrigerators, or adults can open refrigerators. OCCAM randomly selects adults to form a new dispositional attribute[43] (**strong**). The current best hypothesis is that adults are **strong** enough to open a refrigerator (see Figure 4-17 and Figure 4-17). Further examples give a great deal of support to this hypothesis and to the dispositional attribute called

---

[43]To OCCAM it wouldn't matter if this attribute were called **disp-2**.

strength[44].

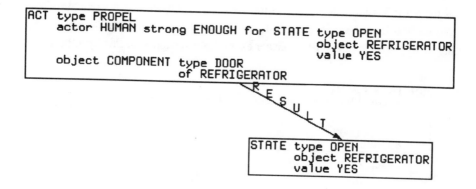

Figure 4-16: A schema that indicates that when a person who is
strong enough to open a refrigerator pulls on the
refrigerator door, the refrigerator door will open.

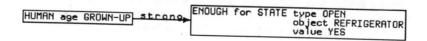

Figure 4-17: The strength dispositional attribute: adults are strong
enough to open a refrigerator.

Once OCCAM has learned a dispositional attribute, future learning is
facilitated. OCCAM is next presented with an example of Mike successfully
inflating a round yellow balloon, while Karen is unsuccessful at inflating a long
blue balloon. This time, two generalization rules apply, one which would
attribute the difference in the result to a difference in the object (round yellow
balloon vs. long blue balloon) and one which would attribute the difference in
the result to the actor (Mike vs. Karen). For the actor difference, the strength
dispositional attribute applies, and the age attribute is selected over other
attributes such as hair color. For the object difference, there is no dispositional
attribute and color is favored randomly over size. There are now two competing

---

[44]Note that an event such as an adult not being able to lift a car would not decrease support for the
existence of the strength dispositional attribute. Only a counterexample such as a child lifting a car
that an adult could not would remove support from this hypothesis since this counterexample would
use the same generalization rule.

hypotheses: adults can inflate balloons or yellow balloons can be inflated. These hypotheses are compared, and since the strength (and, therefore, the age) of the actor has more support than the color of the object,[45] it is favored. The current best hypothesis is that adults are strong enough to inflate balloons (see Figure 4-19 and Figure 4-19). Further examples add support to this hypothesis.

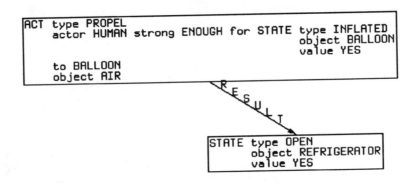

Figure 4-18: A schema that indicates that when a person who is strong enough to inflate a balloon blows air into a balloon, the balloon will be inflated.

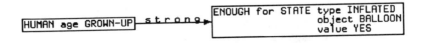

Figure 4-19: The strength dispositional attribute: adults are strong enough to blow up a balloon.

The advantage of using dispositions is that once a disposition has been learned in one situation, such as opening refrigerator doors, learning is easier and fewer examples are required in different situations such as blowing up balloons.

---

[45]Recall that the re-use of a dispositional attribute increases the support for a hypothesis.

4.5.2. Refining a dispositional attribute

In many ways, the evaluation of a dispositional attribute is similar to the evaluation of schemata that are created by similarity-based learning (see Section 3.4) and theory-driven learning. In particular, counters are kept to indicate when the disposition leads to accurate prediction, and when the disposition leads to an incorrect prediction. When a disposition has been useful a number of times, a few exceptions merely decrease support for the disposition rather than cause the disposition to be abandoned. In addition, if there is a regularity to the exceptions, then the disposition is refined to accommodate the exceptions. For example, assume that a few examples of a frail grandmother who is unable to open a jar of jelly are observed. The strength disposition would be revised to indicate that frail persons are not strong. Similarly, after seeing several examples of a child not blowing up balloons, not opening refrigerators, and not opening jars, several examples of a child (Karen) successfully inflating a balloon are seen. Rather than abandoning the relationship between adults and strength, OCCAM modifies the strength disposition to add the fact that Karen is strong enough to blow up balloons. Figure 4-20 illustrates how OCCAM represents that Karen is strong enough to blow up balloons. Note that there is an implicit disjunction since the fact that adults are strong enough to blow up balloons is still in memory (see in Figure 4-19).

Figure 4-20: The modified strength dispositional attribute: Karen is strong enough to blow up a balloon.

4.6. Experimental Results: TDL and SBL

How much of an improvement is theory-driven learning over similarity-based learning? One way to compare the performance of two different approaches to learning is to compare the number of examples each approach requires to find the correct hypothesis. To quantify the improvement in performance of TDL over SBL, I tested OCCAM under various conditions.

In TDL, the number of examples depends upon the number of features used to describe the objects in the event. For example, the generalization in Figure 4-3 states that if similar actions performed on an object have different results, and they are performed by different actors, the differing features of the actor are responsible for the different result. The number of features used to describe the actor and the object influence the number of examples required to learn the concept. However, the number of roles that describe the event does not affect the learning. For example, TDL is not affected if the performance of the stock market, the location of the stars, and the outcome of sporting events is included in the description of an event together with the actor and the object. This is the advantage of TDL since learning is focused on those attributes that are likely to be involved in a causal relationship.

In SBL, performance is dependent on the number of features used to describe each role and the number of roles that describe the event. SBL is adversely affected when additional irrelevant information, such as the performance of the stock market, is included in the input representation.

All learning programs are also affected by the distribution from which the input examples are drawn, and the distribution of feature values in the environment. In the experiment that I ran, half of the examples were positive and half were negative. The concept to be learned is that adults are strong enough to open the refrigerator. The concept is learned when there are no dispositional attributes (e.g., strength) that could assist the theory-driven learner. All of the features that were used to describe the input example were binary features and the value of each feature was selected randomly with equal probabilities. I ran trials in which there were 0, 4 and 10 roles (in addition to actor and the object) used to describe each event. For each of these three conditions, I ran the SBL module and the the TDL module of OCCAM on problems in which each role was described by 3, 5, 10, 20 and 40 features. The results of the experiment are illustrated in Figure 4-21. The values shown for each point is the number of examples (averaged over 25 runs) required to learn the concept as a function of the number of features used to describe each role.

As expected, the performance of TDL was not dependent on the number of roles used to describe the input events. The graph only lists TDL with 10 additional roles because the result does not differ from TDL with 4 or 0 additional roles. The graph clearly shows the advantage that TDL has over SBL. For example, with 10 additional roles and 10 features for each role, theory-driven learning required an average of 4.7 examples to find the correct

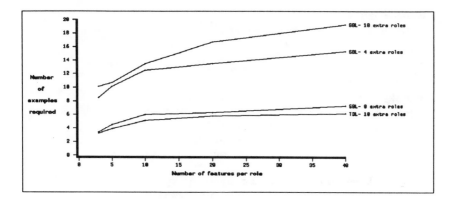

Figure 4-21:   The average number of examples required for similarity-based   learning and theory-driven learning to find the correct hypothesis.

hypothesis. SBL required 13.2 examples. If the consequence of acting upon an incorrect hypothesis are important, or if the number of examples is small, TDL is a significant improvement over SBL.

4.7. Learning Social Theories

In addition to generalization rules that guide the search for laws of physical causality, OCCAM also contains generalization rules for social causation. These generalization rules postulate intentional relationships (Dyer, 1983) between goals, plans and events. They are processed and handled in the same manner as the generalization rules for physical causality. However, I distinguish them mainly to emphasize that there is less empirical support for these generalization rules. Less is known about the constraints on human learning of social knowledge than the learning of physical knowledge. For this reason, OCCAM's coverage of the social domain is much less complete than its coverage of the domain of physical causality.

However, the social generalization rules fit the same pattern and serve the same purpose as generalization rules for physical causality. A generalization rule is a template for a causal or social relationship. For example, one social generalization rule is: *if a goal to perform an action is blocked by a state then the opposite state is an enabling condition for the action.* This generalization rule is displayed in Figure 4-22.

```
(def-gen-rule
  ?state-1 = (state type ?ptype
                     value (no)
                     actor ?actor
                     object ?object)

  blocks
  (goal actor ?actor
        goal ?act-1 = (act type ?atype
                           actor ?actor
                           object ?object))

  ((?act-1 enabled-by (state type ?ptype
                             value (yes)
                             actor ?actor
                             object ?object)))
)
```

Figure 4-22:   An exceptionless generalization rule that applies in a social situation:
if a goal to perform an action is blocked by a state then the opposite
state is an enabling condition for the action.

OCCAM uses this generalization rule to explain why an example of
delta-agency fails.   Recall that in Section 3.4.1 OCCAM acquired a
generalization that indicates that when a person asks a relative to do something,
then the relative will.   What happens, for example, when a persons asks a
relative for an object that the relative doesn't have?   For example, what should
OCCAM do when it encounters **apple-2**?.

- **apple-2**: Karen wants an apple. She asks her mother Chris for
  one and Chris tells her that she doesn't have an apple. The CD
  representation of this indicates that the goal is blocked by Chris not
  having the apple.

Instead of simply decreasing support for **delta-agency**, OCCAM is able
to come up with a hypothesis for why **delta-agency** fails.   The
generalization rule suggests a possible explanation: in order to give an object to
someone, you must possess the object. Note that this explanation is dependent
on the mother informing the child what state is blocking her goal. If the mother
just didn't give the child an apple, then OCCAM would not be able to come up
with an explanation and would decrease support for **delta-agency**. The

inductive leap that OCCAM makes is that the opposite of the state[46] which is blocking the goal is an enabling condition of performing the action that achieves the goal. The warrant that OCCAM has for making this inductive leap is the generalization rule in Figure 4-22. Figure 4-23 illustrates the rule that OCCAM learns in this situation.   A specialized version of **delta-agency** is constructed to account for those situations when asking a relative for an object results in a failure because the relative does not have the object. This schema is displayed in Figure 4-24.

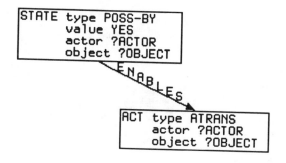

Figure 4-23: A rule acquired by OCCAM when an exception to **delta-agency** is encountered: in order to give an object to someone, you must possess the object.

The generalization rule discussed in the previous example is an exceptionless generalization. Dispositional and historical generalization rules also apply in social situations. For example, there is a generalization rule that states: *if an event (?e) motivates a goal (?g) for someone (?p1), and someone else (?p2) observes the event (?e) and performs an action (?a) that achieves the goal (?g) for ?p1, then the event (?e) motivates the goal (?g) for ?p2.*

This generalization rule is applicable in several situations. For example, we recently purchased a new kitten as a companion for our older cat. When the kitten misbehaved by climbing onto the table while we were eating, we closed it in another room. After the older cat saw us do this, he pushed the door open to let the kitten out. This generalization rule would enable one to hypothesize from

---

[46]i.e., the state that is blocking the goal in this example is " Chris does not have an apple.". The opposite of this state, "Chris has an apple." is required for Chris to give Karen the apple.

```
DELTA-AGENCY the-outcome GOAL-OUTCOME type FAILURE
                                     actor =THE-ACTOR
                                     goal STATE type POSS-BY
                                                    actor =THE-ACTOR
                                                    value NO
                                                    object =THE-OBJ
             the-problem STATE type POSS-BY
                               actor =THE-HELPER
                               value NO
                               object =THE-OBJ
             the-sub-goal GOAL actor =THE-HELPER
                               goal ACT type ATRANS
                                        actor =THE-HELPER
                                        object =THE-OBJ
                                        to =THE-ACTOR
             the-plan PLAN actor =THE-ACTOR
                           plan =THE-MTRANS
             the-goal GOAL actor =THE-ACTOR
                           goal STATE type POSS-BY
                                      actor =THE-ACTOR
                                      value YES
                                      object =THE-OBJ
                           plan PLAN actor =THE-ACTOR
                                     plan =THE-MTRANS
                           outcome GOAL-OUTCOME type FAILURE
                                                actor =THE-ACTOR
                                                goal STATE type POSS-BY
                                                           actor =THE-ACTOR
                                                           value NO
                                                           object =THE-OBJ

             the-mtrans ACT type MTRANS
                            actor =THE-ACTOR
                            to =THE-HELPER
                            object ACT actor =THE-HELPER
             the-helper HUMAN relation IPT type FAMILY-REL
                                           of =THE-ACTOR
             the-actor HUMAN
             the-obj P-OBJ
```

Figure 4-24: The generalized event of a specialization of delta-agency. This schema describes those attempts to use delta-agency that failed because the-helper did not possess the the-obj.

the older cat's actions that the older cat wanted to let the kitten out. In another situation, OCCAM uses this generalization rule when it is given several examples of parents helping their children and strangers not assisting a child. OCCAM hypothesizes that parents have a goal of preserving the health of their children.

Once OCCAM has constructed the rule that parents have a goal of preserving the health of their children, it can use it as background knowledge for EBL. This particular rule is useful in explaining why a parent pays the ransom in a kidnapping episode. A kidnapping schema is created by retaining only those features of the kidnapping episode that are necessary to produce the explanation. This kidnapping schema contains the knowledge that the ransom typically goes to a relative of the hostage because they may be willing to pay money to preserve the health of the hostage. Section 7.5 discusses this example more thoroughly.

There is also a dispositional generalization rule that is useful in another specialization of **delta-agency**. This generalization rule attributes a difference in the outcome to difference in the agent who performs an action that achieves a goal. This rule applies when OCCAM encounters a situation in which **delta-agency** is attempted when the **the-helper** is not a relative:

- **barbie-1**: Lynn asks Tiffany to give her a barbie doll. Tiffany doesn't share the doll with Lynn.

Previously, OCCAM had noticed a similarity between all examples of **delta-agency**. When the **delta-agency** plan is successful, the helper is related to the actor. Now, when it encounters an example when an unrelated person does not assist, a disposition which might be called "caring" is created to account for the different results. The definition of caring in Figure 4-25 states that relatives are caring enough to see that the goal succeeds and unrelated persons are not[47].

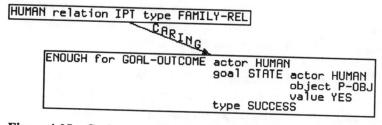

Figure 4-25: Caring: a dispositional attribute. The feature that indicates that a person has this disposition is the presence of an IPT (i.e., an interpersonal theme such as a relative).

A specialized version of **delta-agency** is created to account for those instances of **delta-agency** that fail because the helper does not care if the actor's goal fails. This schema is illustrated in Figure 4-26.

4.8. Summary

This chapter presented the theory-driven learning component of OCCAM. Theory-driven learning determines if an event fits a known pattern for a causal

---

[47]Presumedly, future examples would refine this to accommodate friends, teachers etc.

```
DELTA-AGENCY the-outcome GOAL-OUTCOME type FAILURE
                                      actor =THE-ACTOR
                                      goal STATE object =THE-OBJ
                                                 value YES
                                                 actor =THE-ACTOR
                 ... ...
                 the-helper HUMAN caring ENOUGH for GOAL-OUTCOME type FAILURE
                                                                  actor HUMAN
                                                                  goal STATE object P-OBJ
                                                                             value YES
                                                                             actor HUMAN
                 the-actor HUMAN
```

Figure 4-26: A specialization of `delta-agency` that indicates that `delta-agency` will fail if the helper does not care if the actor's goal succeeds.

relationship. When an events conforms to such a pattern, learning is facilitated because the theory of causality provides an additional constraint on causal relationships. OCCAM represents a theory of causality by a set of *generalization rules* that suggest causal explanations. In addition to being consistent with the examples presented, a hypothesis proposed by the TDL component of OCCAM must be consistent with a theory of causality. For this reason, TDL requires fewer examples than SBL to discover a causal relationship. However, the causal relationships proposed by TDL may prove incorrect when later examples are encountered. Schemata acquired via TDL are evaluated in a manner similar to those acquired via SBL.

This chapter also introduced *dispositions*. Dispositions represent potentials or capacities of people or objects. In the course of learning causal relationships, OCCAM also learns dispositions to account for different outcomes of similar actions. For example, adults can perform many tasks, such as opening a refrigerator, which children cannot. When OCCAM learns this fact about adults, it creates a disposition that might be called "strength" and postulates that adults possess this property. Once OCCAM has acquired a notion of "strength", it is easier for it to learn other relationships, such as adults are strong enough to inflate balloons but children are not.

Chapter 5
Explanation-Based Learning in OCCAM

The information encoded in schemata can be accessed to make predictions about future events. Therefore, a schema should only contain features that an understander has a justification for believing will appear in future events. One justification is that the features have always appeared in previous events. In Chapter 3, I discussed the process of similarity-based learning that utilizes this justification when building generalizations by retaining all features that are common to several examples. In Chapter 4, I illustrated a means of improving on SBL. When a learner has a general theory of what configurations of events might be causally related, correlations that are not consistent with the theory of causality can justifiably be treated as coincidences and ignored. In this chapter, I discuss explanation-based learning that relies on another justification for believing that features which have appeared in previous events will also appear in future events. The justification is to demonstrate deductively that a set of features are sufficient to produce the predicted outcome. This learning method creates a schema by retaining only those features that were necessary to explain why an event occurred. The explanation indicates that when a particular class of events occurs, a particular effect will result. This causal knowledge is associated with the schema and serves as the justification for predicting the consequences of future events.

It is instructive to compare SBL, TDL and EBL on the same problem. Consider the following problem:

- On Monday, Chris is wearing a red shirt. She turns the radio on, takes a jar of peanut butter out of the cabinet and makes a sandwich for Lynn. Lynn likes the sandwich.

- On Tuesday, Mike is wearing a red shirt. He turns the radio on, takes a jar of peanut butter out of the cabinet and makes a sandwich for Lynn. Lynn likes the sandwich.

• On Wednesday, Mike is wearing a blue shirt. He turns the
   television on, takes a jar of peanut butter out of the cabinet, drops
   the jar on the floor, and makes Lynn a sandwich. Lynn gets a cut
   on the roof of her mouth.

If this problem were approached with SBL, all features which are present
when Lynn cuts her mouth and not present when Lynn doesn't cut her mouth on
Monday and Tuesday would be considered as potential causes of Lynn cutting
her mouth. These features include:

1. The jar of peanut butter was dropped.

2. The person who prepares the sandwich is wearing a blue shirt.

3. The television is on.

If the similarity-based learner constructs the most specific conjunctive
generalization consistent with the data, it will hypothesize that when a person
eats a peanut-butter sandwich prepared by someone with a blue shirt after the jar
was dropped while the television is on, then the roof of the mouth will be cut.
Examples of eating sandwiches prepared by persons with blue shirts and
sandwiches eaten while the television is on without unpleasant consequences are
required to arrive at a reasonable hypothesis.

If this problem were approached with theory-driven learning, the examples
would be compared against templates for causal relationships. Two such
templates apply in this situation. One would blame the cut on the different
features of the agent who prepared the sandwich. The other would blame the cut
on the action which preceded the preparation. Two hypothesis would be
consistent with the examples and the theory of causality:

1. The jar of peanut butter was dropped.

2. The person who prepares the sandwich is wearing a blue shirt.

Without any prior knowledge, OCCAM would favor the second hypothesis
initially because dispositional generalization rules are favored over historical
ones. An example of eating a sandwich prepared by persons with blue shirts
without unpleasant consequences would be needed before the correct hypothesis

is considered. The benefit of constraining learning with a theory of causality is that fewer examples are required because fewer hypothesis are considered. In the current example, the hypothesis that the television is responsible for cutting the roof of Lynn's mouth is never considered since it does not fit a pattern for a causal relationship.

If the current problem were approached with explanation-based learning, then the first step is to explain why Lynn cut her mouth. Explanation-based learning requires that the learner have enough knowledge to construct a causal chain that indicates why the outcome occurred. In this example, the causal chain would contain the following information:

- Dropping the jar of peanut-butter caused the jar to shatter.
- When the jar shattered, glass splinters got on the peanut butter.
- When the peanut butter was eaten, glass splinters got in Lynn's mouth.
- A glass splinter cut Lynn's mouth.

To construct a generalization with EBL, the example (Lynn cutting her mouth) is generalized by removing all unessential features. A features is retained if it was relied upon to build the explanation. A generalized explanation is constructed by chaining together several general facts that can be represented as separate schema:

- Dropping a glass object can cause the object to shatter.
- When a glass object shatters, glass splinters can get on nearby objects.
- The contents of a container is near the container.
- When a person eats, the food goes in the person's mouth.
- Glass splinters are sharp.
- If a sharp object touches a person, it can cut the person's skin.

Explanation-based learning creates a new schema by recording the interactions between several previously unrelated facts. Taken together, these facts specify the features of the problem that were required for the explanation to be constructed. The generalized event that is constructed by explanation-based learning in this example indicates that when a person eats a food which was in a glass container that has been dropped, the person's mouth can get cut by glass splinters in the food.

The principle advantage that EBL has over SBL and TDL is that fewer examples are required to arrive at the correct generalization. The idea behind explanation-based learning is quite simple. It is easier to learn that A results in C when P_1 and P_2 are true, if you already know that A results in B when P_1 is true, and B results in C when P_2 is true. Instead of correlating over several examples of A and C under various conditions to arrive at this conclusion, only one example is needed. Note however, that EBL does not add to the knowledge of the learner (Dietterich, 1986). The new schema makes it easier to solve a particular class of problems in the future. Explanation in the future will be a memory search to recognize that a new problem is an instance of the newly learned schema instead of an inference process to chain together several facts. Because of the advantage that EBL has over other forms of learning, it is attempted first in OCCAM. However, because EBL is limited to those situations that OCCAM can explain, SBL and TDL serve important roles.

5.1. Background: Explanation-based Learning

Explanation-based learning (EBL) is a learning method that analytically determines which features of an example are relevant. Explanation-based learning systems (DeJong & Mooney, 1986; Mitchell et al., 1986a) share a common approach to generalization. First, an example problem is solved producing an explanation (occasionally called a justification, or a proof) which indicates what information (e.g., features of the example and inference rules) was needed to arrive at a solution. Next, the example is generalized by retaining only those features of the example which were necessary to produce the explanation. Various systems differ according to the problem solved, and who does the problem solving. For example, in LEAP (Mitchell et al., 1986b) a user designs a VLSI circuit to achieve some specified functionality. LEAP produces a justification that indicates how the circuit implements the specified function. In OCCAM, the reason that an economic sanction incident failed or succeeded in achieving the desired effect determines which features of the incident should be generalized.

5.1.1. GENESIS

GENESIS (Mooney & DeJong, 1985) is a program that utilizes explanation-based learning to acquire schemata. For example, GENESIS learns about arson from the following story:

Arson-1

Stan owned a warehouse. He insured it against fire for $100,000. Stan burned the warehouse. He called Prudential and told them it was burnt. Prudential paid him $100,000.

GENESIS learns from observing others achieve goals. It uses its existing knowledge to understand how a goal was achieved. Then, it creates a general plan to achieve that goal by retaining only those features of the example which were necessary to understand how the goal was achieved. For example, in Arson-1, GENESIS determines that Stan's goal was to acquire money. It constructs an explanation which indicates how Stan achieved this goal (i.e., Prudential paid Stan money because the warehouse was burned. The warehouse was burned because Stan burned it). Next, it generalizes the explanation by removing all details from the example which were not needed to create the explanation. The final plan indicates that a means of acquiring money is to insure a flammable object, and burn it.   GENESIS already had enough knowledge to understand and generalize Arson-1. It creates an arson schema by finding interactions between previously unrelated chunks of knowledge (i.e., if an insured object is destroyed, the beneficiary is paid money and if an object is burned, then the object is destroyed). Explanation-based learning is a useful learning strategy for learning by observation because it is easier to verify that a plan achieves a goal in a particular example than to find a plan to achieve the goal without an example (DeJong, 1986).

5.1.2. Analysis of explanation-based learning

Explanation-based learning is a powerful approach to learning.   It demonstrates that there are benefits in viewing learning as a knowledge-intensive process. In particular, fewer examples are required to acquire a useful schemata. In fact, most EBL systems require just one example. It provides an answer to the problem of determining which features are relevant. The relevant features are exactly those which are needed to arrive at an explanation of why a particular outcome occurred. Of course, in some sense EBL does not learn anything new. It just reformulates existing knowledge into a form that makes future application of that knowledge more efficient.

EBL takes advantage of novel interactions between existing knowledge structures. Previous work in natural language understanding has centered on finding explanations that consist of interactions between existing knowledge structures (Wilensky, 1978). For example, BORIS (Dyer, 1983) finds an interaction between a "divorce" schema and the "ask a friend for a favor" schema when it understands a story in which a distressed husband asks a lawyer who was his college roommate to represent him in a divorce case. EBL adds a generalization step to the process of finding explanations by instantiating existing knowledge structures. EBL finds a general description of the class of situations for which the explanation will apply. This general description becomes a new knowledge structure which can simplify the understanding of that class of situations in the future.

Of course, EBL cannot serve as a general model of human learning. It requires a great deal of existing background knowledge to produce an explanation. It cannot answer the question of how this existing background knowledge is acquired.

5.2. Constructing an Explanation

In most EBL systems (Kedar-Cabelli & McCarty, 1987; Mooney & Bennett, 1986), the search for an explanation can be an expensive process. In these systems, a backward chaining rule system performs depth-first search to arrive at an explanation. In response, to the combinatorics of searching for an explanation, Lebowitz has decided to search for an explanation less frequently in his UNIMEM system. Explanation-based learning in UNIMEM is attempted on generalizations formed with similarity-based learning techniques.

In OCCAM, the problem of producing an explanation is addressed directly. Abstract explanations are first constructed which are then verified with rules associated with schemata. DeJong (DeJong, 1986) has shown that it is computationally less expensive to verify an explanation than to create an explanation. In addition, the work on ABSTRIPS (Sacerdoti, 1974) has demonstrated that in some circumstances problem solving in an abstract search space, followed by refinement in the actual search space, is significantly less expensive than simple problem solving in the actual search space.

In OCCAM, generalization rules serve two purposes. First, as described in Chapter 4, generalization rules suggest explanations that are consistent with a theory of causality. The explanations are tentative hypotheses that can be revised or confirmed when additional examples are encountered. The second purpose that a generalization rule serves is to suggest an explanation for EBL. This explanation is either verified and expanded by specific knowledge or rejected. If the explanation is rejected, then other generalization rules are tried. If no generalization rule produces an explanation that is verified, then EBL is not appropriate because there is not enough knowledge to produce an explanation and TDL is attempted. If the explanation is verified by domain knowledge, then explanation-based generalization is performed.

In some respects, OCCAM's use of generalization rules to come up with an explanation is similar to SWALE's explanation patterns (Leake & Owens, 1986; Schank, 1986). However, there are many more explanation patterns in SWALE than there are generalization rules in OCCAM. In addition, the explanation patterns in SWALE can be quite specific, referring to particular goals, actions and attributes. For example, SWALE contains the following explanation pattern:

```
Being a star performer can result in stress.
Taking drugs can relieve stress.
Taking too much drugs can result in death.
```

In contrast, OCCAM's generalization rules are much more general and refer to relationships between goals and actions. The following generalization rule would suggest an explanation for a situation similar to the one handled by SWALE's explanation pattern:

```
An action that achieves a goal can result in a side effect.
A plan can achieve the goal motivated by the side effect.
Executing the plan results in the failure of another goal.
```

Another difference between SWALE's use of explanation patterns and OCCAM's use of generalization rules is the interpretation process. The explanations produced by SWALE are too specific and must be tweaked (i.e., modified) to apply in future situations. In contrast, the explanations produced by OCCAM's generalization rules are too general and must be refined with additional knowledge. One way to reconcile these two approaches in the future might be to create a hierarchy of explanation patterns. OCCAM's generalization rules would serve as general nodes in the hierarchy and the more specific explanation patterns would be indexed in memory under the generalization rules. Another difference between OCCAM's and SWALE's explanation strategies is that the process of adapting a generalization to a new situation directly supports EBL. However, it is not clear how the process of adapting a specific explanation to a new situation can indicate what features of the new situation are relevant.

5.2.1. Creating a sketchy explanation: An example

In this section, I present a simple example of OCCAM finding a sketchy explanation with a generalization rule. The following example is used to illustrate the explanation process:

Economic-Sanction-1

In 1983, Australia refused to sell uranium to France, unless France ceased nuclear testing in the South Pacific. France paid a higher price to buy uranium from South Africa.

A simplified CD representation of this example is illustrated in Figure 5-1[48]. Representations of the countries (surrounded by asterisks in Figure 5-1) are provided to OCCAM. Figure 5-2 illustrates the representation of South Africa. Information on the imports and exports and other data is derived from the World Almanac (Hoffman, 1986).

In the current example, Economic-Sanction-1 is added to OCCAM's memory, and the most specific schema is found to be the **coerce** schema. However, the coerce schema does not explain the outcome of the economic sanction incident. In this simple example, the outcome is considered to be France possessing uranium[49]. OCCAM attempts to explain this outcome by searching for a generalization rule that would match this situation. To find a generalization rule, OCCAM must change the representation of Economic-Sanction-1 from the macro-schema representation **coerce** to a representation in terms of goals, plans, actions and states. The process that decomposes **coerce** into more primitive elements is described in Section 3.3.5. The results of this decomposition are shown in Figure 5-3. For the purposes of this

---

[48]In Chapter 7, I consider learning from economic sanction incidents in more detail utilizing a more complex coercion schema that OCCAM acquired via SBL.

[49]In the more detailed representation illustrated in Chapter 7, the outcome is a goal failure for Australia when France continues the nuclear testing in the South Pacific.

```
COERCE object COMMODITY type URANIUM
       actor *AUSTRALIA*
       target *FRANCE*
       demand ACT type EXPLODE
                 actor =TARGET
                 object WEAPONS type NUCLEAR
                 location SOUTHERN-HEMISPHERE
                 mode NEG
       threat ACT type SELL
                 actor =ACTOR
                 object =OBJECT
                 to =TARGET
                 mode NEG
       response ACT type SELL
                   actor *SOUTH-AFRICA*
                   object =OBJECT
           .       price MONEY dollars 300000000
                               value >MARKET
                   amount WEIGHT number 1500
                                 unit TONS
                   to =TARGET
       result STATE type POSSESS
                    actor =TARGET
                    value YES
                    object =OBJECT
```

Figure 5-1: Conceptual Dependency representation of Economic-Sanction-1. Country representations (surrounded by asterisks) are omitted to save space. Figure 5-2 illustrates the representation of South Africa.

```
COUNTRY name SOUTH-AFRICA
        language ENGLISH
                 AFRIKAANS
        location SOUTHERN-HEMISPHERE
        business-relationship *US*
                              *JAPAN*
                              =ACTOR
                              =TARGET
                              *UK*
        economic-health STRONG
        government PARLIAMENTARY
        religions CHRISTIAN
        life-expectancy *FIFTIES*
        literacy *SEVENTIES*
        continent AFRICA
        exports =OBJECT
                COMMODITY type GOLD
                COMMODITY type CHROMIUM
                COMMODITY type DIAMOND
        imports COMMODITY type AUTOMOBILES
                COMMODITY type OIL
```

Figure 5-2: OCCAM's representation for South Africa.

example, it is important to note that the primitive representation contains the following information:

- France purchased the uranium from South Africa at an inflated price.

- France purchasing the uranium resulted in France possessing the

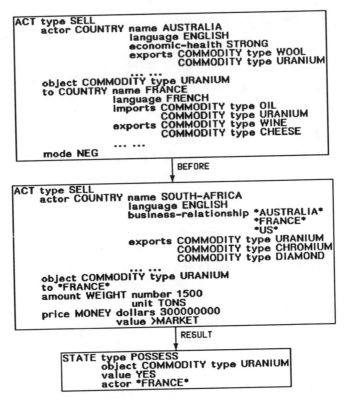

Figure 5-3: Part of the goal representation of Economic-Sanction-1.
This representation was created by decomposing the high-
level coerce representation into more primitive elements.

uranium.

- France purchased the uranium from South Africa after Australia
  refused to sell the uranium.

Figure 5-4 illustrates a generalization rule that fits the current situation.
This generalization rule encodes the following explanatory pattern: if
?action-1 precedes ?action-2 which results in ?state-2, assume
?action-1 results in ?state-1 which enables ?action-2 to produce
?state-2. Note that this is the exact same generalization rule as the one in
Figure 4-4 on page 119. In TDL, this rule suggests that a balloon can be inflated
only after it has been stretched (see the protocol in Figure 4-2 on page 117). In
the balloon example, ?action-1 is Mike deflating the balloon, ?action-2

```
(def-gen-rule
  ?state-2 = (state type ?stype            ;potential effect
                    value ?value
                    object ?object)
    before                                 ;temporal relation
  ?act-2 =   (act type ?atype-2            ;potential cause
                  object ?object)
  ((?act-2 result ?state-2)                ;causal explanation
   (?act-1 result
          ?state-1 = (state object ?object))
   (?state-1 enables ?act-2))
  (:link ?act-2 before                     ;condition
         ?act-1 = (act type ?atype-1
                       object ?object))
)
```

Figure 5-4: A historical generalization rule that matches the situation in Economic-Sanction-1.

is Lynn blowing into the balloon and ?state-2 is that the balloon is inflated. OCCAM does not contain enough knowledge to identify that ?state-2 as the balloon being stretched. Therefore, unlike the current economic sanction example, EBL cannot be applied in the balloon example.

In the current economic sanction example, OCCAM creates a sketchy explanation as indicated by the causal explanation of the generalization rule in Figure 5-4. In this case, ?action-1 is identified as Australia refusing to sell uranium, ?action-2 is identified as France buying the uranium from South Africa, and ?state-2 is France possessing the uranium. The causal explanation of the generalization rule postulates that ?action-1 (refusing to sell the product) resulted in some as yet unidentified ?state-1 that enabled ?action-2 (purchasing the product for more money from a different country) to result in ?state-2 (possessing the product).

The next step is to verify that this sketchy explanation is correct, and to fill in the missing details. In particular, the sketchy explanation leaves ?state-1 unidentified. A more complete explanation would identify this state and indicate the conditions under which this explanation applies. The explanation is verified by consulting rules associated with the schema.

5.2.2. Storing and retrieving rules from memory

Most explanation-based learning systems do not directly deal with the issue of indexing rules in memory. Rather, the rules in these systems are simply stored in a uniform database using the rule storage mechanism of the implementation language. For example, PROLOG-EBG uses PROLOG to index rules according to the predicate name and the number of parameters. In a system such as OCCAM that has a large number of rules dealing with states, it is important to have an efficient retrieval strategy. If a PROLOG type database were used, it would take a long time to find an appropriate rule since many rules would be indexed by **state**. The solution adopted in OCCAM to storing and retrieving inference rules is to index the rules under the most specific schema for the antecedent of the rule. There are, in fact, two different sources of rules in OCCAM. The first source of rules was explained in Section 4.4.2. When TDL creates a new generalized event for a schema, the rule format of the generalized event is created and stored with the schema. The second source of rules in OCCAM is a programmer. Some of the knowledge OCCAM needs to create an explanation has been learned by OCCAM, the remainder is coded by hand. Figure 5-5 illustrates a rule that I implemented so that OCCAM can explain the effects of refusing to sell a product.

```
(def-rule
    refuse-to-sell->demand-increase      ;name
    (act type (sell)                     ;antecedent
         actor (country exports ?y)
         to ?x = (country imports ?y)
         object ?y = (commodity)
         mode (neg))
    result                               ;link
    (state type (demand-increase)        ;consequent
           actor ?x
           object ?y))
```

Figure 5-5:   An economic rule: refusing to sell a product that country-x exports to country-y results in an increased demand for the product by   country-y. This rule encodes part of OCCAM's knowledge about the   relationship between supply and demand.

When a rule such as the one in Figure 5-5 is defined, it is indexed in memory by the most specific schema for the antecedent of the rule. For example, if there was a schema corresponding to "refusing to sell" (i.e., **(act   type   (sell)   mode   (neg)))**, then   the   rule `refuse-to-sell->demand-increase` would be indexed under that schema. Otherwise, it might be stored under a "sell" schema.

When OCCAM needs to make an inference, it retrieves inference rules from memory. For example, if OCCAM needs to find the result of the event "Australia refusing to sell uranium to France", it will search memory for the most specific schema of this event. If this schema has an inference rule that allows a result to be inferred, then that inference rule is used. If there is no inference rule or the inference does not fit in with the rest of the explanation, then schemata that are more general than the most specific schema are searched for inference rules. For example, the **act** schema might have an inference rule that indicates that refusing to do something for another person (or country) might result in the person getting angry. The idea here is that the most specific schema provides a detailed result for that situation, but circumstances may require a more general result. Once again, OCCAM uses the strategy of preferring the most specific information, but relying on more general information when necessary.

The search for an explanation in OCCAM may require OCCAM to explore several alternatives. For example, there are two results of selling an object: the seller possesses money, and the purchaser possesses the object. When OCCAM needs to determine if the result of South Africa selling uranium to France results in a goal failure for Australia, it first checks to see if South Africa possessing money results in a goal failure. Since this does not, OCCAM backtracks and tries the next alternative. The next alternative is France possessing uranium and that does indeed result in a goal failure for Australia.

5.2.3. Refining an explanation: An example

In this section, I continue the example of Section 5.2.1 and illustrate how OCCAM refines a sketchy explanation with domain knowledge. The sketchy explanation is illustrated in Figure 5-6. It indicates that Australia refusing to sell France uranium results in some unidentified state that enables South Africa to sell France the uranium for an inflated price.

The first step in refining the explanation is to specify the unidentified state. The rule `refuse-to-sell->demand-increase` illustrated in Figure 5-5 indicates that Australia refusing to sell the uranium results in France having an increased need for the uranium. The next step is to verify that the result of refusing to sell a product suggested by

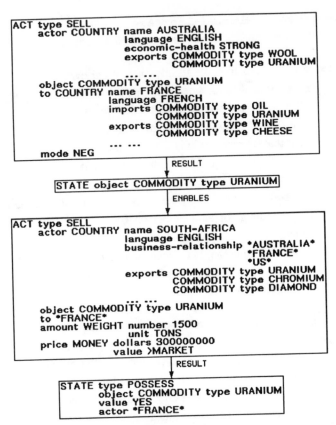

Figure 5-6: The sketchy explanation that postulates how Australia
refusing   to sell uranium to France led to France
purchasing the uranium from South Africa at an inflated
price.

`refuse-to-sell->demand-increase` enables South Africa to sell the
uranium to France at an inflated price. The rule named
`demand-increase->price-increase` illustrated in Figure 5-7 enables
OCCAM to make this inference.

The final step in verifying the explanation proposed by the generalization
rule is to determine that South Africa selling the uranium to France results in
France possessing the uranium. The rule `sell->possess` displayed in
Figure 5-8 allows this inference to be made. The final explanation that chains
together the three inference rules is illustrated in Figure 5-9.

```
(def-rule
    demand-increase->price-increase
    (state type (demand-increase)
           actor ?x = (country economic-health (strong))
           object ?y = (commodity))
    enables
    (act type (sell)
         actor (country exports ?y
                         business-relationship ?x)
         to ?x
         object ?y
         price (money value (>market))))
```

Figure 5-7:   An economic rule that encodes knowledge of supply and
              demand: an increased demand for a product by country-
              x can enable another country to sell country-x the product
              at a price greater than the market price. Country-x is
              required to have a strong economic health so that they can
              afford the inflated price.

```
(def-rule
    sell->possess
    (act type (sell)
         to ?x
         object ?y)
    result
    (state type (possess)
           object ?y
           value (yes)
           actor ?x))
```

Figure 5-8:   A rule that indicates that selling an object to ?x results in
              ?x possessing the object.

5.3. Explanation-Based Generalization

When OCCAM has constructed an explanation for an unexpected outcome, it
also keeps track of the inference rules that were accessed to produce the
explanation. This information is needed to generalize the explanation. The idea
is to find the class of outcomes for which the exact same explanation structure
will apply. Each inference rule that helped produce the explanation has several
constraints that specify the conditions under which the inference rule is
applicable.   For   example,   the   inference   rule
demand-increase->price-increase illustrated in Figure 5-7 indicates
that an increased demand for a product by country-x enables another country to
sell the product at an inflated price. This inference rule only applies if country-x
has a strong economy (so they can afford the price) and the other country

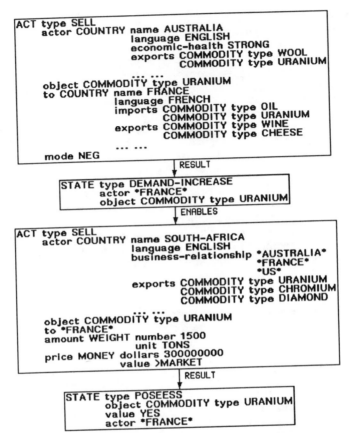

ACT type SELL
    actor COUNTRY name AUSTRALIA
                   language ENGLISH
                   economic-health STRONG
                   exports COMMODITY type WOOL
                           COMMODITY type URANIUM

    object COMMODITY type URANIUM
    to COUNTRY name FRANCE
               language FRENCH
               imports COMMODITY type OIL
                       COMMODITY type URANIUM
               exports COMMODITY type WINE
                       COMMODITY type CHEESE

    mode NEG

| RESULT

STATE type DEMAND-INCREASE
     actor *FRANCE*
     object COMMODITY type URANIUM

| ENABLES

ACT type SELL
    actor COUNTRY name SOUTH-AFRICA
                   language ENGLISH
                   business-relationship *AUSTRALIA*
                                         FRANCE
                                         US
                   exports COMMODITY type URANIUM
                           COMMODITY type CHROMIUM
                           COMMODITY type DIAMOND

    object COMMODITY type URANIUM
    to *FRANCE*
    amount WEIGHT number 1500
                  unit TONS
    price MONEY dollars 300000000
                value >MARKET

| RESULT

STATE type POSEESS
     object COMMODITY type URANIUM
     value YES
     actor *FRANCE*

Figure 5-9: The explanation that OCCAM constructs for Economic-
Sanction-1.   This explanation indicates how Australia
refusing   to sell uranium to France led to France
purchasing the uranium from South Africa at an inflated
price.

exports the commodity and has a business relationship with country-x.

There have been several different algorithms presented for generalizing an explanation structure. For example, Kedar-Cabelli (Kedar-Cabelli & McCarty, 1987) and Hirsh (Hirsh, 1987) present algorithms based on resolution theory proving (Robinson, 1965) and logic programming (Kowalski, 1979). Mooney (Mooney & Bennett, 1986) presents an algorithm (EGGS) based on unification which improves upon the unification-based algorithm used by STRIPS (Fikes et al., 1972). Finally, Mitchell et. al. (Mitchell et al., 1986a) present an algorithm based upon goal regression (Waldinger, 1977). However, none of these algorithms are appropriate for including in OCCAM. The reason for this is the language that OCCAM uses to represent generalized events for schemata is quite constrained. The only mechanism for representing an abstraction in OCCAM is to drop features from a concrete event. In contrast, the above generalization algorithms all introduce variables into the generalization. The simple, feature-based language that OCCAM uses supports the type of generalization-based memory that stores hierarchies of schemata. In particular, traversing memory in OCCAM as well as IPP, UNIMEM, CYRUS, and COBWEB (Fisher, 1987) to find schemata or events involves following indices that are simple features. If pattern matching and unification were required, searching memory would be a more time-consuming process[50]. The role tokens of a macro-schema (see Section 3.3.5) serve much the same purpose that a variable does. In particular, both mechanisms allow objects that appear in more than one event to be constrained to be the same object so that structural concepts can be represented (Bruner et al., 1956; Winston, 1975). However, role tokens are more restricted than variables because role tokens can only refer to the top level roles of a schema.

OCCAM's approach to explanation-based generalization follows closely the intuitive idea of what explanation-based learning should accomplish. A generalized explanation should contain only those features that are required to produce the explanation. The algorithm in OCCAM simply marks a feature name and feature value in the input concept when it has been matched against a feature of an inference rule. In addition, when a CD structure is matched against a variable in an inference rule, the CD structure is given a unique identifier. All CD structures that match against the same variable are given the same identifier[51]. The marking process is performed after the explanation is complete, rather than marking during the explanation. Otherwise, if

---

[50]I have experimented with a version of OCCAM that uses the EGGS algorithm to produce schemata with variables. However, this version does not integrate the learned schemata into memory.

[51]The purpose of these identifiers is to note that the same object is required to play a role in different parts of the explanation. This information is used to create a role token if a macro-schema is formed after generalizing the explanation. Note that when role tokens are created when a schema is formed by SBL, OCCAM is making an inductive leap. That is, in a number of examples, it has seen one object fill two roles in a complex event. Therefore, OCCAM assumes that in future instances of this type of event, these roles will not be filled by two objects. In contrast, with EBL, the explanation indicates when the same object must fill two roles in a complex event. This information is derived analytically from the variables in the inference rules that are chained together to produce the explanation.

backtracking were required to find the explanation, the features of the inferences rules on failed paths would also be marked. Once the marking has determined which features are relevant, the explanation is generalized by removing all features that were not marked. The approach to determining the relevant information is similar to an approach used by SOAR (Laird et al., 1986; Rosenbloom & Laird, 1986).

5.3.1. Explanation-based generalization: An example

In this section, I continue the example of Section 5.2.3 and demonstrate how OCCAM generalizes an explanation and creates a schema with explanation-based learning. In this example, OCCAM has explained how Australia refusing to sell uranium to France led to France purchasing the uranium from South Africa at an inflated price. By generalizing this explanation, OCCAM produces an abstract characterization of the class of situations in which this same explanation will apply. OCCAM first marks the explanation, inserts unique identifiers to indicate that two structures are constrained to be identical since they matched the same variable, and then removes all features that were not needed to produce the explanation. The generalized explanation is shown in Figure 5-10.

In an example, such as this one, where there is a high-level representation that was converted into a more primitive representation, OCCAM must form a generalized event in the high-level representation. This is a simple matter, since the process of marking features for an explanation marks structures that are components of the high level representation. For example, France is the **target** of the **coerce** structure. When the **coerce** structure is decomposed, France becomes the **actor** of a **demand-increase**, the **to** of the a **sell**. Features of France are marked in the explanation because it plays a role in the **demand-increase** and the **sell**. However, since the structure for France is part of the **coerce** structure, features in the **coerce** structure are also marked. To generalize the **coerce** structure, all that is necessary is to remove those features that have not been marked in the explanation. The generalized coerce structure is shown in Figure 5-11.

The generalization in Figure 5-11 indicates that if a country that exports a commodity tries to coerce a wealthy country that imports the commodity by refusing to sell them the commodity, then a response might be to buy the commodity at a higher price from another country. Although this seems like a simple conclusion, there are many examples where economic sanctions have

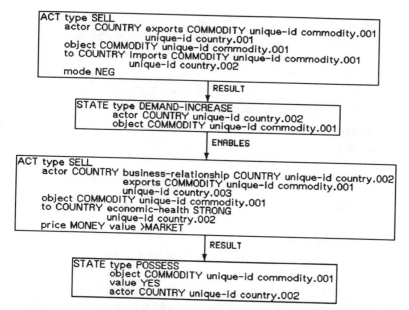

```
ACT type SELL
    actor COUNTRY exports COMMODITY unique-id commodity.001
                  unique-id country.001
    object COMMODITY unique-id commodity.001
    to COUNTRY imports COMMODITY unique-id commodity.001
                  unique-id country.002
    mode NEG
```
                              | RESULT
```
STATE type DEMAND-INCREASE
     actor COUNTRY unique-id country.002
     object COMMODITY unique-id commodity.001
```
                              | ENABLES
```
ACT type SELL
    actor COUNTRY business-relationship COUNTRY unique-id country.002
                  exports COMMODITY unique-id commodity.001
                  unique-id country.003
    object COMMODITY unique-id commodity.001
    to COUNTRY economic-health STRONG
                  unique-id country.002
    price MONEY value >MARKET
```
                              | RESULT
```
STATE type POSSESS
      object COMMODITY unique-id commodity.001
      value YES
      actor COUNTRY unique-id country.002
```

Figure 5-10: The generalized explanation. Only those features of the explanation that were required by the inference rules are included in the generalized event. Additionally, a unique identifier is added to each structure that matches a variable. When two structures have the same unique-id, it indicates that the structures are constrained to be identical by the matching process.

```
COERCE actor POLITY exports =OBJECT
       object COMMODITY
       target POLITY economic-health STRONG
                     imports =OBJECT
       threat ACT type SELL
                  actor =ACTOR
                  object =OBJECT
                  to =TARGET
                  mode NEG
       response ACT type SELL
                  actor POLITY business-relationship =TARGET
                              exports =OBJECT
                  object =OBJECT
                  price MONEY value >MARKET
                  to =TARGET
       result STATE type POSSESS
                  actor =TARGET
                  value YES
                  object =OBJECT
```

Figure 5-11: Generalization of Economic-Sanction-1 produced by OCCAM.

failed for this reason (Hufbauer & Schott, 1985; Brown, 1985) (e.g., in 1980, the

US refused to sell grain to the USSR who purchased it instead from Argentina, and in 1981, the US refused to sell pipeline equipment to the USSR who purchased it instead from France).

A similar conclusion about the effectiveness of sanctions was arrived at by Ian Smith, the former Prime Minister of Rhodesia, which was the target of a decade of economic sanctions following its independence from Great Britain (Renwick, 1981):

> We find that we are compelled to export at discount and import at a premium.

It is interesting to note which features of South Africa were generalized. In Figure 5-11, the only features of the **actor** of the **response** are that it exports the **object** and it has a business relationship with the **target**. Notice that the fact that South Africa has a business relationship with the **actor** was also included in the description of South Africa (see Figure 5-2). However, this feature was not necessary to produce the explanation, so it is not included in the generalization. The features of South Africa that were included are those that matched against the features of the inference rules when the explanation was produced.

Since the **coerce** schema is a macro-schema, its specializations will also need to be a macro-schemata. Explanation-based learning produces the generalized event for the schema. A macro-schema also needs a sequence of events and a pattern to match against new episodes so that the sequence of events can be instantiated. The pattern of a specialized macro-schema is identical to that of the parent schema since they both share the same roles (see Section 3.3.5). The sequence of events could simply be inherited from the parent schema. If this were done, that new specialization would encode enough information to make a specialized prediction, but not enough information to explain the prediction. For example, the **coerce** schema indicates that after the threat is made, the target will make a response that has a result. An explanation of the outcome of an economic sanction incident based on this sequence of events would not be very illuminating. The approach that OCCAM takes to creating a specialized sequence of events is straightforward. The generalized explanation is saved as the sequence of events of the schema. However, first any objects or events in the explanation that refer to roles of the macro-schema are replaced by the corresponding variables. In addition, whatever temporal or intentional links are present in the parent schema are also inserted in the sequence of events. Figure 5-12 illustrates the sequence of events for this simple economic sanction schema.

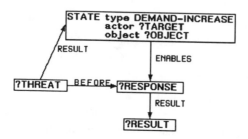

Figure 5-12: **The sequence of events created for an economic sanction schema.**

What does EBL accomplish for OCCAM? In this particular example, OCCAM started with simple knowledge about coercion, and some simple economic knowledge of supply and demand. It finds a useful interaction between coercion and the economic knowledge and saves this as schema. Answering questions about future economic sanction incidents that fit this pattern will be simple since there is an appropriate schema in memory. All that needs to be done is a memory traversal to find the appropriate schema, recognize the new instance as an example of the schema, and instantiate the explanation. In essence, OCCAM is a general problem solving system with domain knowledge of coercion and supply and demand, and after several experiences, it evolves into an efficient specialized expert on economic sanctions.

With some different examples, OCCAM could become expert in a different domain. For example, OCCAM's knowledge of supply and demand might be useful to create a financial expert. If an emerging technology needs a particular commodity, then the demand for that commodity may increase in the future. OCCAM's knowledge of supply and demand would predict that the price of the commodity would increase. Therefore, given an example of an investment in yttrium, a component of many superconductors, OCCAM could create a schema that indicates that an investment in companies that produce materials required by an emerging technology is likely to profitable.

5.4. Explanation-Based Learning and Indexing

How should a new schema or a new event be indexed in memory? There are two sorts of information that could serve as indices. The first is the surface features of the events. An event can be indexed by all features that are easily observed, or commonly associated with the components of an event. For example, Economic-Sanction-1 could be indexed under a coercion by the native language of the actor, or the type of object involved. The problem with indexing by surface features such as these is that inappropriate examples will be retrieved to make predictions and explanations in the future. The fact that two counties involved in economic sanction incidents both speak English will most probably not help an understander predict the outcome of a future incident. Therefore, retrieval on the language feature will result in spurious remindings that offer no assistance in solving any problems.

An alternative to indexing on surface features is to index by the deep features such as goals, plans, and plan interactions that are produced when explaining the outcome of an event (Hammond, 1984; Schank, 1982). Since events that share the same explanation structure will share the same outcome, only relevant information would be retrieved from memory if indices were deep features. However, the extreme view that only deep features are important indices has several problems. First, it is not supported by a number of empirical studies (Getner, 1983; Holyoak, 1985; Skorstad et al., 1987) that appear to demonstrate that effect of surface features is very significant in retrieval of relevant information from memory. Second, indexing entirely on deep goal-based features does not fully address the issue of how these features are identified in events. One cannot observe that an enabling condition for an action is not satisfied in that same manner that one can tell that a car is large or black. Traversing memory to find an appropriate schema to explain an outcome cannot rely on the explanation of the outcome.

It appears that there is a dilemma. If information in memory is indexed by surface features, then much useless information will be retrieved from memory. On the other hand, if information is indexed by deep features of the explanation structure, then an explanation must be derived by some mechanism other than recognition of a known schema. The solution to this problem is to index information in memory by only those surface features that allow the explanation to be inferred. That is, when a schema is constructed with EBL, the generalized event contains only those features that were relevant. I claim that it is exactly these features that make good indexes since they are easily observed and useful in identifying that a saved explanation applies in a future case.

OCCAM does also index by deep goal-based features. These features are not useful in making predictions or explanations. However, they are useful for retrieving exemplars of a class that have a particular explanation. These exemplars might be useful in supporting an argument.

5.5. Operationality

Explanation-based learning can be viewed as a mechanism for operationalizing concept definitions (Keller, 1987a; Keller, 1987b; Mostow, 1987). The idea here is that a learner already has a means of constructing an explanation, but does not have an efficient mechanism to recognize when the explanation applies. For example, when learning about economic sanctions, OCCAM already has enough domain knowledge to explain the outcome of an event. The first time it explains an outcome, it must search for an explanation by brute force techniques of trying various combinations of inference rules. This search for an explanation can be viewed as an inefficient mechanism for recognizing instances of concepts such as "Those economic sanction incidents that will fail to achieve the desired goal because the target will buy the commodity elsewhere". What EBL does for OCCAM is to operationalize concepts such as this by creating an efficient means of recognizing the concept. Operationalizing a concept in OCCAM consists of finding a description of the concept in terms of easily observable features and indexing this description in memory as a schema. In OCCAM, the "observable" features are those features that are used to represent the input examples. For example, the generalization of Economic-Sanction-1 in OCCAM operationalizes the implicit concept "Those economic sanction incidents which will fail to achieve the desired goal because the target will buy the commodity elsewhere". The operational definition of this concept is shown in Figure 5-11. This generalization only references features that were present in the input example to indicate that if a country that exports a commodity tries to coerce a wealthy country that imports the commodity by refusing to sell them the commodity, then a response might be to bid the price of the commodity higher until another country that exports the product is willing to sell the product.

OCCAM has two different mechanisms for creating an explanation of a new event. The first, preferred mechanism is an efficient search of memory for a schema that accounts for the event. The hierarchy of schemata are similar to a discrimination net that indexes stored explanations for events. The second mechanism for finding an explanation is more general, but more expensive. It consists of piecing together an explanation by chaining rules together. Operationalization in OCCAM consists of creating a schema for memory-based explanation by generalizing the explanation found in rule-based explanation. The generalization process finds those surface features of the new event that are useful indices for retrieving a stored explanation.

In OCCAM, the operationality criteria are rather strict, requiring that the feature be present in input examples rather than derivable from the features of the input. For example, OCCAM learns a generalization that contains the threat that a country refuses to sell a product. This threat is directly represented in OCCAM's input. A more general feature might indicate the threat to be any action that results in an increased demand for a commodity. However, this feature is not easily observable and is not included in the representation of an input concept. If a feature such as this were included in a generalization, then an inference process would be needed to traverse memory (see Section 5.4.) There is a trade-off in selecting the operationality criteria. A more specific description of a feature is easy to recognize, but it may also be less generally applicable. For example, if OCCAM represented the threat in an economic sanction schema as any action that results in an increased demand for a commodity, then the schema would apply to more examples, such as increasing demand by destruction of the target's supply, or a naval blockade, or even a natural disaster such as a drought. This feature is harder to recognize, but applies to more cases. Because of its operationality criteria, OCCAM requires a separate schema to handle each method of increasing demand. The benefit that OCCAM derives from its strategy is that it does not require inference to recognize when a saved explanation applies. In addition, there is a potential problem with representing the features more abstractly. The particular instantiation of increasing demand in OCCAM's schema (refusing to sell a product) does not interact with the target's plan to obtain the commodity through other means. Another instantiation of increasing demand such as restricting supply with a blockade might interact with other parts of the explanation such as the ability of another country to supply the commodity. By having a more strict operationality criterion, OCCAM avoids a potential problem that can arise if there is an unforeseen interaction.

5.6. Explanation-Based Learning and Multiple Outcomes

In the examples of EBL presented so far, it has been assumed that an example such as a kidnapping incident or an economic sanction incident has a single outcome. In fact, in most complex situations, there are multiple goals and multiple outcomes. For example, in kidnapping, the actor of the coercion (i.e., the kidnapper) wants to obtain money and the target (i.e., the parent) wants the hostage to be released unharmed. These goals can be resolved independently. For example, if the kidnapper receives the ransom, his goal is achieved, and he may release the hostage, in which case the target's goal is also achieved or he may harm the hostage, in which case the target's goal fails. In essence, in any particular example, it is just a coincidence that the ransom is paid and the hostage is released. Since this is the case, these two explanations should not appear together in a general kidnapping schema. To address this issue, OCCAM creates a separate schema for the resolution of each independent goal. Later examples will create more specialized schemata to deal with resolution of related goals. There are two reasons for learning about independent goals separately. First, since there is no logical relationship between the outcome of the goals, it would be erroneous to construct a schema that indicates that the outcomes of the independent goals are related. Second, it is unreasonable to expect a learner to be able to learn multiple "lessons" from a single example (VanLehn, 1983).

For example, OCCAM is presented with the following kidnapping story:

Kidnapping-4

John, a 10-year-old child, was abducted on his way to church on Sunday morning by a heroin addict. His father, Richard, a wealthy, fair skinned man, received a phone call that evening. The kidnapper threatened that John would be killed unless Richard paid a $100,000 ransom. Monday at noon, Richard left the money in a locker at the train station. Four hours later, his son was released in a wooded area two miles from the train station.

This situation is represented as an instance of coercion to OCCAM. The representation includes the fact that the goal of the coercion was for the kidnapper to obtain money. This goal is achieved. The first problem for OCCAM is to explain how the kidnapper's goal was achieved. The goal was achieved when the father paid the ransom. The father possessing the money (i.e., being rich) is a state that enables the payment. Once OCCAM determines how the father was able to pay the money, the next question to answer is why the father paid the money. OCCAM's domain knowledge indicates that the threat and the demand created a goal conflict for the father. The threat to kill the child motivates a goal to preserve the health of the child (because the father has an interpersonal relationship with the child). The demand motivates a goal for the father to retain his wealth. The action of paying the ransom is a realization of a plan to prefer the achievement of the more important goal: preserving the child's life. Once OCCAM explains the father's action, it can now generalize the plan it observed for obtaining money. The generalized event is shown in Figure 5-13.

```
COERCE goal GOAL goal =GOAL-STATE
                 actor =THE-ACTOR
       outcome GOAL-OUTCOME type SUCCESS
                              goal GOAL goal =GOAL-STATE
                                        actor =THE-ACTOR
                       actor =THE-ACTOR
       goal-state STATE type POSS-BY
                        object =DEMAND-OBJ
                        value YES
                        actor =THE-ACTOR
       the-target-response ACT type ATRANS
                               actor =THE-TARGET
                               object =DEMAND-OBJ
                               to =THE-ACTOR
                               from =THE-TARGET
       plan PLAN actor =THE-ACTOR
                 plan =THE-ASK
       the-ask ACT type MTRANS
                   actor =THE-ACTOR
                   to =THE-TARGET
                   object COND If =THE-DEMAND
                               else =THE-THREAT
       the-demand ACT type ATRANS
                      actor =THE-TARGET
                      object =DEMAND-OBJ
                      to =THE-ACTOR
                      from =THE-TARGET
       demand-obj P-OBJ type MONEY
                       amount DOLLARS relative-number LARGE
       the-threat ACT type KILL
                      actor =THE-ACTOR
                      object =THREAT-OBJ
       threat-obj HUMAN
       the-target HUMAN relation IPT type FAMILY-REL
                                    of =THREAT-OBJ
                        Income-class RICH
       the-actor HUMAN
```

Figure 5-13: The kidnapping schema formed from generalizing Kidnapping-4.

The kidnapping schema in Figure 5-13 explains how the kidnapper achieved the goal of obtaining money and constrains the roles to have certain values. The **the-actor** (i.e., the kidnapper) does not have to be a heroin addict as in the example, but can be any human. The **threat-obj** can also be any human and **the-target** must be a wealthy human related to the `threat-obj`. The `demand-obj` is a large amount of money. In addition, the following events are specified: the goal is for `the-actor` to possess the `demand-obj`. `the-outcome` is that the goal succeeds. The `plan` `the-actor` follows is to tell `the-target` that he will perform `the-threat` if `the-target` does not meet `the-demand`. `the-demand` is for `the-target` to give `the-actor` the `demand-obj` and `the-threat` is for `the-actor` to kill the `threat-obj`.

When OCCAM first created this schema, I thought that there was a bug in the program because it did not include the preparation (i.e., abducting the hostage) in the schema. After some thought, I realized that in the explanation that OCCAM has constructed, it is not necessary to abduct the hostage. It would work just as well to threaten to kill the child without abducting the child. With more sophisticated domain knowledge, a better explanation can be constructed. For example, abducting the child makes the threat more believable. In particular, an important precondition for killing the child is satisfied since the kidnapper knows where the child is. In addition, abducting the child prevents the target from pursuing counterplans such as hiring a bodyguard or sending the child out of the country. Still, I am mystified why there are not more examples of this sort of blackmail without abduction[52].

Once OCCAM has acquired a schema that indicates how the kidnapper's goal is achieved, it can now focus on explaining how the target's goal was achieved. When OCCAM encounters the following episode, it initiates an explanation process to determine how the target achieves his goal:

---

[52]The explanation is that there are in fact more examples. Blackmail of this sort is a less serious crime than kidnapping, is not reported as widely, and makes less interesting detective shows for television. There have only been 236 cases of ransom kidnapping in the U.S. between 1874 and 1974 (Alix, 1978). There were 284 blackmail cases reported between 1920 and 1940 (Hepworth, 1975). Since I started working on OCCAM I have encountered two persons who "had friends or neighbors" who were victims of this sort of blackmail, but I have never encountered anyone who had even second-hand knowledge of a kidnapping for ransom in the US.

Kidnapping-5

Mary, a 18-year-old college student was dragged into a car while waiting for a bus. Her grandmother, Linda, a wealthy, fair skinned woman, received a note two days later that indicated that Mary would be killed unless she paid a $50,000 ransom. The grandmother instructed her butler to leave the money in a trash can in the men's room at a local park. Mary was released unharmed the next day.

The explanation for how the target's goal is achieved is quite simple. When the hostage is released, the goal is achieved. OCCAM's domain knowledge indicates that the kidnapper was following the plan of keeping a bargain since the ransom has been paid. A specialized schema of kidnapping is formed and indexed in memory under the schema in Figure 5-13. The specialized schema is illustrated in Figure 5-14.

5.7. Psychological Investigations of EBL

A second experiment I ran with Professor Mort Friedman of the Psychology Department at UCLA investigated how specific causal knowledge facilitates learning.

In this experiment, we investigated how existing causal knowledge affects the number of trials required to make accurate predictions. This experiment involved one subject population (introductory psychology students) and two different tasks. Each task used the same examples, a set of cards containing a photograph of a child performing an action on a balloon (either stretching or measuring the balloon). On different cards the balloons varied in shape (long or round) and color (blue or yellow). One task was to make a prediction about whether or not the child would be able to inflate a balloon. Prior causal knowledge can assist in this task. The second task was to determine whether or not the card belonged to an arbitrary category. This second task is a classic concept identification task (Bower & Trabasso, 1968) with the exception that the data are more natural stimuli[53]. Of course, prior causal knowledge cannot help the second task.

---

[53]Instead of determining that an "alpha" is a triangle, subjects had to learn that an "alpha" is a child measuring a balloon.

```
COERCE goal GOAL goal =GOAL-STATE
              actor =THE-ACTOR
      outcome GOAL-OUTCOME type SUCCESS
                           goal GOAL goal =GOAL-STATE
                                     actor =THE-ACTOR
                               actor =THE-ACTOR
           goal-state STATE type POSS-BY
                           object =DEMAND-OBJ
                           value YES
                           actor =THE-ACTOR
           the-target-response ACT type ATRANS
                                 actor =THE-TARGET
                                 object =DEMAND-OBJ
                                 to =THE-ACTOR
                                 from =THE-TARGET
           plan PLAN actor =THE-ACTOR
                     plan =THE-ASK
           the-ask ACT type MTRANS
                        actor =THE-ACTOR
                        to =THE-TARGET
                        object COND if =THE-DEMAND
                                   else =THE-THREAT
           the-demand ACT type ATRANS
                             actor =THE-TARGET
                             object =DEMAND-OBJ
                             to =THE-ACTOR
                             from =THE-TARGET
           demand-obj P-OBJ type MONEY
                                 amount DOLLARS relative-number LARGE
           the-threat ACT type KILL
                             actor =THE-ACTOR
                             object =THREAT-OBJ
           threat-obj HUMAN
           the-target HUMAN relation IPT type FAMILY-REL
                                           of =THREAT-OBJ
                            income-class RICH
           the-actor HUMAN
```

│ the-actor-response, the-prep etc.

```
COERCE the-target-outcome GOAL-OUTCOME goal GOAL goal STATE value YES
                                                       type P-HEALTH
                                                       object =THREAT-OBJ
                                             actor =THE-TARGET
                                   actor =THE-TARGET
                                   type SUCCESS
       the-actor-response ACT to =THE-TARGET
                              from =THE-ACTOR
                              object =THREAT-OBJ
                              actor =THE-ACTOR
                              type ATRANS
       the-ask ACT object COND then =THE-ALTERNATIVE
       the-alternative ACT type ATRANS
                           actor =THE-ACTOR
                           object =DEMAND-OBJ
                           to =THE-TARGET
                           from =THE-ACTOR
       the-prep ACT type ATRANS
                    actor =THE-TARGET
                    object =DEMAND-OBJ
                    to =THE-ACTOR
```

Figure 5-14: A specialization of the kidnapping schema formed from generalizing Kidnapping-5. This specialization indicates how the target's goal of preserving the health of the child was achieved. The specialization is indexed in memory under the kidnapping schema.

The subjects in this experiment were 120 undergraduates fulfilling a requirement for an introductory psychology course. Subjects were divided into two conditions:

- Inflate: those who had to predict whether the child would be able to inflate the balloon.

- Alpha: those who had to predict whether the card belonged to an artificial category called alpha.

Subjects were presented with a card, asked to make a prediction, and then informed of the correct answer. Trials continued until the subject was able to predict correctly on every card. We recorded the number of the last trial on which the subject made an error. In the "Inflate" condition, we predicted that subjects would be able to use their existing causal knowledge about balloons (i.e., stretching a balloon makes it easier to inflate the balloon). We predicted that existing causal knowledge would facilitate learning to make the correct prediction when the data were consistent with existing knowledge and hinder learning when the data were not consistent with existing knowledge. In the "Alpha" condition, knowledge of what makes a balloon easier to inflate should neither facilitate or hinder classifying the cards.

Subjects in each condition were subdivided into groups who had to predict based upon the action performed on the balloon. (In the "Inflate" condition, some subjects saw examples that indicated the child could only inflate a balloon if she stretched it; others saw examples that indicated the child could only inflate a balloon if she measured it. In the "Alpha" condition, some subjects saw examples that indicated that alpha is a child stretching a balloon; others saw examples that indicated that alpha is a child measuring a balloon.)

There are two major findings of this experiment. The results are significant at the .05 level ($F(3,44) = 6.03$):

- Subjects required fewer trials to learn to predict that a balloon which had been stretched could be inflated (2.1 trials) than to predict that a balloon which had been measured could be inflated (6.1 trials). This finding indicates that knowledge of an existing causal relationship facilitates learning. Note that there are a small number of hypotheses consistent with the existing causal knowledge (i.e., the child can inflate all balloons, the child can inflate no balloons, and the child can inflate stretched balloons.) Subjects required a small number of examples to determine which hypothesis is correct. On the other hand, if the correct answer is inconsistent with prior causal knowledge, many more hypotheses are possible (e.g., the child can inflate only blue balloons, the child can only inflate measured balloons, etc.). In this situation, more examples are required before finding the correct hypothesis.

- Subjects required approximately the same number of trials to determine that a balloon being stretched is an alpha (3.9 trials) or to determine that a balloon being measured was an alpha (3.0 trials). Subjects in the "Alpha" condition are presented with the same data as the "Inflate" condition. Since existing knowledge cannot help in the "Alpha" condition, there is no significant difference between the group that learned that stretching is an alpha and the group that learned that measuring is an alpha. The alpha group serves as a control group. Differences in the "Inflate" condition cannot be explained by factors such as greater perceptual salience of stretching as opposed to measuring. Otherwise, these same differences would appear in the "Alpha" condition.

In this experiment, we have demonstrated that the process of learning to predict outcomes is not simply a matter of comparing and contrasting examples. If this were true, then the results in the "Inflate" condition would not differ from the "Alpha" condition. Instead, existing causal knowledge facilitates learning in the "Inflate" condition when the data are consistent with the prior knowledge so that fewer examples are needed to arrive at the correct hypothesis.

5.8. Summary

This chapter provided details of explanation-based learning in OCCAM. The process of explanation-based learning consists of three steps:

1. Generalization rules suggest a causal relationship between an example event and its outcome.

2. Existing knowledge verifies and refines (or denies) postulated relationships.

3. A generalized event is created by retaining only those features of the example that were needed to establish causal relationships.

Explanation-based learning creates schemata by identifying the class of situations for which the explanation created for a single example event will apply. When the underlying cause can be identified, the conditions under which the causal relationship will hold can be derived analytically rather than empirically. OCCAM is unique among explanation-based learning systems in that it has the ability to acquire the knowledge needed for analytical learning via empirical techniques.

Chapter 6
Integration of Learning Methods

In this chapter, I review the architecture that OCCAM uses to integrate similarity-based, theory-driven, and explanation-based learning algorithms. I describe the role that each learning method plays in a general theory of learning causal relationships. Then, OCCAM is compared to other systems that combine learning methods.

6.1. OCCAM's Architecture

An important facet of artificial intelligence research is to determine which method is best suited for a given problem. In OCCAM, I am primarily interested in the learning method that will create a schemata that makes accurate predictions with fewest number of examples. The central role of OCCAM is to determine which learning method to apply in a given situation.

The top-level control structure of OCCAM is quiet simple. OCCAM is an incremental learning system. As each new example comes in, OCCAM first determines if there is one existing schema that can adequately explain the outcome of the new example. If there is such a schema, OCCAM does not need to learn and simply stores the example for future retrieval. Otherwise, OCCAM attempts explanation-based learning. Explanation-based learning can only be accomplished if OCCAM can chain together two or more existing schemata to explain the example. If OCCAM cannot explain the example, theory-driven learning is attempted. Theory-driven learning can only operate the new example and previous recalled examples conform to known pattern for causal relationships. If theory-driven learning does not apply, then similarity-based learning is attempted. For similarity-based learning to create a new generalization, OCCAM must be able to detect a correlation among previous examples similar to the new example. Finally, if similarity-based learning fails, OCCAM simply stores the new example so that in the future a correlation may be detected.

Clearly, if the prior knowledge is accurate, then explanation-based learning will require fewer examples than similarity-based learning and theory-driven learning. Similarly, theory-driven learning requires fewer examples than similarity-based learning to create schemata that make accurate predictions. Only a subset of the hypotheses consistent with a set of examples will be consistent with the set of generalizations rules. Similarly, only a subset of the hypotheses consistent with a set of examples and the set of generalizations rules will be consistent with the domain theory.[54] The more knowledge-intensive learning algorithms search a hypothesis space that is smaller than the hypothesis space searched by the more data-intensive algorithms. Therefore, it is more likely that an accurate hypothesis will be selected from the smaller set of hypotheses, provided that the desired hypothesis is contained in the smaller set. OCCAM has a means of determining when the hypothesis is not in the smaller set of hypotheses. When this is detected (i.e., the example cannot be explained or the example doesn't match a generalization rule), a less knowledge-intensive learning algorithm that searches a larger set of hypotheses is attempted.

Other sets of learning algorithms also have the property that the hypothesis space of one is embedded in the hypothesis space of the other. For example, the hypothesis space of a multi-layer neural network (Rumelhart et al., 1986) is a superset of the hypothesis space of a single layer network. If a learning problem is capable of being solved by the one layer network, then the one-layer network is more accurate than the multi-layer network after a limited number of examples. Similarly, linear discriminants are more accurate than quadratic discriminants when the additional power of the quadratic discriminant is not needed. One difference between the embedding of hypotheses spaces in OCCAM and these methods is that OCCAM automatically switches between learning methods when it becomes apparent that the desired hypothesis is not in the smaller set.

The learning methods interact through a common memory. The results of all learning methods are added to the hierarchy of schemata. The hierarchy of schemata is used by the explanation-based learning method to constrain future learning.

---

[54]Recall, that explanations are proposed by generalizations rules and verified by the domain theory.

The learning methods also interact more subtly. Similarity-based learning is only attempted on examples that OCCAM cannot explain. Therefore, if the domain theory is only partially complete, some examples will be processed by explanation-based learning and other examples will be processed by similarity-based learning. Reducing the number of examples processed by similarity-based learning reduces the possibility that the aggregation method used by the similarity-based method will be led astray by surface similarities between the explained and the unexplained event. In effect, this combined strategy focuses the similarity-based aggregation process to acquire schemata to complete the partial theory.

6.2. Comparing EBL and SBL on Economic Sanction Data

How much of an improvement over SBL is EBL? To answer this question, I compared EBL and SBL on the same economic sanction data. I varied the number of training examples and measured how accurate OCCAM was at predicting the outcome of the remaining data and predicting the outcome of five hypothetical sanction incidents. A political analyst from the Rand Corporation was consulted to predict the outcome of the five hypothetical incidents. There were a total of at most 15 training instances presented to the learning programs. While this may seem like a small amount of data, there have not been many major sanction incidents.

The number of training instances (N) varied between 3 and 15. For each N, I ran 64 trials of selecting N instances at random from the set of actual sanction incidents, and then measured how accurately the resulting hierarchy of schemata classified the remaining actual and all the hypothetical cases. Each condition was repeated 64 times because the SBL module is sensitive to the order of examples. Of course, both learning strategies are sensitive to the specific subset of examples selected as training examples. To test the SBL module of OCCAM, I deleted the knowledge base of political and economic rules so that EBL was not applicable.

Figure 6-1 plots the mean percentage of correct predictions made by OCCAM with EBL and SBL as a function of the number of training examples. The graph clearly illustrates the superiority of EBL over SBL for this class of data. For example, with 5 examples SBL predicts an average of 14% correctly, with 10 examples 17% are predicted correctly, and 25% are predicted correctly with 15 examples. EBL makes an average of 54% correct with 5 examples, 83% with 10 examples, and 100% with 15 examples. Of course, fifteen is a small number of examples for an empirical learning program and in this situation EBL has a clear advantage over SBL. With all fifteen actual examples, the EBL program always creates the same schemata that are sufficient for making correct predictions on the five hypothetical cases. The actual and hypothetical cases are listed in Appendix A.6.

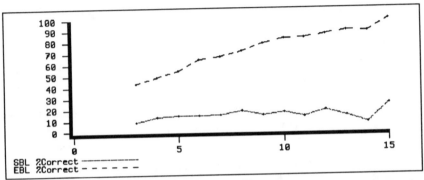

SBL %Correct ————————————
EBL %Correct — — — — — —

Figure 6-1: Percent of correct predictions made by OCCAM with EBL and SBL as a function of the number of training examples.

In this experiment the explanation-based learning module of OCCAM does not make any incorrect predictions. This is a consequence of OCCAM having domain knowledge that is complete enough, and accurate enough to create schemata that account for the actual and hypothetical cases. When OCCAM is asked to make a prediction, it searches memory for the most specific schemata and instantiates the outcome of that schemata. When there are no economic sanction schemata that apply, then the more general coercion schemata is used. However, the coercion schemata has a very vague prediction about the outcome of coercion incidents. It predicts that after the threat is made, the target will perform a response that will result in an outcome. The specializations of coercion provide more specific predictions. For example, one schema formed by EBL indicates that when a country refuses to sell a commodity to a target country with a strong economy, then the target country's response will be to purchase the commodity at a higher price from another country that exports the commodity, and the outcome will be a goal failure. When using SBL on the same data, OCCAM makes a small number of incorrect predictions. Figure 6-2 plots the percent of unclassified examples (i.e., those which do not predict a failure or a success) and the percent of incorrect predictions.

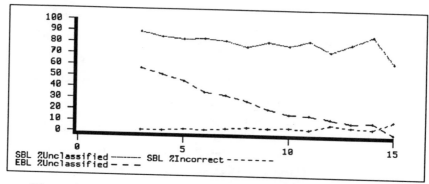

**Figure 6-2:   Percent of unclassified examples and incorrect predictions
made by OCCAM with EBL and SBL as a function of the
number of training examples. EBL does not make any
incorrect predictions on this set of data.**

Of course, one should not forget that there are important qualitative
differences between EBL and SBL. The most important difference is that the
schemata formed by EBL provide the knowledge needed to create an
explanation of why a prediction is made. The schemata formed by SBL cannot
support this task.

6.3. The Accuracy of EBL While Learning a Domain Theory

The economic sanction domain is a good domain in which to use EBL in
because there are not many economic sanctions (so empirical methods may not
work well) and there are many opportunities to acquire the necessary
background theory for this activity. For example, the relationship between
demand and price may be acquired through formal instruction, or it may be
induced from examples of the price for a commodity increasing when the
demand increases. Typically during a corporate takeover attempt, the price
offered for the shares of stock is considerably higher than the market price.

In this section, I report on several experiments in which the domain theory
is being acquired by empirical methods at the same time that it is being used by
explanation-based methods. The experiments vary the ratio of two types of
training examples. In a system that integrates similarity-based and explanation-
based learning algorithms, two kinds of training examples can be distinguished:

- **Foundational.** Examples from which background domain knowledge can be learned. For example, OCCAM is presented with examples of parents helping their children and examples of strangers not assisting others' children. From these foundational examples, it acquires a schema that indicates that parents have a goal of preserving the health of their children. This schema explains why a parent pays a ransom to a kidnapper.

- **Performance.** These training examples are instances of the performance task. In OCCAM, one performance task is to infer the outcome of a kidnapping incident. For this performance task, examples of actual incidents are used as performance examples. Because OCCAM has learned the relevant background knowledge, it can use explanation-based learning on these performance examples.

Note that the classification of an example as a performance or foundational example is relative to a particular performance task. For example, if the performance task were to predict who might be a potential candidate for purchasing ransom insurance, kidnapping incidents would serve as foundational examples. The foundational examples differ from the performance examples in that they can be viewed as subproblems of the performance task.

In this section, I report on three experiments that compare SBL applied alone, EBL applied only on the performance examples (and SBL applied on the foundational examples), and OCCAM (which prefers EBL for the performance examples, but uses SBL on the performance examples if the domain theory does not explain the outcome of a new example). The experiments vary the ratio of performance to foundational examples.

The experiments were run on artificial data created as follows: Each training example consists of 100 Boolean attributes. The performance rule to be acquired, AC, has a precondition that consists of a conjunction of 10 of these attributes, the remaining 90 attributes are irrelevant. The probability that an irrelevant attribute appears in a training example was 0.5. There are two foundational rules to be acquired, AB and BC. Each of these rules consists of a conjunction of 5 Boolean attributes and the remaining 95 attributes are irrelevant. In these experiments, the domain theory to be learned from foundational examples by SBL is:

```
A and AB causes B
B and BC causes C
```

The accuracy of the three learning methods as a function of the total number number of examples (performance and foundational) will be computed on acquiring the rule:

```
A and AC causes C
```

Here, I am assuming that **AB** and **BC** are not known, but they can be learned by SBL from the foundational training examples. The general idea is that when one is told that **A causes C**, there are often other conditions that are unstated. For example, **A** might represent striking a object, **B** might represent the object breaking and **C** might represent the owner of the object getting angry. The goal of the learning is to acquire the concept **A and AC causes C**: "If a person strikes an expensive fragile object, then the owner of the object will get angry." Explanation-based learning on this task is possible if two rules in the domain theory are acquired empirically: "If a fragile object is struck, the object will break" and "If an expensive object breaks, the owner will be angry."

I varied the ratio of performance to foundational examples and computed the accuracy of each algorithm at predicting the outcome of a set of 100 test examples. I anticipated that EBL would converge on an accurate rule for AC more quickly than SBL when there are significantly more foundational examples than performance examples in the training data. Under these circumstance, SBL will acquire an accurate domain theory from the foundational examples and EBL will make use of the domain theory. I anticipated that SBL would converge on an accurate rule for AC more quickly than EBL when there are significantly more performance than foundational examples. Figure 6-3 show the mean difference in accuracy (N = 200) between EBL and SBL (i.e., the accuracy of EBL minus the accuracy of SBL) as a function of the total number of training examples for several ratios of performance examples.

The results of this experiment were as expected. With fewer foundational and more performance examples, SBL converges on an accurate rule more quickly than EBL. With few performance examples and many foundational examples, EBL finds an accurate predictive rule more quickly than EBL. Both

N	10%	30%	50%
10	0.0	-4.5	-40.6
20	28.3	-19.0	-90.1
30	50.1	-23.5	-62.8
40	66.3	-6.0	-32.3
50	52.5	-3.6	-4.0
60	43.3	-2.0	-3.5
70	23.6	-1.0	-3.5
80	10.8	-1.8	-1.5
90	11.0	-2.5	-2.1
100	8.0	-1.6	-2.8
110	8.1	-2.6	-1.6
120	5.1	-1.1	0.0
130	0.0	0.0	0.0

Figure 6-3:   The difference in accuracy between EBL and SBL as a function of the number of training examples. 10% means that one tenth of the training examples were performance examples and the remaining nine tenths were evenly divided between the two sets of foundational examples.

learning algorithms eventually find an accurate rule. The central difference is how accurate each algorithm is between the fifth and eightieth training example. This experiment indicates that the strategy of always relying on explanation-based learning to acquire concepts that are implications of domain theory is not always more effective than using SBL to acquire these concepts. When the domain theory is inaccurate (e.g., if the domain theory is learned by SBL from few examples), it is best to ignore the domain theory.

In the next two experiments, I compare the combination of EBL and SBL argued for in this book and implemented in OCCAM with each strategy applied alone. The experimental design is the same as the earlier experiment. Figure 6-4 shows the difference in accuracy between OCCAM and EBL. In this experiment, as soon as a rule learned by either EBL or SBL is shown to be inaccurate on a new example, the rule is deleted and a new rule is learned. It can occur that a rule created by EBL is deleted and a new rule is formed by SBL. This occurs when the domain theory was accurate enough to explain an earlier training example, but the generalization formed by EBL fails to make a correct prediction on a new training example and the domain theory does not explain the new training example.

N	10%	30%	50%
5	0.1	0.1	0.3
10	0.2	3.5	14.3
15	0.4	24.4	41.8
20	0.9	46.4	60.3
25	1.0	43.8	56.4
30	1.6	25.6	48.4
35	1.4	18.8	33.0
40	0.9	9.6	19.8
45	1.0	5.8	12.0
50	-0.8	3.6	5.3
55	-1.2	0.2	4.2
60	-1.1	0.8	1.4
65	-1.0	0.2	1.2
70	-0.8	-0.2	0.6
75	-0.9	-0.4	0.6
80	0.0	0.0	0.2

Figure 6-4: The difference in accuracy between OCCAM and EBL as a function of the number of training examples.

In almost all cases, OCCAM is as accurate or more accurate than EBL. The greater accuracy of OCCAM is attributable to the fact that OCCAM uses SBL when the domain theory is not accurate enough to explain a training example. In this situation, EBL cannot produce a hypothesis at all. OCCAM relies on SBL primarily when there are more performance examples than foundational examples. In this case, it is unlikely that the domain theory is accurate enough to explain a training example, or that the hypothesis produced by explaining one training example is accurate enough to make the correct prediction on later training examples. Note that OCCAM does not explicitly contain a test for the ratio of performance to foundational examples. Rather OCCAM simply decides to use EBL when the domain theory is accurate enough to explain one example and OCCAM retains this hypothesis if it makes accurate predictions on future examples.

In the final experiment, I compared OCCAM to SBL. The experimental design is identical to the earlier two experiments. Figure 6-5 shows the difference in accuracy of OCCAM and SBL.

In almost all cases, OCCAM is as accurate or more accurate than SBL. However, when there were 50% performance examples, after 25 examples SBL was 0.36% more accurate than OCCAM. The greater accuracy of OCCAM is attributable to the fact that OCCAM uses EBL when the domain theory is accurate enough to explain a training example. In this situation, SBL must rely on correlation and does take advantage of the domain theory. When there are significantly more foundational examples than performance examples, the domain theory is likely to be accurate and the generalizations formed by EBL from this domain theory are more accurate than the generalizations produced by SBL.

The surprising result of the last two experiments is that the simple decision to use EBL when the domain theory is accurate enough to explain a single training example (and to abandon this hypothesis when it fails to make accurate predictions) is a sufficient test to produce rules that are in almost all circumstances at least as accurate as EBL or SBL applied alone.

6.4. Integrated Learning Systems

To appreciate the strengths and weaknesses of the learning strategy proposed in this book, it is worthwhile to compare this strategy to alternative means of integrating SBL and EBL. One such strategy is to first use SBL to form a correlational generalization, and then use EBL to verify that the generalization is consistent with existing knowledge. Those parts of the correlational generalization that are not supported by the existing knowledge are discarded. Figure 6-6 illustrates this approach. This strategy is employed by the UNIMEM program (Lebowitz, 1986a; Lebowitz, 1986b; Lebowitz, 1986c) .

N	10%	30%	50%
5	0.0	0.0	0.0
10	0.0	0.0	0.0
15	3.0	2.8	0.0
20	16.4	10.6	0.0
25	32.4	16.0	-0.3
30	48.2	13.5	1.0
35	63.0	11.0	0.0
40	68.9	8.3	0.0
45	65.5	5.6	0.0
50	66.8	1.6	0.0
55	58.2	1.0	0.0
60	56.1	0.0	0.0
70	45.0	0.0	0.0
80	35.4	0.0	0.0
90	25.0	0.0	0.0
100	19.2	0.0	0.0
140	3.4	0.0	0.0
180	0.5	0.0	0.0
220	0.0	0.0	0.0

Figure 6-5: The difference in accuracy between OCCAM and SBL as a function of the number of training examples. With more than 40% performance examples, there is little or no difference between the two algorithms.

There is one important benefit of this strategy. Rather than explaining individual events, generalized events are explained. Generalized events encode an observed regularity between events. Many of the features of the individual events are not included in the generalized event, so the search for an explanation is more focused. However, there are two weaknesses of this strategy. First, the EBL program is limited by the biases of the SBL program. For example, the similarity-based learning module of UNIMEM is limited to uncovering the situation in which one feature predicts the presence of another feature. It cannot

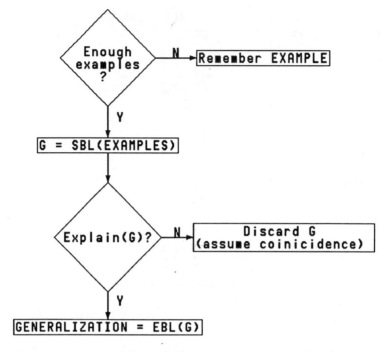

Figure 6-6:   Preferring similarity-based to explanation-based learning.

produce a generalization that indicates that a combination of features is predictive due to the amount of storage that a similarity-based program would require to perform this task. However, it is trivial for an explanation-based learning program to perform this task.   Additionally, the similarity-based program limits the explanation-based program by relying on a syntactic clustering algorithm for the aggregation of events into useful clusters. The second weakness of this strategy is that the explanatory power of the learner does not increase. Since the results of the similarity-based module are filtered through the explanation-based learning module, only generalizations that are implications of existing knowledge are created[55]. Finally, this strategy is not consistent with findings in psychology that indicate that people overlook correlations that are not anticipated by existing knowledge (Nisbett & Ross, 1978). However, this strategy has been employed in domains that are typically more data-intensive than the tasks that people commonly encounter (Lebowitz, 1987). For example, one domain in which UNIMEM operates is finding and

---

[55]In Diettrich's terms, there is no learning at the knowledge level.

explaining correlations between the voting records of United States senators. In this domain, the program performs a task that would be difficult or impossible for many people. The program is presented with data on how 100 senators voted on 15 issues in addition to 20 features describing each senator, and builds predictive generalizations. In such a domain, the benefits of this strategy outweigh its weaknesses.

Another strategy that combines existing knowledge and correlational information would be to use existing knowledge to explain an event. However, rather than using EBL for the generalization, SBL can find regularities between events and their explanations. Figure 6-7 illustrates this approach. Such a strategy has been implemented in the WYL program (Flann & Dietterich, 1986) that performs inductive generalization on explanation structures. In Purpose-Directed Analogy (Kedar-Cabelli, 1985), the explanation of a new example is produced by analogy with a known example and a generalized concept definition is formed by combining common parts of the explanation.

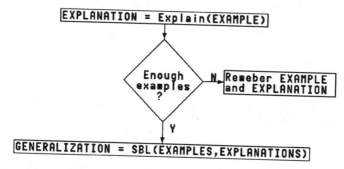

Figure 6-7: Similarity-based learning of explanation structures.

One important benefit of this strategy is that the learning system does not have to have enough knowledge to be able to produce the explanation. The explanation may be supplied by some external agent. For example, a parent might tell a child "You can't have a cookie now because it's too close to suppertime and it might spoil your appetite." Although a parent might give an explanation, the principles from which the explanation was derived are rarely given (e.g., "One hour before supper is too close" or "Foods with more than 100 calories are filling"). In a situation such as this, EBL is not applicable. Of course, if the explanation is derived from the learner's knowledge, or even verified by the learner's knowledge, it is more effective to use EBL to generalize explanations. Otherwise, irrelevant coincidental information is likely to appear in the generalized explanations.

The final alternative I consider is the one proposed in this book and implemented in OCCAM. In this approach, EBL is applied if applicable and similarity-based learning is used as a last resort[56]. This approach is illustrated in Figure 6-8.

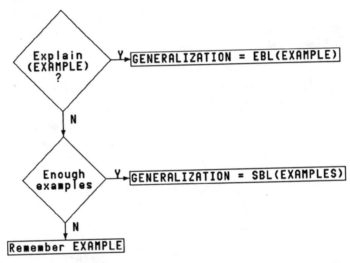

Figure 6-8: OCCAM: preferring explanation-based to similarity-based learning.

The primary benefit of this approach is that the knowledge necessary to perform EBL can be acquired by the learning system. EBL is preferred, but if there is not enough knowledge to produce an explanation, SBL can acquire this knowledge. The primary disadvantage of this approach is that knowledge that is needed to make generalizations can be incorrect. This is a consequence of using SBL that makes unjustified inductive leaps to acquire this knowledge. It is important to realize that OCCAM is much more than a switch that decides when to run each type of learning program. The separate parts of OCCAM cooperate by utilizing the same memory for learning and explanation. Figure 6-9 illustrates the flow of information in OCCAM. Schemata are formed by SBL or EBL and serve as background knowledge for EBL.

---

[56]For the moment, I am ignoring the theory-driven learning component of OCCAM.

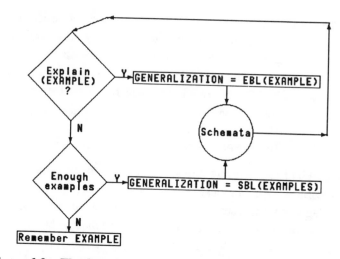

Figure 6-9: **The flow of information in** OCCAM. **Schemata are formed by similarity-based or explanation-based learning and serve as background knowledge for explanation-based learning.**

6.5. Comparisons to Related Work

In the previous section, I compared OCCAM's learning strategy to alternative means of combining prior knowledge and correlational information. In this section, I compare OCCAM to a number of different approaches to learning.

6.5.1. Empirical learning

In machine learning, empirical techniques that create a concept definition from a number of examples have been extensively studied (Michalski, 1977; Mitchell, 1982; Winston, 1975). There are serious problems with considering an empirical learning method to be the only mechanism for learning causal relationships. In particular, empirical learning methods cannot distinguish between relevant similarities and coincidences. In addition, empirical learning methods cannot account for the fact that relationships consistent with current beliefs are easier to detect (see Section 7.7.1), or that it is easier to learn relationships that are consistent with a general theory of causality (see Section 4.2.1). Furthermore, empirical learning programs are sensitive to biases that might affect the collection of data. For example (Shell, 1987), in one study it was found that people in a hospital with pancreatic cancer had consumed more coffee than a control group of hospital patients with other illnesses. This might suggest that heavy coffee use increases the chances of pancreatic cancer. However, further investigations showed that over thirty percent of the control group were hospitalized for digestive ailments and were less likely to consume coffee for this reason. This example illustrates one manner in which prior knowledge can assist SBL: by reasoning about how well the observed cases represents the entire population.

6.5.2. Explanation-based learning

Explanation-based learning provides a solution to the central problem of empirical learning. All empirical learning programs must make an unjustified inductive leap when it is assumed that a regularity that has been true in the past will be true in the future. In contrast, EBL is an analytical technique that makes justifiable generalizations. When the underlying causes for a regularity are known, the exact conditions under which the regularity will hold can be derived.

However, there would be several problems with the claim that EBL is the only mechanism necessary to learn causal relationships. In particular, EBL cannot answer the question of how the underlying knowledge of causality is learned. In OCCAM, it is the role of SBL and TDL to create this knowledge.

A further problem with EBL is that most researchers have considered an explanation to be a deductive proof (Hirsh, 1987; Kedar-Cabelli & McCarty, 1987). However, in many instances explanation cannot properly be viewed as a deductive process (Charniak & McDermott, 1985; Josephson et al., 1987; McDermott, 1986). Instead, explanation should be viewed as an abductive process (Peirce, 1932) that generates hypotheses to account for facts. Explanation cannot be deduction, because in the typical case, information is missing that would allow a deductive proof to be completed (Rajamoney & DeJong, 1987). This problem has been called the incomplete theory problem (Mitchell et al., 1986a). When a domain theory is incomplete, missing information must be assumed, and multiple inconsistent explanations arise because it is possible to make multiple inconsistent assumptions. A crucial problem is deciding between alternative explanations.

While it is true that the explanation-based learning component of OCCAM suffers from the problem of treating an explanation as a deductive proof, OCCAM does address the issue of selecting between alternative explanations in its theory-driven learning component. The theory-driven learning component of

OCCAM can be thought of as explanation-based learning with a weak, incomplete domain theory. For example, in TDL, it is often the case that more than one generalization rule may apply in a situation. In this case, OCCAM does not have enough knowledge to determine which of the possible explanations is correct. However, OCCAM has two strategies for selecting a hypothesis from the set of alternatives:

- Select the simpler hypothesis. The generalization rules in OCCAM are ordered in increasing complexity of the explanation. Exceptionless generalization rules have the highest priority, followed by dispositional generalization rules which attribute different outcomes to different features of the objects, and finally historical generalization rules which attribute different outcomes to different histories of the objects.

- Dispositions. When other factors are equal, OCCAM selects explanations that utilize the distinctions that have been useful in previous explanations.

One important aspect of EBL with incomplete theories that is addressed in TDL is the evaluation of explanatory hypotheses and the revision of incorrect hypotheses. OCCAM is unique among EBL programs in dealing with this issue.

6.5.3. Case-based reasoning

Recently, there has been a large amount of interest in case-based reasoning (Hammond, 1987; Kass, 1986; Kolodner, 1987; Leake & Owens, 1986). Case-based reasoning is to a large extent compatible with the theory of memory in which OCCAM is embedded. According to Schank's MOP theory (Schank, 1982), understanding a new event consists of finding the best knowledge structure in memory that accounts for the event, and using the knowledge structure for inferences, predictions, and explanations. There are two primary differences between OCCAM and most case-based reasoning systems. First, case-based reasoning systems to date have focused on SBL to acquire new generalizations. Second, in case-based reasoning, sometimes the best knowledge structure is a specific experience in memory, rather than a generalized experience. When the best knowledge structure can be a specific case, there are two problems that must be solved:

- Finding the best case in memory. In OCCAM the most specific schema to account for a new event cannot contradict any of the features of the new event. This is no longer true in case-based reasoning, since a specific case is bound to differ on some (irrelevant) details.

- Adapting the explanation of a previous case to fit a new situation. For example, one system (Alterman, 1985), modifies a plan for riding on the subway system in San Francisco to ride on the subway in Washington D.C.

A critical issue for case-based reasoning systems is finding a good previous case. Clearly, a plan to ride the subway in Washington D.C. could not be easily constructed by modifying a plan to visit the Lincoln Monument in Washington D.C. This crucial problem for case-based reasoning has been addressed by OCCAM since it contains a mechanism for determining which features are relevant to solving a goal. This mechanism could be used by a case-based reasoning system to select which features to index an event by so that the event can be recalled when relevant. The second issue addressed by case-based reasoning systems, dynamically modifying old explanations to fit new situations, is not addressed in OCCAM. Instead, OCCAM generalizes explanations when they are added to memory, so that they can be specialized when needed for a new case.

6.5.4. Discovery systems

An area of research that is related to the learning of causal relationships in OCCAM is the discovery of scientific laws (Langley et al., 1986). There are, however, a number of differences between OCCAM and scientific discovery systems. Most scientific discovery systems operate on data that do not include irrelevant attributes. For example, in a version of BACON (Langley et al., 1983) that discovers the ideal gas law, the system is presented cases representing the pressure, volume, and temperature of various gases. If the system were also presented with data indicating the height and age of the experimenter, the size of the search space would be increased considerably. A general theory of causality, such as the one implemented in OCCAM, could help to rule out irrelevant attributes.

The second difference between OCCAM and discovery systems is that most discovery systems have looked for quantitative laws that summarize numerical relationships (e.g., the velocity of a falling object increases at 9.81 meters per second). In contrast, OCCAM focuses on qualitative laws (e.g., all objects except helium balloons fall toward the ground).

6.6. Limitations of OCCAM

In this section, I point out some inadequacies of OCCAM that may be more difficult to address in the current framework.

6.6.1. Nondeterministic concepts

One class of concepts that is difficult for OCCAM to learn is nondeterministic causal relationships that appear in concepts such as "dangerous" or "slippery." Part of the problem is that these concepts are awkward to represent in the conceptual dependency framework. It would be trivial for OCCAM to learn when things are slippery if the input were that "On Monday, it was snowing and the road was slippery and on Tuesday the road was clear and it wasn't slippery." However, more realistically, OCCAM's input shouldn't refer to "slippery," but some observable result of slipperiness. For example, OCCAM might be presented with input data about the weather and information about cars driving by. Suppose that when the roads are clear, one out of every fifty thousand examples describes a car that drives by and swerves off the road. When it is snowing, one out of every thousand examples of a car going by indicates that the car swerves off the road. A problem arises because the learning of these concepts conflicts with OCCAM's method for judging the accuracy of a learned rule. The fact that a road is slippery is not enough to predict that a car will have an accident. It really means that a car is *more likely* to have an accident. OCCAM has a fixed threshold that indicates whether or not a prediction is usually true. A more flexible technique might look for conditions under which a prediction is more likely to be true. However, such a technique might be prone to discovering more coincidences than actual tendencies.

6.6.2. Simplicity and accuracy

OCCAM's method of evaluating the accuracy of learned rules can cause an additional problem. There is a tradeoff between the accuracy of a rule and the simplicity of a rule. OCCAM currently selects the simplest explanation for an event that does not introduce too many errors. A problem arises because a slightly more complex explanation might make significantly fewer errors. It might be possible to extend OCCAM to look for a more complex explanation when a prediction fails, and to favor a more complex explanation that produces more accurate predictions. However, one must be careful not to "overfit" the data if the exception to a simple rule may be a noisy data point.

6.6.3. Learning about unobserved states

The general philosophy behind OCCAM is to try the most knowledge-intensive form of learning first and resort to weak methods when the knowledge-intensive methods fail. OCCAM demonstrates this by learning complex schemata through knowledge-intensive analytic techniques. The background knowledge necessary for knowledge-intensive techniques is acquired empirically. However, OCCAM does not acquire this background knowledge from complex examples. Instead, OCCAM is presented with simple input examples in which there is an observable action and an observable consequence of that action. By comparing similarities and contrasting differences, OCCAM can empirically acquire the conditions under which a cause results in an effect. For example, OCCAM does not learn the background knowledge for kidnapping from examples of kidnapping. Instead, OCCAM acquires this knowledge from examples such as parents helping hurt children.

A more difficult problem for an empirical learning program is the acquisition of knowledge about unobserved intermediate states. For example, from examples of glass cups breaking when dropped, it's easy enough for OCCAM to learn that glass objects break. What is more difficult is to induce that glass cups break and the person setting the table knew that children are likely to drop their cups and wanted to avoid a broken cup, from an example of a table setting in which the children have plastic cups and the adults have glass cups.

6.6.4. Partitioning the input

OCCAM currently assumes that its input is the description of an important situation. Learning in OCCAM makes the understanding of similar situations easier in the future. A problem arises if the input describes a unique event that may never occur again. For example, if OCCAM were presented a complete novel or even a complex short story, such as those understood by BORIS (Dyer, 1983), then OCCAM would attempt to generalize the particular explanation structure of that story. OCCAM probably will never see another story with the exact same explanation. However, future examples may share part of that explanation structure because subgoals may be achieved in the same manner.

To deal with this sort of situation, a mechanism could be added to OCCAM that identifies "important" subgoals, and creates schemata to deal with the resolution of these subgoals. This mechanism would serve two purposes:

- To avoid learning from events that one may never encounter again.

- To partition an event, so that learning can occur from more than the description of a top-level event.

6.6.5. Learning concepts without operational descriptions

Researchers in AI have proposed knowledge structures that cannot be recognized simply as a conjunction of surface features that describe an event. For example, Thematic Abstraction Units (TAUs) (Dyer, 1983) have been proposed as knowledge structures that encode information about planning errors. TAUs are not recognized by a set of surface features, but rather by a certain configuration of goals and plans connected by intentional links. If OCCAM is presented with examples of a TAU-like situation, it does not learn the general form of the TAU. For example, OCCAM finds a flaw in kidnapping because when the kidnapper abducts the hostage, the hostage sees the kidnapper and can identify him later (see Section 7.6). This is a special case of TAU-CONFUSED-ENABLEMENT, in which a plan to achieve one goal causes the failure of another goal. However, OCCAM does not learn the TAU from this situation because the TAU cannot be represented as a conjunction of the surface features of the event. If OCCAM is presented another example of the same TAU, such as the Aesop fable of the Fox and the Crow, then it would learn another special case of the TAU. However, OCCAM does not ever learn the general description of this class of situations.

One approach to learning TAUs has been implemented in the CRAM system, (Dolan & Dyer, 1985). This approach composes complex TAUs by noticing the interactions among simpler TAUs. However, CRAM does not address the issues of how these simpler TAUs might be learned. One approach to acquiring TAUs is to use a similarity-based program to find the commonalities between the explanation structure of special cases of the TAU. In OCCAM, these special cases can be represented in the same manner as any other schema (e.g., see Figure 7-17 on page 238.)

6.6.6. Consolidating multiple descriptions of the same event

OCCAM currently assumes that its input is a complete description of an event. However, one typically does not find out all the details about a situation all at once. For example, there might be several newspaper stories about a kidnapping incident. Individual stories might report on the abduction, the ransom demands, the release of the hostage, the arrest of a suspect, and the trial. It is not clear how this would affect the learning component of OCCAM, but a number of interesting issues are raised for the memory component and the hypothetical natural language understanding component:

- How should a partial description of an event be represented and indexed in memory? Should the representation of a partial event contain "questions" which could be answered by later information?

- How can one recognize that two partial descriptions of a story are referring to the same event?

- How should conflicts between multiple descriptions of the event be resolved?

- When should inferences be made and what mechanism should there be to retract erroneous inferences?

Chapter 7
Experiments in Integrated Learning

In this chapter, I discuss several examples of OCCAM acquiring schemata in several different domains. These examples illustrate in detail the points made in the book. So far, I have described OCCAM's similarity-based learning mechanism in Chapter 3, OCCAM's theory-driven learning mechanism in Chapter 4 and OCCAM's explanation-based learning mechanism in Chapter 5. In this chapter, I show how these mechanisms can work together in an integrated learning system. SBL and TDL acquire schemata that can serve as background knowledge for EBL in OCCAM. Several examples are illustrated:

- Acquiring a coercion schema with SBL. The coercion schema provides a framework (and representation) for understanding economic sanction incidents and kidnapping stories.

- Acquiring economic sanction schemata with explanation-based learning. OCCAM relies on the coercion schema and hand-coded political and economic knowledge to explain individual events that are generalized.

- Answering questions about the possible outcomes of economic sanction incidents. OCCAM utilizes the schemata acquired via EBL to perform this task.

- Theory-driven learning of the social knowledge needed to explain the goals of the target in kidnapping.

- Acquiring a kidnapping schema and some specializations of kidnapping with EBL. The coercion schema that OCCAM uses was acquired via SBL and some social knowledge was acquired via TDL.

Finally, I conclude this chapter by evaluating OCCAM as a cognitive model of the acquisition of causal relationships. I report on several experiments that influenced the design of OCCAM. In addition, I describe how the integration of learning methods accounts for empirical findings in human learning:

- When subjects have detailed knowledge of a causal mechanism, they are not misled by temporal or spatial cues that conflict with the known mechanism.

- Faster learning rates have been observed on prediction tasks when the prediction is consistent with specific world knowledge.

- Hypotheses that are not consistent with prior knowledge are ignored when a hypothesis consistent with prior knowledge is available.

OCCAM contributes to the understanding of human learning by defining an integrated learning process that accounts for the influence of prior knowledge in learning. The goal of this chapter is to provide examples of how the learning strategies interact in OCCAM and to evaluate how well this integration accounts for human learning.

7.1. Learning About Coercion

The process that OCCAM goes through to learn about coercion is identical to the process that OCCAM goes through to learn **delta-agency**. The only differences are the complexity of the domain and the complexity of the examples. The **coerce** domain is more complex than **delta-agency** because more goals and participants are involved. For example, **apple-1** is an instance of **delta-agency** while **broccoli-1** is an instance of **coerce**.

- **apple-1**: Karen wants an apple. She asks her mother, Chris, for one and Chris gives her one.

- **broccoli-1**: Chris wants Karen to eat her broccoli. Chris tells Karen that if Karen eats her broccoli, then Chris will let Karen have some soda to drink. Otherwise, Chris will give Karen water. Karen has a goal conflict between avoiding a food she doesn't like and not eating a food she does like. Karen decides to eat her broccoli and

Chris gives Karen some soda.

The event, **broccoli-1**, contains a goal for Chris as well as two goals for Karen. **coerce** is also more complex than **delta-agency** because more objects are involved. There is a different object involved in the threat (drink water), the demand (eat broccoli) and the alternative (drink soda). Earlier, I chose to illustrate similarity-based learning with **delta-agency** for two reasons. First, it is less complex so that figures of the intermediate stages are not cluttered with too many details to fit on a single page. Second, it provides support for the claim that the learning mechanisms in OCCAM are general because the representation formalism and learning procedures have been applied in several domains.

Learning **coerce** is more difficult than learning **delta-agency** due to the greater complexity of the **coerce** examples. In **delta-agency**, all of the initial examples were examples of goal success. Some of the **coerce** examples illustrate failures as well as successes. For instance, one example presented to OCCAM is the following event:

• **ball-1**: Mat and Sam are playing football. Sam tells Mat that if he doesn't allow Sam to kick the ball, Sam will take his ball and go home. Mat decides that he does not want to play with Sam, and that he will go buy a frisbee. Mat goes to the store, but finds that he does not have enough money to buy a frisbee. Both Sam's and Mat's goals fail.

The greater variety of examples results in a more general **coerce** schema that does not predict the outcome of a coercion incident. Instead, specializations in various domains, such as economic sanctions and kidnapping, allow the outcome to be predicted.

The input to OCCAM in the coercion examples is represented in terms of primitive CD goals, actions, and states. Since coercion is sufficiently complex, OCCAM will create a macro-schema when it encounters a number of coercion examples. A third coercion example is all that is needed to start the generalization process:

• **swing-1**: Brian tells Ben that unless Ben gets off the swing and

gives Brian a turn, Brian will hit Ben with a stick. Ben doesn't get
off so Brian hits him.

Once OCCAM has encountered three coercion examples (broccoli-1,
ball-1 and swing-1) it finds the common features of the three events and
their subordinate goals and plans. A simple schema that is a specialization of
the goal schema is formed. In addition, a macro-schema that I call coerce
(for its mnemonic value) is created. The generalized event for the coerce
schema is shown in Figure 7-1.

```
COERCE the-actor HUMAN hair BROWN
        the-bene HUMAN age KID
        the-target HUMAN eyes BLUE
                         age KID
        demand-obj P-OBJ
        threat-obj P-OBJ
        the-alt-obj P-OBJ
        response-obj P-OBJ
        goal GOAL outcome =OUTCOME
                  plan =PLAN
                  goal =GOAL-STATE
                  actor =THE-ACTOR
        goal-state STATE actor =THE-BENE
        outcome GOAL-OUTCOME goal GOAL goal =GOAL-STATE
                                       actor =THE-ACTOR
                             actor =THE-ACTOR
        plan PLAN plan =THE-ASK
                  actor =THE-ACTOR
        the-ask ACT type MTRANS
                    actor =THE-ACTOR
                    object COND if =THE-DEMAND
                                then =THE-ALTERNATIVE
                                else =THE-THREAT
                    to =THE-TARGET
        the-prep ACT actor =THE-ACTOR
        the-demand ACT actor =THE-TARGET
                       object =DEMAND-OBJ
        the-threat ACT actor =THE-ACTOR
                       object =THREAT-OBJ
                       to =THE-TARGET
        the-alternative ACT actor =THE-ACTOR
                            object =THE-ALT-OBJ
                            to =THE-TARGET
        the-sub-goal GOAL-CONFLICT actor =THE-TARGET
                                   goal1 GOAL-OUTCOME-LINK goal-b GOAL actor =THE-TARGET
                                                           goal-a GOAL actor =THE-TARGET
                                   goal2 GOAL-OUTCOME-LINK goal-b GOAL actor =THE-TARGET
                                                           goal-a GOAL actor =THE-TARGET
        the-sub-plan PLAN plan =THE-TARGET-RESPONSE
                          actor =THE-TARGET
        the-target-response ACT object =RESPONSE-OBJ
                                actor =THE-TARGET
        the-actor-response ACT actor =THE-ACTOR
        the-target-outcome GOAL-OUTCOME actor =THE-TARGET
```

Figure 7-1:   The initial coerce schema.

The coerce schema contains a number of different roles[57]:

---

[57]Recall that a user types a name for these roles. Names such as role.17 would have the same
semantics to OCCAM. All OCCAM knows about a role such as the-threat is that structurally it can
be found as the filler of the else role of the filler of the object role of an mtrans and that
the-threat will lead to a goal failure for the-target. the-target is simply the to of an
mtrans. As a convention, the feature names of the coerce schema start with "the" if there is the
possibility of confusing the feature name with a primitive feature in Conceptual Dependency.

- **the-actor**: the person who has a goal and plans to make a threat to achieve the goal. In the generalized event, the features of the actor are those features that Chris, Mat, and Brian have in common.

- **the-bene**: the person who benefits if the goal of the actor is achieved. Typically, this is the actor, however in **broccoli-1**, it is Karen who benefits since Chris has a goal of making sure Karen eats a healthy meal.

- **the-target**: the person who the actor threatens. In the **coerce** generalized event, **the-target** is a composite of Karen, Sam, and Ben.

- **demand-obj**: The object involved in the demand. In the **coerce** generalized event, this is generalized from broccoli, a football, and a swing.

- **threat-obj**: The object involved in the threat. The **threat-obj** is a composite of water, a ball, and a stick.

- **the-alt-obj**: The object involved in the alternative. **the-alt-obj** is generalized from soda, a ball, and a stick.

- **response-obj**: The object involved in the response to the actor's demand. In the **coerce** generalized event, this is a composite of broccoli, a frisbee, and a swing.

The generalized event contains abstract goals, plans and events in addition to the people and objects that participate in coercion. In the **coerce** generalized event in Figure 7-1 these roles are:

- **goal**: The goal that the actor wishes to achieve.

- **goal-state**: The state that would be true if the actor achieves his goal.

- **outcome**: The outcome of the actor's goal.

- **plan**: The plan the actor has to achieve his goal. In **coerce** the plan is to tell a target that if he meets a demand then the actor will do **the-alternative**, otherwise the actor will do **the-threat**.

- **the-ask**: The actual act of asking the target to do the demand.

- **the-prep**: The preparation that is necessary for the actor to carry out the plan.

- **the-demand**: The act the actor wants the target to perform. This act will achieve the actor's goal.

- **the-threat**: The act the actor will do if the target meets the demand.

- **the-alternative**: The event that will occur if the target does not meet the demand. The alternative is sometimes that the actor will not perform the threat (as in **ball-1** and **swing-1**) but it can also be that the actor will do something else (as in **broccoli-1**).

- **the-sub-goal**: A goal of the target that is motivated by the actor making the demand. In **coerce**, this goal is the goal conflict caused by the target linking the outcome of the demand, to the outcome of the threat.

- **the-sub-plan**: the plan the target pursues to resolve **the-sub-goal**.

- **the-target-response**: The action the target performs that realizes **the-sub-plan**. This response may be meeting the demand, ignoring the demand, or pursuing some plan that mitigates the effect of the threat.

- **the-actor-response**: The action that the actor performs in response to **the-target-response**.

- **the-target-outcome**: The outcome of the target's goal.

When OCCAM forms a macro-schema such as **coerce**, it also constructs a sequence of events that records the temporal, causal, or intentional relationships

(Dyer, 1983) between the various components of the event. In Figure 7-2 the sequence of events for the **coerce** schema is illustrated.

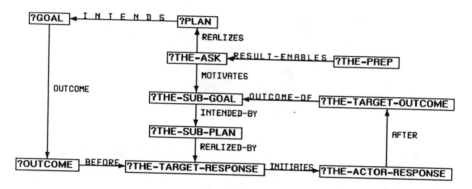

Figure 7-2: The sequence of events for the coercion schema.

Like any schema formed with similarity-based learning, the coercion schema is subject to revision when further experiences are encountered. Once the initial coercion schema has been constructed, future examples refine the schema, removing details that were just coincidences. For example, the initial coercion schema indicates that the target is a child with blue eyes and the actor has brown hair. These features are deleted after OCCAM processes more events. The final version of the coercion schema that OCCAM specializes to create kidnapping and economic sanction schema is displayed in Figure 7-3. This schema removes all constraints on the possible actors and participants. For example, after OCCAM is presented with a Berenstain Bears story in which the Mother Bear coerces the Father Bear (Berenstain & Berenstain, 1985), the constraint that the actor and target are human is removed.

7.2. Economic Sanctions

When OCCAM learns about economic sanction incidents, it utilizes the coercion schema in two ways. First, the input representation to OCCAM is in the high-level language of coercion rather than the primitive goals and plans. I am assuming that the understanding process which would parse accounts of economic sanction incidents would have access to the representational transfer created when OCCAM creates the **coerce** schema. This assumption is not too unrealistic: in Section 7.3, I demonstrate OCCAM's question answering capabilities, which include parsing questions into a CD primitive representation.

```
COERCE goal GOAL outcome =OUTCOME
              plan =PLAN
              goal =GOAL-STATE
              actor =THE-ACTOR
     goal-state STATE actor =THE-BENE
     outcome GOAL-OUTCOME goal GOAL goal =GOAL-STATE
                                    actor =THE-ACTOR
                          actor =THE-ACTOR
     plan PLAN plan =THE-ASK
               actor =THE-ACTOR
     the-ask ACT type MTRANS
             actor =THE-ACTOR
             object COND if =THE-DEMAND
                         then =THE-ALTERNATIVE
                         else =THE-THREAT
             to =THE-TARGET
     the-prep ACT actor =THE-ACTOR
     the-demand ACT actor =THE-TARGET
                    object =DEMAND-OBJ
     the-threat ACT actor =THE-ACTOR
                    object =THREAT-OBJ
                    to =THE-TARGET
     the-alternative ACT actor =THE-ACTOR
                         object =THE-ALT-OBJ
                         to =THE-TARGET
     the-sub-goal GOAL-CONFLICT actor =THE-TARGET
                          goal1 GOAL-OUTCOME-LINK goal-b GOAL actor =THE-TARGET
                                                  goal-a GOAL actor =THE-TARGET
                          goal2 GOAL-OUTCOME-LINK goal-b GOAL actor =THE-TARGET
                                                  goal-a GOAL actor =THE-TARGET
     the-sub-plan PLAN plan =THE-TARGET-RESPONSE
                       actor =THE-TARGET
     the-target-response ACT object =RESPONSE-OBJ
                             actor =THE-TARGET
     the-actor-response ACT actor =THE-ACTOR
     the-target-outcome GOAL-OUTCOME actor =THE-TARGET
```

Figure 7-3: **The final refined version of the generalized event for the
coerce schema.**

The process of searching memory converts the CD primitive representation to
the high level representation.

OCCAM is provided with a large amount of domain knowledge that helps it
to learn about economic sanction incidents. This knowledge is of two sorts:

- economic knowledge: inference rules that indicate the effects of
  decreases in supply, increases in price, etc.

- political knowledge: inference rules that indicate the goals of
  political entities. For example, one inference rule states that
  countries have the goal of reducing the influence of their
  adversaries.

In addition, OCCAM starts with some pre-existing schemata representing
Conceptual Dependency goals, states, and actions (see Figure 3-3 on page 78).

These inference rules can explain the outcomes of economic situations and
infer the goals of the participants. With this knowledge, EBL is possible and
OCCAM does not need to rely on correlational information. Furthermore, this

knowledge prevents OCCAM from indexing events in memory based on simple surface features. For example, consider the following two economic sanction stories:

Economic-Sanction-1

In 1983, Australia refused to sell uranium to France, unless France ceased nuclear testing in the South Pacific. France paid a higher price to buy uranium from South Africa and continued nuclear testing.

Economic-Sanction-3

In 1961, the Soviet Union refused to sell grain to Albania if Albania did not rescind economic ties with China. Albania continued the ties with China, and China sold Albania wheat imported from Canada.

If these two episodes were in memory, which episode would be considered more similar to Economic-Sanction-2?

Economic-Sanction-2

In 1980, the US refused to sell grain to the Soviet Union unless the Soviet Union withdrew troops from Afghanistan. The Soviet Union paid a higher price to buy grain from Argentina and did not withdraw from Afghanistan.

Economic-Sanction-2 has more surface similarities in common with Economic-Sanction-3 than Economic-Sanction-1. In both Economic-Sanction-2 and Economic-Sanction-3, the commodity in dispute is grain and the target is a communist country. However, clustering these two episodes together would ignore the goals of the country who assisted the target. In particular, in Economic-Sanction-2, Argentina sold the grain to make a profit:

While Argentina had apparently scheduled deliveries of its grain to its traditional customers the deals had not been finalized and the contracts had not been signed. As the Soviets began bidding up the price of grain the Argentines reneged on these informal understandings with other countries and sold almost all their grain to the Soviets. (Brown, 1985, p. 341)

However, in Economic-Sanction-3, the goal of China was not to monetarily profit from the incident but to reduce the influence of the Soviet Union in Albania:

> As part of an Albanian-Chinese trade and assistance agreement signed in early 1961, Chinese agreed to extend $123 million to Albania. That is $118 million more than the amount promised by the Soviet Union. China also buys 60,000 tons of Canadian wheat and has it shipped to Albania. (Freedman, 1970, p. 77)

Because of these different goals, Economic-Sanction-2 and Economic-Sanction-3 should not be treated as similar. The goal of South Africa is identical to the goal of Argentina since they both profit from the sanction incidents.

Even if a correlational learner were to properly cluster Economic-Sanction-1 and Economic-Sanction-2, it would face a more serious problem of determining which of the similarities between these two events are relevant. If a schema were formed encoding all of the similarities between these two events, it would indicate that when an English speaking democracy that imports oil threatens a country in the Northern Hemisphere that has a strong economy and exports weapons, then the sanction will fail because a country in the Southern Hemisphere will sell the product.

Explanation-based learning solves both the problem of selecting the relevant features and the problem of classifying events. Rather than treating all features identically, similarity relationships are only based on relevant surface features (i.e., those which are essential in explaining the goals and actions of the countries involved).

In the domain of economic sanctions, OCCAM was presented with examples in the twentieth century in which economic sanctions were not accompanied by covert or overt military operations[58]. In total, 15 incidents were presented to OCCAM. However, because many of the sanction incidents had identical explanation structures, OCCAM did not acquire 15 different schemata with

---

[58]In addition, I did not present OCCAM with a number of examples of sanction incidents involving the sale of fuel for nuclear reactors.

explanation-based learning. For example, once OCCAM acquired a schema from Economic-Sanction-1, it merely recognized that Economic-Sanction-2 was an instance of that same schema.

7.2.1. A detailed example

In this section, I provide a detailed example of OCCAM acquiring an economic sanction schema with EBL. In Section 7.2.2, I sketch the generalizations that OCCAM builds from a number of other examples. The detailed example I present is Economic-Sanction-4:

Economic-Sanction-4

In 1948, the Soviet Union threatened to stop granting economic aid to Yugoslavia if Yugoslavia continued its attempts at political independence from the Soviet Union. The United States offered $35 million in economic aid to Yugoslavia which continued to distance itself from the Soviet Union.

```
COERCE the-actor POLITY type COUNTRY
                       name USSR
                       ideology COMMUNIST
                       language RUSSIAN
                                SLAVIC
                       location NORTHERN-HEMISPHERE
                       continent ASIA
                       economic-health STRONG
                       political-relationships ANTAGONISTIC with =RESPONSE-OBJ
                                ...
                       business-relationship =THE-TARGET
                                             =RESPONSE-OBJ
                                             POLITY type COUNTRY
                                                    name FINLAND
                                ...
                       exports COMMODITY type MANUFACTURED-GOODS
                               COMMODITY type GAS
                                ...
                       imports COMMODITY type FOOD
                               COMMODITY type CONSUMER-GOODS
                       life-expectancy *SEVENTIES*
                       literacy *NINTIES*
                       religions RUSSIAN-ORTHODOX
                                 MUSLIM
           the-bene =THE-ACTOR
           the-target POLITY type COUNTRY
                             name YUGOSLAVIA
                             economic-health WEAK
                             business-relationship =THE-ACTOR
                             strategic-importance HIGH
                                ... ...
           threat-obj MONEY dollars 35000000
           the-alt-obj =THREAT-OBJ
           response-obj POLITY type COUNTRY
                               name US
                               economic-health STRONG
                               location NORTHERN-HEMISPHERE
                               ... ...
```

Figure 7-4:   The countries and objects that participate in Economic-Sanction-4.

Figure 7-4 contains OCCAM's representation for the objects and countries that participate in this episode. Figure 7-5 continues the representation of Economic-Sanction-4 by illustrating the events. Note that these two figures do not contain all of the features of the coercion schema. There are two reasons for this. First, some of the features take their values from the general coercion schema. For example, the **plan** in Economic-Sanction-4 is the same as the general coercion **plan**: to make a demand of the target. Second, some of the feature values are unknown. In particular, Economic-Sanction-4 does not indicate the reason that the United States helped out or why Yugoslavia adopted this plan. The features **the-sub-goal** and **the-sub-plan** are not specified for this reason. These features are the same as the ones from the **coerce** schema, but the values of the features are too abstract to be useful. For example, the value of **the-sub-plan** in **coerce** is that the target has a plan that leads to the **outcome**. The mechanism with which events take default values from a schema is rather simple: OCCAM finds the most specific schema for an event. If the event does not contain a feature of the most specific schema, then the feature value of the most specific schema is used for the feature value of the event. Although OCCAM maintains a hierarchy of schemata, it does not need an inheritance mechanism to find values from more general schemata. Instead, when a schema is specialized, all information from the more general schema is copied to the more specific schema. This implementation detail could easily be changed to inherit the information when needed.

OCCAM is relying on a hypothetical natural language interface to build the representation in Figure 7-5. Of course, OCCAM does not deal with issues such as ellipsis, pronominal reference, or word sense disambiguation. OCCAM can accept its input in either the high-level coerce representation, or the CD representation of goals and actions. If the input is in the primitive goals and actions, the memory search converts it to the **coerce** representation. Section 7.3 presents an example of changing representations. In this section, I deal with the **coerce** representation because it is more compact and easier to read.

When Economic-Sanction-4 is added to OCCAM's memory, it must determine if it can account for the outcome of the new event. OCCAM finds that the coercion schema is the most specific schema in memory for this event. However, it does not account for the event's outcome: a goal failure for the Soviet Union.

Since the coercion schema does not predict the outcome of this event,

```
COERCE the-threat ACT type ATRANS
                      actor =THE-ACTOR
                      object =THREAT-OBJ
                      to =THE-TARGET
                      mode NO
        the-alternative ACT type ATRANS
                          actor =THE-ACTOR
                          object =THE-ALT-OBJ
                          to =THE-TARGET
                          mode YES
          the-demand ACT type CHANGE-RELATIONSHIP
                        actor =THE-TARGET
                        to DOMINATED with =THE-ACTOR
            the-target-response ACT type AGREEMENT
                                actor =THE-TARGET
                                object =RESPONSE-OBJ
                                agreement ACT type ATRANS
                                             actor =RESPONSE-OBJ
                                             object =THREAT-OBJ
                                             to =THE-TARGET
                                             mode YES
        goal-state STATE type RELATIONSHIP
                         actor =THE-BENE
                         object DOMINANT with =THE-TARGET
          outcome GOAL-OUTCOME type FAILURE
                               actor =THE-ACTOR
                               goal GOAL actor =THE-ACTOR
                                         goal =GOAL-STATE
            the-actor-response ACT type ATRANS
                               actor =THE-ACTOR
                               object =THREAT-OBJ
                               to =THE-TARGET
                               mode NO
```

Figure 7-5:   The events that occur in Economic-Sanction-4.

OCCAM must search for an explanation by identifying the circumstances that led to this goal failure. OCCAM constructs the following chain of events to explain the outcome:

1. When the Soviet Union issues the threat to halt the economic aid to Yugoslavia, this motivates conflicting goals for Yugoslavia. In effect, the threat of the Soviet Union has linked together the outcome of two goals. Either (a) the goal of maintaining economic health will fail and the goal of achieving political freedom will succeed, or (b) the goal of maintaining economic health will succeed and the goal of achieving political freedom will fail.

2. Yugoslavia has a plan to undo the linkage between the two conflicting goals. Its plan is to find another means of maintaining economic health and to continue on the path toward political freedom.

3. Since the United States is an adversary of the Soviet Union, it has a goal of reducing the political influence of the Soviet Union.

4. Providing economic assistance to Yugoslavia will reduce influence of the Soviet Union.

5. Since the United States has a strong economy, it can afford to give economic aid to Yugoslavia.

6. When the United States gave aid to Yugoslavia, Yugoslavia's goal of economic health was achieved.

7. Since Yugoslavia's goal of economic health was achieved by the United States, the Soviet threat will not cause a goal failure.

8. When Yugoslavia continued to distance itself from the Soviets, the Soviet goal of dominating Yugoslavia was thwarted.

```
COERCE the-actor POLITY political-relationships ANTAGONISTIC with =RESPONSE-OBJ
       the-target POLITY economic-health WEAK
                         strategic-importance HIGH
       the-threat ACT type ATRANS
                      actor =THE-ACTOR
                      object =THREAT-OBJ
                      to =THE-TARGET
                      mode NO
       response-obj POLITY economic-health STRONG
       the-target-response ACT type AGREEMENT
                               actor =THE-TARGET
                               object =RESPONSE-OBJ
                               agreement ACT type ATRANS
                                             actor =RESPONSE-OBJ
                                             object =THREAT-OBJ
                                             to =THE-TARGET
                                             mode YES
       outcome GOAL-OUTCOME type FAILURE
                            actor =THE-ACTOR
                            goal GOAL actor =THE-ACTOR
                                      goal =GOAL-STATE
```

Figure 7-6: The generalization that OCCAM acquires in Economic-Sanction-4.

Once OCCAM has constructed the explanation, it can create a schema by deleting those features of the example that were not needed to explain the failure of the Soviet Union's goal. The generalized event that OCCAM constructs for this situation is displayed in Figures 7-6 and 7-7. Figure 7-6 contains abstract descriptions of the participants and events. This is the most general description of the episode for which the explanation found by OCCAM is applicable. The following constraints are placed on the coercion structure so that this explanation applies:

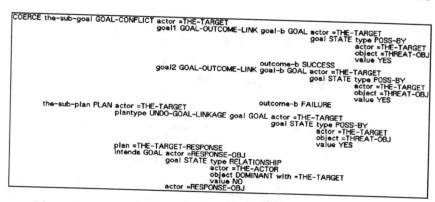

Figure 7-7: **The generalized goal and plan of the target in an economic sanction schema.**

- **the-actor** must have an adversarial relationship with the **response-obj**. This feature is required for the **response-obj** to have a goal of reducing the influence of **the-actor**.

- **the-target** must have a weak economy. This is required so that the threat will harm **the-target**. In addition, **the-target** must have high strategic importance so that it is worthwhile for the **response-obj** to intervene.

- the **response-obj** must have a strong economy so that it can afford to intervene.

- **the-threat** is that **the-actor** will not give **the-target** the **threat-obj**.

- **the-target-response** is for **the-target** to make an agreement with the **response-obj** for the **response-obj** to give **the-target** the **threat-obj**

- the **outcome** is that the goal of **the-actor** will fail.

In the process of constructing the explanation, OCCAM also infers the goal of Yugoslavia and the plan Yugoslavia was undertaking in pursuit of its goal. Since the goal and plan are features of the coercion schema, they are also included in the generalized event for the economic sanction schema.

the-sub-goal and **the-sub-plan** are illustrated in Figure 7-7. The generalized goal indicates that the target has a conflict between some unspecified goal and the goal of obtaining the **threat-obj**. The plan that the target took to resolve this conflict was to find a different means of obtaining the **threat-obj**.

When OCCAM creates a specialized version of a macro-schema such as **coerce** it also updates the sequence of events for the schema. For example, the coercion schema states that the outcome of the actor's goal comes after the target's response (see Figure 7-2). In this type of economic sanction incident, the sequence of events is specialized to indicate that the target's response thwarts the actor's goal so the outcome is a failure. Figure 7-8 shows the modified sequence of events for this economic sanction schema.

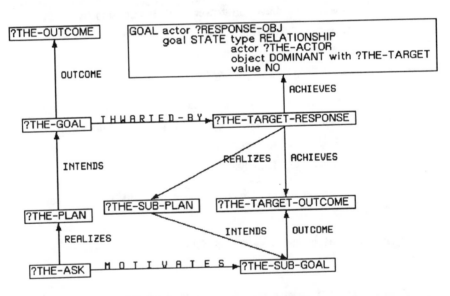

Figure 7-8:   The sequence of events of an economic sanction schema. This sequence of events elaborates on the relationships specified in the   coercion schema. For example, the subgoal that   ?THE-TARGET-RESPONSE achieves is specified.

The schema acquired from explanation-based learning on Economic-Sanction-4 accounts for several other incidents. For example, consider the following two episodes:

Economic-Sanction-5

In 1948, the Soviet Union threatened to block the import of goods into West Berlin to prevent the formation of a West German government. The United States agreed to airlift supplies to West Berlin.

Economic-Sanction-6

In 1960, the United States cut off all exports to Cuba in retaliation for the nationalizing of oil refineries. The Soviet Union then shipped goods and extended credit to Cuba.

Both of these incidents fit the same general pattern as Economic-Sanction-4. When OCCAM encounters these examples, it can already predict their outcomes and there is nothing for OCCAM to learn. Furthermore, OCCAM can easily infer the goals of the target countries and the motivation of the supporting country by simply instantiating the explanation saved with the schema. However, the schema does not account for the following economic sanction incident:

Economic-Sanction-7

In 1983, South Africa threatened to block the import of goods into Lesotho (a small country completely surrounded by South Africa) if Lesotho did not expel members of the African National Congress. Twenty-two members of the African National Congress left within two weeks of the implementation of the blockade.

There are several reasons the schema acquired from the Soviet threat to Yugoslavia does not fit this pattern. First, South Africa does not have a wealthy adversary who would gain politically by helping Lesotho. Second, the strategic importance of Lesotho is minimal. Its location is of no military importance and it has little mineral reserves. This example does demonstrate that in the proper circumstances, economic sanctions can be effective. In the words of Lesothoan Foreign Minister Evaristus Sekhonyana in the *Washington Post* on August, 12 1983:

> *But unless some kind of pressure can be brought to bear on South Africa there is nothing we can do. We have to comply with the demands. We have no other options.*

From this example, OCCAM acquires another economic sanction schema which indicates that when a country is of low strategic importance, poor economic health, and the actor does not have a wealthy adversary, then a threat to cut off imports will produce the desired effect.

7.2.2. Summary of economic sanction schemata

OCCAM acquires a total of seven economic sanction schemata. In this section, I summarize a few of the economic sanction incidents and the lessons that OCCAM learned from the incidents.

OCCAM learns that there is an alternative means for the target to acquire the commodity. From Economic-Sanction-4 OCCAM acquires a schema that indicates that another country might supply the commodity to satisfy a political goal. From Economic-Sanction-1 (repeated below), OCCAM learns that the helper may be pursuing an economic goal.

Economic-Sanction-1

In 1983, Australia refused to sell uranium to France, unless France ceased nuclear testing in the South Pacific. France paid a higher price to buy uranium from South Africa and continued nuclear testing.

From this example, OCCAM acquires a schema that indicates that if a country that exports a commodity tries to coerce a wealthy country that imports the commodity by refusing to sell them the commodity, then a response might be to buy the commodity at a higher price from another country. This schema also applies to the US grain embargo (Economic-Sanction-2) and 1981 incident in which the US refused to sell pipeline equipment to the USSR.

In addition to the Lesotho example, economic sanctions have been effective in two other types of circumstances in the examples that OCCAM has encountered. First, in the 1960's there were a number of incidents of the nationalization[59] of American companies. The following example is typical:

---

[59]Note that OCCAM does not treat verbs such as "expropriate" and "nationalize" as primitive elements. These are represented in terms of the primitive **atrans**.

Economic-Sanction-8

In 1962, Brazil expropriated the national telephone company, a subsidiary of the ITT corporation valued at $7 million dollars. The United States threatened to cut off foreign aid totaling $173 million and Brazil agreed to reimburse ITT.

From this example, OCCAM acquires a schema that indicates that if a threat to cut off aid is for an amount that is greater than a demanded payment, the target country will agree to the demand. OCCAM comes up with the schema through a rather simple cost-benefit analysis of choosing between two goals. Once acquired, this schema applies to a number of cases, such as Ceylon's expropriation of oil companies in 1961, and Peru's nationalization of oil and sugar companies in 1968. In response to a series of similar incidents, the US Congress approved the Hickenlooper amendment that requires a termination of US aid to countries that do not settle expropriation disputes. This amendment was quite successful in producing favorable settlements (Hufbauer & Schott, 1985).

Another example of an economic sanction incident in which the desired goal was achieved is also the first example in modern times. It is also noteworthy because it is an example of stopping a military aggression with economic sanctions:

Economic-Sanction-9

In 1921, the League of Nations voted to stop all exports including food supplies to Yugoslavia in retaliation for an invasion of Albania. Yugoslavia yielded to the threat before the sanctions were implemented.

The schema that OCCAM acquires in this case indicates that if the withheld commodity is essential and not manufactured internally, and the target economy is weak (to prevent the country from bidding up the price of the product until it finds a supplier), then the goal will be successful. OCCAM's domain knowledge determines the relevant features of this schema. This same schema also applies to another threat by the League of Nations which stopped Greece from invading Bulgaria in 1925. Despite the best intentions, not all League of Nations sanction incidents were successful:

Economic-Sanction-10

In 1935, Italy invaded Abyssinia (Ethiopia). The League of Nations refused to sell Italy weapons if it continued its conquest. Italy, which had the capability of manufacturing its own weapons, ignored the threat and quickly occupied Abyssinia.

From this example, OCCAM learns that if a threat is made to refuse to sell a country a commodity that is manufactured by that country, the threat will be ignored.

There is a common theme in OCCAM's mastery of the domain of economic sanctions. The understanding of a novel episode requires a great deal of search of a rule base consisting of domain knowledge and general knowledge of plans and goals. Once this work is performed, the result of the search is saved as a schema. The schema serves as a quick, efficient method of recognizing when a general explanation applies. Once a set of economic sanction schemata is acquired, OCCAM can function as an economic sanction expert system.

7.3. Question Answering

OCCAM demonstrates its knowledge of economic sanctions by answering questions about the effectiveness of applying economic sanctions in hypothetical circumstances. It is not designed to predict whether or not a nation will implement a program of economic sanctions. Indeed, this would be a much more difficult problem because it appears that economic sanctions are often attempted when there is no hope of success[60].

OCCAM's question answering capabilities are quite limited. It only deals with one type of question: the user requesting OCCAM to predict the outcome of an event. All of OCCAM's questions start with "What would happen if...". In addition, the only subject that OCCAM deals with is economic sanctions. This question answering capability was developed to demonstrate that the knowledge that OCCAM acquires can be accessed to solve a useful problem. An overview of the issues in question answering and a taxonomy of question types is presented in (Lehnert, 1978) and extended in (Dyer, 1983). In Lehnert's taxonomy, OCCAM answers concept completion questions. In this type of question, the

---

[60]One reason that economic sanctions are proposed when they cannot bring about the desired goal becomes apparent when one considers the alternatives: doing nothing or military retaliation.

question describes some details of a situation and asks for additional details. OCCAM answers these questions by finding the most specific schema associated with the question and filling in the default value for the missing information. In the questions presented to OCCAM, the missing information is the outcome of the hypothetical event.

The process of question answering has a number of steps involved. First, OCCAM must parse the user's question to represent the meaning of the question in terms of CD goal, plans, and events. Next, OCCAM must search memory to attempt to recognize the question as referring to an instance of a known schema. The process of searching memory can re-represent the meaning of the question by creating a high-level representation. There are three possible results of the memory search:

1. OCCAM does not have any schemata that can help answer the question. In this case, OCCAM simply replies that it does not know the answer to the question. One could think of extending OCCAM so that it attempts to construct an explanation when it cannot find an appropriate schema in the same manner that it builds an explanation to acquire schemata with EBL. However, during question answering, the search to construct an explanation would be more difficult. During learning, examples presented to OCCAM contain a problem statement and a resolution, and OCCAM must explain the resolution in terms of information in the problem statement. During question answering, however, only a problem statement is given. Since it is easier to verify that a plan achieves a goal than to find a plan to achieve a goal, searching for an answer to a question would be computationally more expensive. However, if OCCAM were capable of this task, it would raise the interesting issue of learning when answering a question.

2. There is exactly one schema in memory that accounts for the situation. In this case, OCCAM instantiates the sequence of events of the schema with information from the question. This instantiation process provides an answer for the question and OCCAM's justification for the answer.

3. There is more than one applicable schema in memory. In this case, OCCAM cannot decide on a correct answer to the question. For example, if the United States were to try to threaten Kuwait by refusing to sell a necessary commodity, there are two schemata that apply: Kuwait might be willing to pay a higher price for the commodity and ignore the threat, or Kuwait might approach an adversary of the United States such as the Soviet Union for assistance. OCCAM cannot decide among these explanations and offers both.

When OCCAM finds an answer and a justification, these are represented in Conceptual Dependency. OCCAM must select some of this information to tell the user. Finally, a response is generated by converting the CD representation of the answer to English.

An example will help to illustrate this process of question answering. OCCAM is presented with the following question:

Question: What would happen if the US refused to sell computers to South Korea unless South Korea stopped exporting automobiles to Canada?

The four separate tasks of parsing, memory search, instantiation, and generation will be illustrated on this example.

7.3.1. Parsing

OCCAM has a simple expectation-based parser based loosely on CA (Birnbaum & Selfridge, 1981) and DYPAR (Dyer, 1983). The interested reader is referred to either of these references for a more detailed treatment of this type of parser. The parser in OCCAM is driven by word definitions. A definition of a word typically adds a template concept that represents the meaning of the word to a local memory, and associates a number of <u>requests</u> with the concept. The requests implement expectations. A request looks for other concepts in certain positions and connects them together. Typically, the definition of a noun simply adds a representation of an object to the local memory. The definition of a verb adds an action representation to memory and looks for objects to fill the roles of the action.

The results of parsing the question "What would happen if the US refused to sell computers to South Korea unless South Korea stopped exporting automobiles to Canada?" is shown in Figure 7-9. The representation indicates that the US has a goal and the outcome of the goal is in question. The plan the US is pursuing to achieve the goal is to tell South Korea that the US will not sell computers to South Korea unless it stops the exporting of automobiles to Canada.

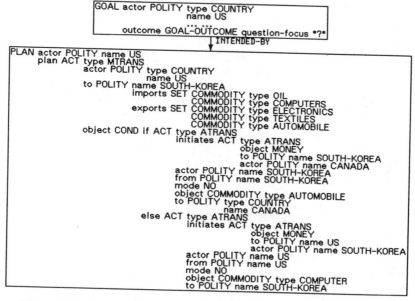

Figure 7-9: The result of parsing the question, "What would happen if the US refused to sell computers to South Korea unless South Korea stopped exporting automobiles to Canada?" Many features of the countries are not shown to conserve space.

7.3.2. Finding an applicable schema

Once the question has been parsed, the next step is to traverse memory to find a schema that can answer the question. In the current example, the memory traversal starts at the top of the goal hierarchy. Following an index of the plan feature, OCCAM arrives at a simple schema that represents those goals whose plan is to issue a threat. This schema has no specializations, but it contains a representational transfer that can convert the **goal** representation to a **coerce** representation. The question is re-represented in a higher-level representation.

```
COERCE the-actor POLITY type COUNTRY
                        name US
                        imports COMMODITY type OIL
                                COMMODITY type ELECTRONICS
                        exports =THREAT-OBJ
                                COMMODITY type WEAPONS
                                COMMODITY type ELECTRONICS
                                COMMODITY type MANUFACTURED-GOODS
           the-target POLITY type COUNTRY
                        name SOUTH-KOREA
                        exports COMMODITY type ELECTRONICS
                                COMMODITY type TEXTILES
                                =DEMAND-OBJ
                        imports COMMODITY type OIL
                                =THREAT-OBJ
                        continent ASIA
                        economic-health STRONG
           threat-obj COMMODITY type COMPUTER
           demand-obj COMMODITY type AUTOMOBILE
           the-threat ACT type ATRANS
                        actor =THE-ACTOR
                        object =THREAT-OBJ
                        to =THE-TARGET
                        from =THE-ACTOR
                        mode NO
                        initiates ACT actor =THE-TARGET
                                      to =THE-ACTOR
                                      object MONEY
                                      type ATRANS
           the-demand ACT type ATRANS
                        actor =THE-TARGET
                        object =DEMAND-OBJ
                        from =THE-TARGET
                        to POLITY type COUNTRY
                                 name CANADA
                        mode NO
                        initiates ACT actor POLITY type COUNTRY
                                                   name CANADA
                                      to =THE-TARGET
                                      object MONEY
                                      type ATRANS
           goal GOAL actor =THE-ACTOR
                        outcome GOAL-OUTCOME question-focus *?*
```

Figure 7-10: **The new representation for the question created during memory traversal.**

The new high-level representation for the schema is illustrated in Figure 7-10. This representation indicates that **the-actor** is the US, **the-target** is South Korea, **the-threat** is to refuse to sell computers and **the-demand** is to stop selling cars to Canada. The outcome of the **goal** is the focus of the question. OCCAM continues memory traversal with the new representation, following indices from the general coercion schema formed by SBL. There are many schemata indexed under the coerce schema, including the kidnapping schema (which is not appropriate since the threat is not to kill someone), and several economic sanction schemata. Only one economic sanction schema is appropriate. This schema (which is displayed in Figure 7-11) indicates that since **the-target** has a strong economy, its response would be to buy the commodity at a higher price from another country that exports the commodity. Notice that the schema in Figure 7-11 contains a general description of the target's response, the target's plan (**the-sub-plan**) and the goal outcome.

This information will be specialized with information from the question to form
an answer.

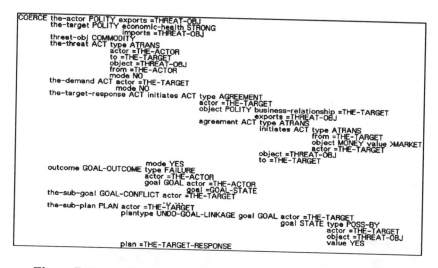

Figure 7-11:   The schema that provides a general explanation to
answer the question, "What would happen if the US
refused to sell computers to South Korea unless South
Korea stopped exporting automobiles to Canada?" This
schema is a more complex version of the schema
presented in Figure 5-11. It indicates that if a country
that exports a commodity tries to coerce a country that
imports the commodity by refusing to sell them the
commodity, then a response might be to buy the
commodity at a higher price from another country.

7.3.3. Instantiation

Once a schema with a general explanation has been found, the next step in
the process of question answering in OCCAM is to specialize the general
explanation so it applies to the particular circumstances described by the
question. In OCCAM, all that is needed is to match the input event against a
pattern, binding a number of variables. Typically, there is one variable for each
feature of the macro-schema. The values of these variables are substituted into
the general explanation to produce a particular explanation that applies in the
current situation.

The explanation in the current example (which is partially illustrated in

Figure 7-12) indicates that the threat motivated a goal conflict in the South Koreans by linking together the success of their goal to export automobiles and the failure of their goal to possess computers. A plan to resolve the conflict is to find another means of possessing computers. Importing computers from another country is one such plan to obtain computers. This will result in the failure of the US goal.

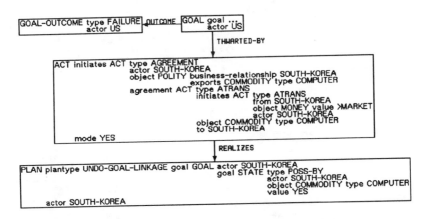

Figure 7-12: **Part of the explanation that indicates why the US goal will fail.**

7.3.4. Generating a response

Once OCCAM has found the CD representation of the answer, it must generate the answer in English. There are two subproblems: deciding how much information the user should be told and converting the CD representation of the answer to English. OCCAM does not have novel solutions for either of these problems.

OCCAM has a number of simple heuristics for deciding what information to tell the user. First, OCCAM always tells the user the concept that is the direct answer to the question. Next, if the direct answer is a goal failure, then OCCAM reports the action that led to the goal failure. This simple heuristic is adequate for selecting the information to report in the current example.

After selecting the content of the answer, OCCAM must generate an English sentence. This is accomplished by simple recursive application of patterns that transform CD representations into English. A pattern is matched against a CD structure, binding a number of variables. Each pattern has an action that indicates that certain words be output and that the generation process should recurse on the value of some variables. Although quite simple, such patterns are sufficient to generate understandable English replies to questions. The following illustrates how OCCAM translates the CD from Figure 7-12 into English.

> Question: What would happen if the US refused to sell computers to South Korea unless South Korea stopped exporting automobiles to Canada?

> OCCAM: **The goal of the United States that South Korea not sell automobiles to Canada will fail and South Korea will agree to purchase computers from a country that exports computers.**

There are a number of possible extensions to the question answering capabilities of OCCAM. For example, OCCAM finds an abstract specification of the country that would sell computers to South Korea: "a country that exports computers". A simple scheme to find such a country could be implemented so that OCCAM might be able to generate "some country, such as Japan, which exports computers" for this concept. In addition, since the schema that produces the answer is already located, it should be simple to retrieve an example to help make the point:

> OCCAM+:   **The goal of the United States that South Korea not sell automobiles to Canada will fail and South Korea will agree to purchase computers from a country that exports computers in the same manner as the Soviets purchased grain from Argentina during the US grain embargo.**

Finally, a more elaborate question answering capability might provide for a more interactive dialogue. OCCAM currently cannot adjust the level of detail it includes in an answer. Although the instantiated explanation for the question contains information about supply and demand, OCCAM currently has no means of articulating this information. For example, the answer that OCCAM finds for this question is similar to the answer provided by an expert political analyst with the Rand Corporation:

> **Question:** What would happen if the US refused to sell computers to South Korea unless South Korea stopped exporting automobiles to Canada?
>
> **Answer:** S. Korea will probably buy computer equipment from some other country.

Although OCCAM has the necessary information, it is not able to continue the dialogue in the same manner as the political analyst:

> **Question:** Why?
>
> **Answer:** If the US restricts S. Korea's supply of computers, they would be willing to pay a higher price for the computers and some other country would move in.

In spite of the limitations of OCCAM's language capabilities, I believe that the approach outlined in this book is a promising means of creating knowledge-based systems to perform useful functions. OCCAM directly addresses the issue of knowledge acquisition for knowledge-based systems. In Section 7.5, I demonstrate how OCCAM acquires the knowledge needed for EBL.

7.4. Kidnapping: An Example of Integrated Learning

The primary advantage of the approach to learning advocated in this book is that the learner gets better at learning. At first, the learner relies on similarity-based and theory-driven learning. As a consequence, learning is slow and requires many examples to rule out incorrect hypotheses that are consistent with initial observations. However, the knowledge that the learner acquires through these data-intensive mechanisms focuses later learning. Once the learner has sufficient background knowledge, explanation-based learning, a knowledge-intensive learning mechanism, is possible.

OCCAM demonstrates the advantage of this strategy by acquiring a kidnapping schema. Much of the knowledge needed to explain why a ransom is paid in kidnapping is learned by empirical means. In addition, the coercion schema that provides a general framework for understanding kidnapping (and economic sanctions) is acquired through similarity-based means (see Section 7.1). An important issue arises when relying on empirical learning techniques to provide the background knowledge for EBL. The background knowledge may be incorrect. Therefore, the schemata that are acquired by EBL may also be incorrect and are subject to revision. In this section, I demonstrate how OCCAM deals with this problem. First, I demonstrate how OCCAM acquires the knowledge used to produce an incorrect explanation of why the ransom is paid. Next, I demonstrate how it is possible to create an incorrect kidnapping schema by relying on an incorrect theory. Then, I demonstrate how OCCAM revises its background knowledge when it encounters more examples. Finally, I show how OCCAM detects that a schema formed by EBL relied on an incorrect theory and how OCCAM revises the schema to reflect a change in the background knowledge.

7.4.1. Acquiring background knowledge for kidnapping

OCCAM acquires two rules that are needed to explain why the ransom is paid by the kidnapper. The first is the simple rule discussed in Section 4.7. This rule states that in order to give someone an object, you must first possess the object. OCCAM uses this rule to explain why the target in kidnapping is required to be wealthy. Only a wealthy person can afford to pay the ransom. OCCAM acquires this rule when an example of **delta-agency** fails to achieve the goal, because the helper does not possess the object. This rule explains why the target would be able to pay the ransom.

The second rule explains why the target would want to pay the ransom. OCCAM must acquire a rule that indicates that a certain class of persons have a goal of preserving the health of another class of persons. This rule will explain why the target pays the ransom, since paying the ransom in kidnapping is a means of preserving the health of the hostage. OCCAM is presented with two similar examples of a small child who is hurt when she falls off a swing:

- **aid-1**: Lynn is playing on the swing and she falls off and scuffs her knee. Her mother, Chris, gets a band-aid and puts it on her knee.

- **aid-2**: Lynn is playing on the swing and she falls off and scuffs her knee. Her neighbor, Tiffany, gets on the swing and rides it.

OCCAM contains a dispositional generalization rule to deal with these two cases. The generalization rule states: *if an event (?e) motivates a goal (?g) for someone (?p1), and someone else (?p2) observes the event (?e) and performs an action (?a) that achieves the goal (?g) for ?p1, then the event (?e) motivates the goal (?g) for ?p2.* The dispositional generalization rule tries to account for counterexamples by focusing on ?p2 when a person observes the event, but does not assist. In this example, OCCAM postulates that a difference between Chris in **aid-1** and Tiffany in **aid-2** is responsible for the different goal and, therefore, the different behavioral response. However, without any knowledge to favor one feature over another, OCCAM selects one feature at random: height. OCCAM constructs a dispositional attribute (**disp-17**) and indicates that tall persons have this disposition. Furthermore, it constructs a rule that indicates that when a person with **disp-17** observes an action that motivates a goal of preserving the health of another person, then the person with **disp-17** will also have a goal of preserving the health of that person. The dispositional attribute is illustrated in Figure 7-13 and the rule is illustrated in Figure 7-14.

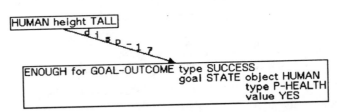

Figure 7-13: A dispositional attribute: tall persons have a potential called **disp-17**. This attribute is postulated to be responsible for the different reactions in **aid-1** and **aid-2**.

7.4.2. Explanation-based learning with an incorrect theory

Once OCCAM has acquired some background knowledge, it can use that knowledge to perform EBL. When OCCAM has learned rules that indicate that tall people have a goal of preserving the health of others and in order to give someone an object, you must first possess the object, it is capable of producing an explanation of the actions in a kidnapping incident. Of course, since there is an incorrect rule, the resulting explanation will also be incorrect. For example,

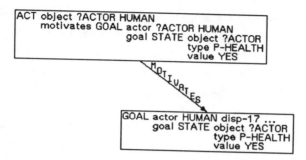

Figure 7-14:   A rule that indicates that persons with disp-17 (i.e., tall people) have a goal of preserving the health of others.

after forming an incorrect theory, OCCAM is presented with Kidnapping-4, repeated below:

Kidnapping-4

John, a 10-year-old child, was abducted on his way to church on Sunday morning by a heroin addict. His father, Richard, a wealthy, fair skinned man, received a phone call that evening. The kidnapper threatened that John would be killed unless Richard paid a $100,000 ransom. Monday at noon, Richard left the money in a locker at the train station. Four hours later, his son was released in a wooded area two miles from the train station.

The first problem for OCCAM is to explain how the kidnapper's goal of obtaining money was achieved. The following explanation chain is constructed:

1. The goal was achieved when the target paid the ransom.

2. The target possessing the money (i.e., being rich) is a state that enables the payment.

3. The threat to kill the child motivates a goal to preserve the health of the child (because the father is tall).

4. The demand motivates a goal for the target to retain his wealth.

5. The action of paying the ransom is a realization of a plan to prefer the achievement of the more important goal: preserving the child's life.

The knowledge OCCAM acquired from empirical learning techniques was responsible for producing the second and third steps in this explanation. Once OCCAM explains the target's action, it can now generalize the plan it observed for obtaining money by retaining only those features that were needed to produce the explanation. For example, the target is required to be rich, so that he can afford the ransom, and the target is required to be tall so that he is willing to pay the ransom. The generalization that OCCAM constructs is illustrated in Figure 7-15.

```
COERCE goal GOAL goal =GOAL-STATE
               actor =THE-ACTOR
        the-target-response ACT type ATRANS
                               actor =THE-TARGET
                               object =DEMAND-OBJ
                               to =THE-ACTOR
                               from =THE-TARGET
        the-demand ACT type ATRANS
                      actor =THE-TARGET
                      object =DEMAND-OBJ
                      to =THE-ACTOR
                      from =THE-TARGET

     ... ...
     demand-obj P-OBJ type MONEY
                        amount DOLLARS relative-number LARGE
        the-threat ACT type KILL
                      actor =THE-ACTOR
                      object =THREAT-OBJ
        threat-obj HUMAN
        the-target HUMAN height TALL
                          income-class RICH
        the-actor HUMAN
```

Figure 7-15: The kidnapping schema formed from generalizing
             Kidnapping-4 with an incorrect domain theory. Note
             that OCCAM's incorrect theory indicates that the target
             should be tall, because tall persons have a   goal of
             preserving the health of others.

This example illustrates a danger of learning with an incorrect theory. Simply stated, if the theory is incorrect, then explanation-based learning will produce incorrect generalizations. OCCAM does contain a mechanism to revise a rule that makes incorrect predictions. In addition, generalizations formed with an incorrect theory also need to be updated.

7.4.3. Revising an incorrect domain theory

As described in Section 4.4.1, OCCAM contains a mechanism to evaluate its knowledge. First, OCCAM must detect that an inference rule is making an incorrect prediction. Confidence is reduced in an incorrect inference rule until it is finally eliminated and a new hypothesis that is consistent with the data is created. For instance, after OCCAM creates an incorrect inference rule from **aid-1** and **aid-2**, it is presented with the following example:

- **aid-3**: Lynn is playing on the swing and she falls off and scuffs her knee. Tiffany's mother, Loreli, who is eating an ice cream by the swing does not help.

Since there was very little support for the inference rule that predicts that Loreli will help because she is tall, it is abandoned. When the inference rule is abandoned, OCCAM no longer has a justification for believing that tall people are good targets in kidnapping. Should OCCAM discard its kidnapping generalization at this point?

There have been a number of techniques proposed in artificial intelligence for withdrawing conclusions of erroneous beliefs (De Kleer, 1984; Doyle, 1979; McDermott, 1983). It would be possible to incorporate such a truth maintainance technique in OCCAM. However, there are two problems with all of these approaches. First, they are very expensive computationally (Charniak et al., 1980). Second, there is much evidence from psychology experiments that indicates that people maintain erroneous beliefs after the initial support for the belief has been discredited (Anderson et al., 1980; Hoenkamp, 1987; Nisbett & Ross, 1978). A recent article on weight-loss is an excellent example of a failure to revise "compiled" knowledge when the underlying facts change (Hosansky, 1987). The article advised against drinking diet soda because the consumption of diet soda results in water retention. This was good advice when diet sodas were sweetened with sodium saccharin. However, most diet sodas are now sweetened with aspartame and the caution is unjustified since the sodium was responsible for the water retention.

Rather than performing an expensive truth maintainance task when an inference rule is abandoned, OCCAM utilizes a less expensive technique that may introduce a few errors. OCCAM does not abandon or update a schema until it makes an incorrect prediction[61]. Recall that when a schema makes an incorrect

---

[61]A more conservative (and more expensive) strategy would check each schema before it is used to verify that schema is justified by the current theory. However, in OCCAM, I am willing to tradeoff accuracy for efficiency. Much more research in psychology needs to be done to determine the exact conditions under which a person's beliefs do change.

prediction, OCCAM attempts to explain why the incorrect prediction is made. One reason that a schema makes an incorrect prediction is that the schema was formed with an incorrect theory.   Therefore, when a schema formed by explanation-based learning makes an incorrect prediction, OCCAM checks to see if it can verify the explanation saved with the schema with its current theory. If it cannot, then the schema is abandoned, and an attempt is made to explain and generalize the new example.

In the current example, after abandoning the hypothesis that tall people have the goal of preserving the health of others, OCCAM must come up with a new hypothesis. Unfortunately, the new hypothesis is not much better than the first. One difference between Chris who helped Lynn and Loreli and Tiffany who did not is that Chris has brown hair while Loreli' and Tiffany both have blond hair. Once again, this illustrates the hazards of guessing: one is likely to guess wrong. This example also illustrates why it would not be a good idea to update the kidnapping schema with the new hypothesis. The expensive process of rederiving the kidnapping schema would only create another incorrect schema that indicates that a good target for kidnapping is a rich person with brown hair.

Finally, OCCAM is presented with another example that forces it to formulate a correct hypothesis:

- **aid-4**: Karen falls off her bike and bruises her lip. Her sister,
  Lynn, gets an ice cube to put on Karen's lip.

In this example, since the person who helped (Lynn) also has blond hair, the inference rule that indicates that blonds will not help must be discarded. OCCAM finds another difference between those people who helped and those who did not in these examples. In all the cases that a person helped, they were related to the person who was injured. OCCAM creates a new dispositional attribute that might be called "caring". The feature that one person has a family relationship with another is used to indicate when the caring disposition applies. Additionally, a new rule is created that indicates that when a person cares for another, then they have a goal of preserving their health[62]. Once OCCAM has

---

[62]One should not forget that OCCAM doesn't have a complete notion of caring. Perhaps, I should have said "Additionally, a new rule is created that indicates that when a person has disp-18, then they have a goal of preserving the health of their relatives".

acquired this rule, it is in a position to learn a correct kidnapping schema. The reason that OCCAM took a number of examples to acquire this rule is that without any prior knowledge OCCAM must simply randomly select one hypothesis from the set that is consistent with the data. If there were a dispositional attribute already present, then it would have been much simpler for OCCAM to arrive at the correct conclusion. In fact, in Section 4.7, I showed how OCCAM acquired the "caring" disposition in another manner. That example showed that the caring disposition was also useful in **delta-agency** for distinguishing those people who give a desired object when asked[63]. If OCCAM is first presented with the **delta-agency** examples, it learns the caring disposition in that domain. Then, OCCAM can reach the correct conclusion from fewer examples in the playground domain and the incorrect version of the kidnapping schema is not formed.

7.5. Detecting and Correcting an Incorrect Generalization

Once OCCAM has acquired an updated domain theory, it is in a position to update its incorrect kidnapping schema. It requires an example of an incorrect prediction to make it evaluate the schema. The following example will cause an incorrect prediction since the ransom is not demanded of a tall person:

Kidnapping-5

While filming a television show for the new season, Webster was interrupted with an important phone call. His mother was being held hostage and the kidnapper demanded $50,000. Webster had his chauffeur deliver the money immediately.

This example does not conform to the prediction of the incorrect kidnapping schema. The target of the coercion is predicted to be a tall, wealthy person. Instead, the target is Webster, a wealthy child actor, who is quite small. Instead of simply reducing confidence in the kidnapping schema, OCCAM attempts to identify the source of the erroneous expectation. It determines that the intentional link that indicates that tall persons have a goal of preserving the health of others is no longer supported by the domain theory. The kidnapping

---

[63]The disposition applies in this situation because the same class of generalization rule is involved (i.e., those which attribute a difference in goals to a difference in a feature of the actor).

schema is abandoned and OCCAM initiates EBL on the new problem.

Now that OCCAM has a correct domain theory (from our point of view), it can correctly explain why the target pays the ransom. Instead of indicating that the target is motivated to preserve the health of the hostage because he is tall, the explanation indicates that the target wants to save the hostage because he is related to the hostage. The new kidnapping schema correctly indicates that the target should be a rich person related to the hostage (see Figure 7-16).

```
COERCE goal GOAL goal =GOAL-STATE
                 actor =THE-ACTOR
       the-threat ACT type KILL
                     actor =THE-ACTOR
                     object =THREAT-OBJ

       ... ...
       threat-obj HUMAN
       the-target HUMAN relation IPT type FAMILY-REL
                                     of =THREAT-OBJ
                        income-class RICH

       the-actor HUMAN
```

Figure 7-16:   **Part of the kidnapping schema formed from generalizing Kidnapping-5 with a correct domain theory. Note that now the target is required to have an interpersonal relationship with the hostage (i.e., the `threat-obj`).**

The principle limitation of the approach to revising schema outlined in this section is that it does not deal with the situation in which a schema formed via EBL makes an incorrect prediction, but the domain theory has not been revised. This is a sign that the domain theory is incorrect. However, OCCAM currently has no mechanism to assign blame to a particular rule. One direction for future research is to record and exploit the dependencies between a relevant operational feature and the specific rule that determines the feature's relevance. Another potential problem could arise if OCCAM uses a schema formed by explanation-based learning with an incorrect theory as part of the explanation for another schema. For example, suppose OCCAM learns that tall people want to help others, and then creates the kidnapping schema that indicates that the ransom note should go to a tall, rich person. When presented with a counterexample, OCCAM can retract the rule that indicates that tall people want to help others. However, the incorrect implication of this rule is present in the kidnapping schema. The kidnapping schema might be used as part of an explanation to explain some other incident. For example, some companies offer ransom insurance to pay the ransom in kidnapping. OCCAM might learn that tall rich people should buy this insurance. To avoid this possibility, OCCAM should be extended to check to see if the support for a schema has been retracted when the schema is used in an explanation.

7.6. Specializations of Kidnapping

Once OCCAM has formed a kidnapping schema, it is ready to learn about some specializations of kidnapping. Since kidnapping is a complex event, there are many goals involved. For example, in addition to the central goal of the kidnapper (to obtain money) and the target (to ensure the safety of the hostage), the kidnapper also wants to avoid going to jail, the hostage wants to remain alive, the police want to arrest the kidnapper, etc. The specializations of kidnapping will focus on the features of the various agents that determine the outcome of these subordinate goals.

For example, OCCAM forms a specialization of kidnapping when it is presented with the following episode (Alix, 1978):

Kidnapping-6

In May 1933, Mary McElroy, twenty-five-year-old daughter of the city manager of Kansas City, Missouri was abducted. The abductors demanded $60,000 for her safe return. They accepted a $30,000 ransom and released the hostage unharmed from a farm in Kansas where she had been held for twenty-nine hours. The kidnappers were arrested by the FBI. The testimony of the victim was largely responsible for their conviction. The kidnappers received a sentence of life in jail.

In this episode, the kidnappers' goal of preserving their freedom was thwarted when they received the punishment of life in jail. To create a specialized kidnapping schema, OCCAM must identify the circumstances that led to this goal failure. A possible explanation is suggested by the following generalization rule: *if a preservation goal is thwarted after an action that is needed to perform a plan that achieves a goal, then the action results in a state that enables the preservation goal to fail.* This generalization rule suggests that abducting the hostage results in a state that enables the conviction of the kidnappers. OCCAM's domain knowledge is needed to complete the explanation. The complete explanation indicates that abducting the hostage results in the hostage seeing the kidnapper that enables the hostage to testify against the kidnapper. OCCAM generalizes this explanation and uncovers an inherent flaw in kidnapping: the hostage sees the kidnapper when he is abducted and can testify against the kidnapper. A new schema is created (see Figure 7-17) and indexed in memory under the kidnapping schema. The explanation is saved as the sequence of events for the specialized kidnapping schema (see Figure 7-18).

```
COERCE the-prep ACT type ATRANS
                    actor =THE-ACTOR
                    to =THE-ACTOR
                    object =THREAT-OBJ
                    after ACT type $TRIAL
                              defendant =THE-ACTOR
                              verdict GUILTY
                              witness =THREAT-OBJ
                              thwarts GOAL actor =THE-ACTOR
                                           goal STATE type P-FREEDOM
                                                        actor =THE-ACTOR
```

Figure 7-17: A specialized version of kidnapping that represents an inherent flaw: the hostage sees the kidnapper when he is abducted and can testify against the kidnapper.

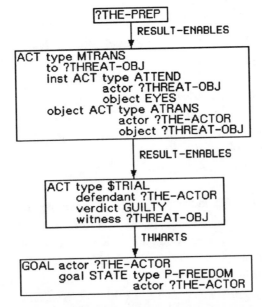

Figure 7-18: Part of the generalized explanation stored with a specialization of kidnapping. Since the hostage sees the kidnapper during the abduction, the hostage can testify against the kidnapper.

Another kidnapping episode results in a different specialization of kidnapping that avoids the problem of the previous incident (Moorehead, 1980):

Kidnapping-7

On June 2, 1920, Blakely Coughlin, the thirteen-month-old son of a wealthy Pennsylvania family vanished from his bedroom. A ladder was found abandoned near the window to the nursery. Several nights later, a ransom letter arrived and instructed Mr. Coughlin to throw $12,000 from a moving train when he saw a white flag being waved.

When this kidnapping episode is added to memory, a generalization rule suggests an explanation for the selection of the hostage: *if a preparation is performed on an object, look for other schemata that have a goal failure. Postulate the preparation avoids the goal failure.* OCCAM searches memory and finds the specialization of kidnapping in which the kidnapper is convicted by the testimony of the hostage. Since the hostage does not testify in this case, the generalization rule suggests that this particular victim was chosen to avoid the goal failure. OCCAM next tries to determine if the hostage in this episode would be able to testify against the victim. However, the explanation that worked in the previous case will not work in this case because the hostage is an infant. Therefore, OCCAM constructs an explanation that indicates that the kidnapper selected this particular hostage as a plan to avoid the failure of the kidnapper's goal to preserve his freedom. The generalized event that OCCAM constructs for this situation is illustrated in Figure 7-19.

```
COERCE threat-obj HUMAN age INFANT
       the-prep ACT type ATRANS
                    actor =THE-ACTOR
                    to =THE-ACTOR
                    object =THREAT-OBJ
```

Figure 7-19: **A specialized version of kidnapping that avoids a potential problem with kidnapping by selecting an infant as the hostage.**

The new specialized kidnapping schema is indexed under the original kidnapping schema by the age of the hostage and the preparation (i.e., abducting the hostage) since these are the only features needed to construct the explanation. Alternative examples might focus on other reasons that the hostage might not be able to testify by interfering with other locations in the causal chain. For example, by killing the hostage the kidnapper can prevent the hostage from testifying as well as preventing the hostage from assisting the police by providing information that might lead to the kidnapper's capture.

7.7. Learning Causal Relationships: Empirical Investigations

In this section, several experiments assessing the role of prior knowledge in learning are reviewed. Early models of concept formation (Bruner et al., 1956) did not consider the role of prior knowledge. More recent models have improved on this work. The early concept learning work has been criticized (Rosch, 1978) because it assumed that features are distributed randomly in world. Rosch argues that in the world, features are correlated. For example, the features "has wings", "flies" and "lays eggs" often co-occur. Rosch proposed a *prototype* representation of concepts where a prototype is a central tendency of a concept, representing what examples of the concept are generally like. One representation of a prototype is a set of typical features weighted by importance (Smith & Medin, 1981). Since features are not uniformly distributed, natural clusters of features occur. It has been suggested (Rocsh et al., 1976) that *basic* level categories are formed where the maximum number of features overlap between examples of that category. The basic level categories also minimize the feature overlap between other categories[64].

However, prototypes and basic categories have their limitations as well. One criticism of the work on prototypes and basic categories is that it does not address the issue of why certain features co-occur, and how people can make use of knowledge that certain features co-occur because they are causally related (Murphy & Medin, 1985; Schank et al., 1986). The experiments reviewed in this section demonstrate that any theory of concept learning that does not take into account the prior knowledge of the learner is flawed.

The design of OCCAM was influenced by psychology studies that assess how people learn causal relationships. The theory of learning causal relationships proposed in this book integrates a number of findings from psychology. There are several specific claims made in this book about the process of learning causal relationships. These claims include:

• When learning a causal relationship people exhibit a preference for

---

[64]Rosch has proposed three levels of categories: superordinate (e.g., furniture), basic (e.g., chair) and subordinate (e.g. rocking chair).

using existing knowledge instead of correlating features over a number of examples. There are a number of different ways to establish this claim. First, one could demonstrate that it takes more examples to learn when there is no prior knowledge of a domain than when there is prior knowledge. Second, one could show that in an ambiguous situation, where there are several possible causes, people choose a cause that is consistent with their prior knowledge. Finally, one could show that people will perceive a causal relationship that is consistent with their prior beliefs even if such a relationship is not present in the data. Note that this does not imply that people never use correlation. In the absence of prior knowledge, people certainly make use of correlation. Similarly, if there is an overwhelming amount of correlational evidence, people revise their knowledge to be consistent with this evidence.

- Learning a causal relationship in the absence of prior causal knowledge is guided by a general theory of causality. This can be established by showing that people require fewer trials to learn a causal relationship that conforms to a standard pattern for causal relationships. In addition, one could demonstrate that when the data do not conform to a causal pattern, people will not induce a causal relationship. Many investigations in developmental psychology have been conducted to uncover the principles that guide the learning of causal relationships by small children.

- People naturally and typically try to find an explanation for a single event. Therefore, explanation-based learning is not an expensive process because much of the effort is essential for other tasks.

- Finally, some investigations on the revision of beliefs after presentation of new evidence support the claim in OCCAM that a schema that has an explanation as its justification is more resilient in the face of contradictory evidence.

7.7.1. Illusory correlation

A series of tests were performed (Chapman & Chapman, 1967) to determine why practicing clinical psychologists believe that certain tests with no empirical validity are reliable predictors of personality traits. In one study, clinical psychologists were asked about their experience with the Draw-a-Person test (DAP). In this test, a patient draws a picture of a person that is analyzed by the psychologist. The DAP test has repeatedly been proved to have no diagnostic value (i.e., there is no valid correlation between features in the picture drawn and an underlying illness). Their results illustrate the phenomenon of **illusory correlation**, when the correlation between two classes of events is reported by observers to differ from the actual correlation:

- Of the psychologists who responded to a survey, 80% reported that in their practice, men worried about their manliness draw a person with broad shoulders and 82% stated that persons worried about their intelligence draw an enlarged head.

- In the second experiment in this study, the Chapmans asked subjects (college undergraduates) to look at 45 DAP tests paired with the personality trait of the person who (supposedly) drew them. The subjects were asked to judge what sort of picture a person with certain personality traits did draw. Although the Chapmans paired the pictures with traits so that there would be no correlation, 76% of the subjects rediscovered the invalid diagnostic sign that men worried about their manliness were likely to draw a person with broad shoulders and 55% stated that persons worried about their intelligence drew an enlarged head.

- In another experiment in this study, the Chapmans asked another set of subjects about the strength of associations between personality traits and body parts. For example, subjects reported a strong association between shoulders and manliness, but a weak association between ears and manliness. For four of the six personality traits studied, the body part that was the strongest associate was the one most commonly reported as having diagnostic value by clinical psychologists and subjects.

- In the final experiment of this study, subjects were presented DAP tests that were negatively correlated with their strong associates (e.g., small shoulders paired with patients worried about their manliness). Subjects still found a correlation between personality traits and their strong associates but to a lesser degree (e.g., 50% rather than 76% reported that broad shoulders was a sign of worrying about manliness).

There are several interesting aspects to the results of this study. First, the invalid diagnostic signs discovered by the undergraduate subjects were similar to those used by practicing clinical psychologists. Second, the subjects perceived correlation when it did not exist between the tendency to draw a picture emphasizing certain parts of the body and traits strongly associated with these body parts. It appears that due to the semantic association between body parts and traits, the subjects expected certain correlations and their perception was biased by this expectation. Finally, even when negatively correlated, the semantic expectations were strong enough to perceive a positive correlation.

A similar finding was obtained for particular Rorschach cards which have no validity (Chapman & Chapman, 1969). These experiments clearly demonstrate that covariation may be perceived when it is not actually present if there is a reason to suspect covariation. Conversely, actual covariation may go undetected if it is unexpected. Due to the phenomenon of illusory correlation, Kelley has qualified the covariation principle to apply to perceived rather than actual covariation.

Some people have proposed that illusory correlation is responsible for beliefs in astrology (Dean, 1986) and racial stereotypes (Allport, 1954). That is, people do not conclude that certain ethnic groups are lazy because they have observed many people of various races working and one group stands out as the laziest. Rather, it is hearsay or rumors of laziness, perhaps motivated by fear of economic competition, which form a belief that biases the analysis of the data. Once a belief is present, a few examples can be found to support the belief. Any counterexamples can be viewed as "exceptions which prove the rule". Prior theories determine what is considered the exception and what is considered the rule. For example, some might say "All X's are lazy, but there are a few who work hard" while others might say "All X's work hard, but there are a few who are lazy", given the same set of data but different prior beliefs. Even when the data clearly indicate a correlation, prior knowledge can influence the perceived cause of the correlation. For example, some person's causal theories could explain the high crime rate in certain areas due to the racial make-up of the area. Others' causal theories will place the blame on the high unemployment in the area.

Should a computer program exhibit the same biases that people do? After all, prejudices and beliefs in astrology[65] are not the most desirable characteristics. Yet, these are some of the implications of preferring prior knowledge and expectations to covariation information. The alternative however, is a learning system that requires so much time and space that it is not practical.

There are benefits, of course, in allowing prior theories to bias learning. The experiments in Sections 7.7.2 through 7.7.4 demonstrate how prior theories facilitate learning.

The danger in looking for correlations everywhere is that some correlations may just turn out to be coincidences. For example, in 1965 with the aid of a computer, Gerald Hawkins (Hawkins, 1965) correlated the alignments between 165 holes and stones at Stonehenge and significant astronomical locations. Hawkins concluded that Stonehenge was a primitive astronomical observatory capable of determining the summer solstice and predicting lunar eclipses. While there is little doubt that the alignment which marks the location of the sunrise on the year's longest day is deliberate, most of the other proposed alignments are coincidences (Murphy, 1987). Indeed, the system proposed by Hawkins predicts only a small fraction of the eclipses observable from Stonehenge and predicts several eclipses which are not visible from Stonehenge (or anywhere else on earth) (Hoyle, 1972).

There are many amusing coincidences which have been found between seeming unrelated events such as the outcome of major sporting events, stock prices, presidential elections, and hem lengths:

---

[65]In defense of utilizing existing knowledge to bias learning, I should point out that the results of learning are as accurate as the prior knowledge. One must start out with the belief that the alignments of the sun, moon, and planets influence human behavior to accept a few anecdotes that purport to prove astrological theories.

- When a team from the old AFL football league wins the Superbowl, the stock market has a bad year, but when a team from NFC wins the stock market has a good year[66].

- When a baseball team from the American League wins the World Series, a Republican is elected president. When a team from the National League wins, a Democrat is elected. This rule did not hold true in 1980 when Ronald Reagan was elected, but since a president who is elected in a year which is a multiple of 20 always dies in office, it's possible that the Democrats didn't want to win.

- When Billy Martin is appointed coach of the New York Yankees, the stock market has a decline. This has happened five times.

- When hemlines go up (i.e., women wear short dresses) the stock market goes up. When hemlines go down, the stock market goes down.

If these were anything but coincidences, one would expect political action committees to supply funds to baseball teams so that they could attract superstars, and one would see the crash of the stock market in October 1987 blamed on uncertainty of the outcome of the Superbowl due to unknown football players replacing the striking players or the refusal of some women to wear short skirts.

7.7.2. The effect of differences in prior knowledge

In one study (Ausubel & Schiff, 1954), kindergarten students and sixth grade students were asked to predict which side of a teeter-totter would fall when the correct side was indicated by a relevant feature (length) or an irrelevant feature (color). They found that the kindergarten children learned to predict on the basis of relevant or irrelevant features at approximately the same rate (3.7 trials for relevant, 3.4 trials for irrelevant). However, the older children required significantly fewer trials (.83 trials) to predict on the basis of a relevant

---

[66]When I first heard this, it was simpler. When an AFC team wins, the stock market has a bad year. When a NFC team wins the stock market has a good year. However, since then, an AFC team won the Superbowl, but the stock market had a good year. However, the team was an expansion team who was not in the old AFL, so the rule was revised a little.

feature than an irrelevant one (3.1).

Presumedly, the older children had a prior causal theory which facilitated their learning: a teeter-totter falls on the heavier side and the longer side is likely to be the heavier side. The younger children had to rely solely on correlation. Their performance on learning in the relevant and irrelevant conditions were comparable to the older children in the irrelevant condition. In this experiment, the difference in the number of trials could be attributed to the difference in the prior knowledge of kindergarten and sixth grade students.

7.7.3. Selecting a cause consistent with prior knowledge

Another way to demonstrate that existing causal knowledge influences the learning of new causal relationships is to present subjects with ambiguous stimuli. For example, there might be two potential causes that consistently covary with an effect. If one potential cause is consistent with prior knowledge, then subjects may prefer that cause. Such an experiment was run (Bullock, 1979).

In Bullock's experiment, a small metal ball rolled down an inclined plane toward a jack-in-the-box. At the same time, a series of lights turned on and off following the motion of the ball[67]. When the ball and the light appeared to reach the jack-in-the-box, the jack jumped up. Adults, when presented with this situation, typically indicate that the ball caused the jack to pop up. This cause is preferred to the light because a light reaching an object does not result in a force being applied to the object. Children as young as three also indicated that the cause of the jack jumping up was the ball rather than the light. If only covariation information was used by subjects in this experiment, then the light would be just as likely as the ball to be selected as the cause. Instead, existing knowledge constrained the selection of the cause.

Another experiment (the "unconnected" condition) was run that was similar to the above experiment. The only difference was that the ball and light both stopped about 6 inches away from the jack-in-the-box. In the first experiment, close to 80% of the children indicated that ball was the cause of the jack popping up. In the unconnected condition, the children were just as likely to choose the light as the ball as the cause. In the unconnected condition, there is

---

[67]In fact, the ball caused the lights to go on and off by completing an electrical circuit.

no possible mechanism for the ball to cause the jack to pop up. This finding is consistent with the view that specific knowledge is applied when appropriate to select the cause in an ambiguous situation.

7.7.4. Feature correlations in conceptual representation

A series of experiments were run (Murphy & Wisniewski, 1986) to assess how prior theories affect the accuracy and confidence in learning new concepts. In one experiment, subjects were presented with descriptions of fictitious foods, furniture, flowers, or vehicles. Some of these concepts were coherent in that pairs of features could be related by prior knowledge (e.g., a "plapel" has a hard surface and is designed for writing on). Others were incoherent because they contained pairs of features that violated normal expectations, (e.g., has a cushioned surface and is designed for writing on). Subjects were presented with 12 examples each of two concepts of the same type (i.e., two fictious types of furniture). Each example was constructed by selecting three features from a set of four features that are consistently associated with one concept and two features from a set of three that could be associated with either concept. For the coherent concepts, the set of consistent features included the two features that were related by prior knowledge while for the incoherent concepts, the set of consistent features included two pairs of features whose co-occurrence violated prior knowledge.

After seeing 12 examples of two concepts, the subjects were asked to indicate the conceptual category of 16 new examples. For the coherent concepts, subjects made the correct classification 90% of the time while for the incoherent concepts the correct classification was made 80% of the time. In addition, subjects were more confident in the correctness of their classification of coherent concepts. In a similar experiment, (Barrett & Murphy, 1986) with first and fourth grade students (instead of college undergraduates), children correctly identified 90% of the examples of coherent concepts, but only 53% of the examples of incoherent concepts. If subjects did not pay attention to their prior causal knowledge, the results would be identical for coherent and incoherent concepts.

This experiment demonstrates that when subjects must override their existing world knowledge, learning is a difficult correlational task. On the other hand, learning is facilitated when existing knowledge anticipates certain correlations in the data.

7.7.5. Forming and utilizing theories

The order in which examples are presented can affect what is learned by a series of examples. When subjects approach a new problem without any *a priori* expectations, they form an initial theory from an initial set of data and this initial theory affects the interpretation of later data. This phenomenon is similar to illusory correlation except that the subject acquires the knowledge in the experiment rather than bringing the knowledge to the experiment.

In one experiment (Jones et al., 1968), subjects observed a person solve 30 multiple-choice analogy problems. In all cases, 15 of the problems were solved correctly. One group of subjects saw the person solve more problems correctly in the first half and another group saw the person solve more problems correctly in the second half. The group that saw the person perform better on the initial examples rated the person as more intelligent and recalled that he had solved more problems correctly. The explanation for the difference is that one group formed the hypothesis that the person was intelligent on the initial set of data, while the other group formed the opposite opinion. Once this hypothesis is formed, when contradictory evidence is presented it can be discounted by attributing later performance to some other cause such as chance or problem difficulty.

This is an important finding with respect to OCCAM because it describes how OCCAM operates. When OCCAM has little or no domain knowledge, it empirically creates explanatory schemata that represent new causal knowledge. Later, these schemata influence the interpretation of new examples by selecting the relevant features of examples.

7.8. Spontaneous Causal Search

A crucial difference between OCCAM and UNIMEM is that OCCAM attempts empirical learning techniques only when explanation-based techniques fail and UNIMEM applies explanation-based learning techniques to generalizations formed by empirical means. Lebowitz claims that explanation-based techniques are too complex to apply to single examples because the search for a causal explanation is too expensive. However, the results of several studies indicate that causal attribution is a spontaneous activity (Weiner, 1986). There are several different ways to explore this issue. One procedure involves coding written material such as newspaper articles or business reports for causal attributions (Lau, 1984). Another approach involves analysis of verbal materials

(Nisbett & Ross, 1978). A final approach is to demonstrate that specific cognitive processes require search for causal explanations. For example, after succeeding or failing at a particular task, the expectancy of future success is a function of the perceived cause of success or failure. If the perceived cause of a failure is stable, then the expectancy of future success decreases (Weiner et al., 1971). The results of these studies clearly indicate that causal search is elicited by several conditions, such as an unexpected event or the failure of a goal. In addition, Weiner has hypothesized that an outcome important to the learner is more likely to result in a search for an explanation (Weiner, 1986). Similarly, Lebowitz has suggested that interest is an important factor in learning (Lebowitz, 1984).

7.9. Perseverance of Beliefs in the Face of New Evidence

What should happen when new evidence is encountered that contradicts existing knowledge? The answer to this question depends upon the reason for believing the existing knowledge. In OCCAM, if there is a justification for a schema (i.e., the schema was formed by explanation-based learning), then contradictory evidence is given little weight. However, if a schema merely summarizes a trend which has occurred in several examples, a few counterexamples can be enough evidence to abandon the schema.

The perseverance of explained generalizations is supported by a study (Anderson et al., 1980) in which subjects, who were requested to explain a relationship showed a greater degree of perseverance after additional information than those who were not requested.

The ability to spontaneously generate explanations accounts for the findings of another study (Nisbett & Ross, 1978). Subjects were asked to distinguish real suicide notes from fake suicide notes. Subjects were given false feedback to indicate that they were exceptionally good or exceptionally poor at this task. Later, the subjects were told that the feedback was false and they had been randomly chosen to receive the feedback. Nonetheless, subjects who were given "poor" feedback thought they would do more poorly at distinguishing real suicide notes from fake suicide notes than subjects who were given "good" feedback. The reason for this phenomenon is that subjects who did well were able to explain their excellent performance to themselves (e.g., "I am good at figuring out people's true feelings."). Similarly, the subjects who did poorly were able to find an explanation for their poor performance (e.g., "I have never known anyone who has committed suicide."). These explanations remain true even though the reason for creating the explanation has gone away. Therefore, these explanations can influence the rating on how well a subject would do in a similar task in the future. Findings such as these influenced the approach to revising current schema when faced with new evidence that was implemented in OCCAM.

7.9.1. OCCAM as a cognitive model

The integration of learning techniques in OCCAM explains three empirical findings on human learning.

1. If people have a reason to expect a correlation, they perceive one even if there is none. Conversely, people overlook unexpected correlations. OCCAM exhibits these properties as a result of preferring analytical learning strategies to empirical strategies.

2. If there is a known cause and effect relationship, learning is facilitated in that fewer examples are required. This result explains why people prefer analytical learning strategies to empirical strategies: analytical strategies, when applicable, arrive at the correct conclusion sooner. In OCCAM, the space for hypotheses consistent with the data and prior knowledge is smaller than the space of hypothesis consistent with only the data. As a consequence, fewer examples are required to locate an accurate hypothesis with analytical techniques than empirical techniques.

3. If there is a cue for a causal relationship, learning is facilitated. This demonstrates that people possess a general theory of causality. When examples are consistent with this theory of causality, learning is more focused because those hypotheses which are not consistent with the theory of causality need not be considered. The theory-driven learning component of OCCAM specifies a computational process that makes use of a theory of causality to constrain and facilitate learning.

7.10. Summary

This chapter presented examples of schemata acquired by OCCAM. The primary benefit of the theory of learning proposed in this book is demonstrated. In familiar domains in which OCCAM has the relevant background knowledge, learning is quick. New schemata that encode novel interactions among existing knowledge are created via explanation-based learning. In unfamiliar domains, learning is slower as OCCAM uses empirical techniques to acquire new knowledge. Simple causal relationships acquired via empirical techniques, can be combined analytically to form more complex relationships. For example, via empirical techniques, OCCAM acquires a coercion schema and a rule that indicates that members of the same family have a goal of protecting other family members. OCCAM uses explanation-based learning to create a kidnapping schema from only one example. The kidnapping schema is a specialization of coercion that indicates that a relative is willing to pay the ransom of the hostage so that the hostage is not harmed.

OCCAM has been used to create the knowledge-base for a system that predicts the outcome of economic sanction incidents. The system accepts questions in English, searches memory for the relevant schema, and constructs an English answer.

We have reviewed the psychological evidence on the influence of prior knowledge on human learner. OCCAM is able to qualitatively predict differences in the number of trials required by human learners to acquire an accurate hypothesis. In addition, OCCAM is able to predict which hypotheses people will prefer if more than one hypothesis is consistent with the data, but only one hypothesis is consistent with prior knowledge.

Chapter 8
Future Directions and Conclusions

What has been accomplished in this book? First and foremost, I have proposed a theory of learning causal relationships that integrates two different sources of information: the experiences the learner observes and the knowledge the learner possesses when the observations are made. Furthermore, the theory claims that analytical learning techniques that make use of prior knowledge are to be preferred to empirical learning techniques when both are applicable. Section 7.7 reviews the psychological evidence that supports the claim that people exhibit this same preference. In Chapters 6 and 3, I indicate the computational reasons for this preference. In addition, I have argued that people possess a general theory of causality to assist in learning causal relationships, and demonstrated how a machine learning system can benefit from this source of knowledge.

8.1. Future Research on Integrated Learning

Numerous directions exist for future research on integrating empirical and analytical learning methods. Additional research directions include the acquisition of generalization rules and the use of empirical learning techniques to complete an explanation.

8.1.1. Learning generalization rules

Currently, in OCCAM there is a fixed set of generalization rules that never changes as the program learns. When the program starts, it has its complete theory of causality. While there is evidence that very young infants are able to perceive causal relationships (Leslie & Keeble, 1987), there is no question that older children are better at attributing causality than younger children (Bullock, 1979; Piaget, 1930). It might be better if OCCAM started with a few very simple generalization rules, and learned the more complex generalization rules. Certainly, I would not want to claim that the more complex social rules are innate in humans (e.g., *If an event (?e) motivates a goal (?g) for someone (?p1), and someone else (?p2) observes the event (?e) and performs an action (?a) that achieves the goal (?g) for ?p1, then the event (?e) motivates the goal (?g) for ?p2).*

How might a general theory of causality be acquired? The answer is that it can be learned from experience. For example, it might be possible to start with a very simple theory of causality with only one generalization rule:

```
If an event (?e) is followed by a result (?r),
Then ?e causes ?r
```

This generalization rule is necessary to warrant the inference of a causal relationship from a temporal relationship.

This simple generalization rule doesn't contain any constraints between causes and effects. Although, it will make some correct causal inferences, it also allows a number of mistakes. For example, if the cat meows shortly before the doorbell rings, the inference that the cat caused the doorbell to ring will be made. Eventually, with further examples of the doorbell ringing without the cat meowing and the cat meowing without the doorbell ringing, this mistake will become apparent. Other proposed causal relationships will be confirmed after a large number of examples have been observed. If similarities could be detected between the examples in which the simple generalization rule successfully proposes causal relationships, then the generalization rule could be specialized. This scheme alters the definition of generalization rules slightly. In OCCAM, a generalization rule is intended as an encoding of a causal theory. In the empirical scheme for specializing generalization rules sketched here, a generalization rule is a commonly encountered pattern of causal relationships. By equating these two definitions, an answer emerges to the question of how a theory of causality could be learned: by noticing common patterns in established causal relationships.

To illustrate how this scheme would work consider the following example. A causal relationship is noticed about balloons: when air is blown into balloons, they get bigger. This relationship is illustrated in Figure 8-1. Other examples suggest another causal relationship: when a glass object is struck, it shatters. This relationship is illustrated in Figure 8-2.

By noticing the common features between these two generalizations, a new generalization rule could be created. Such a scheme has been implemented and the result is shown in Figure 8-3. This generalization indicates that one pattern of causal relationships occurs when the destination of an action changes as a

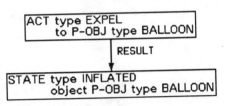

Figure 8-1: A causal relationship: a balloon is inflated when air is blown into it.

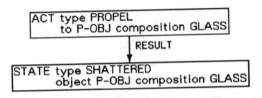

Figure 8-2: A causal relationship: a glass object shatters when it is struck.

result of the action. When a number of such patterns have been detected and confirmed, future learning can be focused by first considering only those regularities that have proved useful in the past. Figure 8-4 shows the flow of information when generalization rules are acquired through SBL.

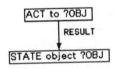

Figure 8-3: A generalization rule formed by detecting the common features of the generalizations in Figures 8-1 and 8-2.

However, this scheme for acquiring generalization rules is not yet integrated into OCCAM and OCCAM does not use the generalization rule illustrated in Figure 8-3. A number of questions remain. How many examples should be encountered before a causal relationship is confirmed? How many examples of confirmed causal relationships are needed before a generalization rule is formed? What sort of clustering algorithm would find useful patterns in causal relationships?

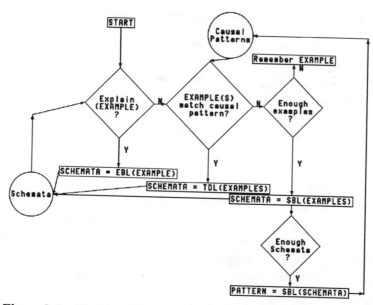

Figure 8-4: The flow of information in an extended version of OCCAM. Background knowledge for explanation-based learning is acquired through similarity-based or theory-driven learning. Generalization rules are learned by similarity-based learning.

The ability to acquire new causal patterns to guide generalization would enable OCCAM to adapt to new domains. These causal patterns would suggest causal mechanisms for state changes. For example, one would not want to claim that people are born with a theory of electric switches. However, as adults, we are more likely to attribute a change in an electronic device to a pushing of a button or the flicking of a switch than to another random action (such as a cat meowing). This is true even if the wires are hidden (as in a light switch) or the connection is not observable (as in the remote control for a television). This knowledge could be acquired by noticing similarities among the control of electrical devices and could be represented as a new causal pattern:

```
If a switch is pressed
immediately before a state change of an electronic device
then pressing the switch results in the state change.
```

8.1.2. Learning inference rules when failing to explain

Must a learner resort to empirical learning techniques when there is not enough knowledge to complete an explanation? Currently, in OCCAM, if it is not possible to produce a complete inference chain, EBL is not attempted. This is a problem because OCCAM's domain knowledge is ignored even if only one inference rule needed to complete an explanation is missing. Ideally, one would want to use the existing incomplete domain knowledge to focus the learning process on acquiring the missing inference rule.

There is a serious problem that must be addressed in acquiring a missing inference rule: there are typically many possible ways to complete an inference chain. To illustrate, suppose that OCCAM does not contain an inference rule that indicates that an increased demand for a product by one country can enable another country to sell the product at a price greater than the market price. Now when it is presented with Economic-Sanction-1 (repeated below) it is not able to explain the outcome.

Economic-Sanction-1

In 1983, Australia refused to sell uranium to France, unless France ceased nuclear testing in the South Pacific. France paid a higher price to buy uranium from South Africa.

In this situation, there are several inference rules that indicate some implications of refusing to sell a product (e.g., France will have an increased demand for the product, and Australia will still have the product) and there are rules associated with France obtaining the uranium (e.g., France obtaining the uranium is a result of France purchasing the uranium, France purchasing the uranium is enabled by France having $30,000,000, and France purchasing the uranium results in South Africa not possessing the uranium). The problem is that there is no connection between Australia refusing to sell the uranium, and France obtaining the uranium from South Africa. This situation is illustrated in Figure 8-5.

Furthermore, there are numerous connections that could be made if one were to propose any possible connection as a new inference rule. For example, one could propose that Australia refusing to sell the uranium results in France possessing the money. If intermediate states and events could also be proposed, then there are an infinite number of ways to complete an explanation. For

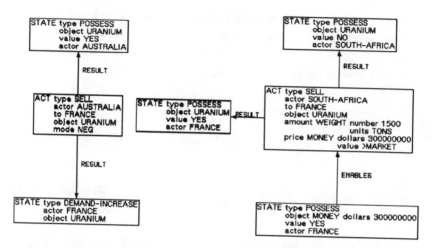

Figure 8-5:   **The situation when there is some domain knowledge, but
not enough to complete an   explanation. There is no
inference rule that connects the two events in bold:
Australia refusing to sell uranium to France and France
obtaining the uranium.**

example, Australia refusing to sell uranium could result in the existence of pigs
that fly that could be an enabling condition of France purchasing the uranium
from South Africa. The problem here is that without any structure to judge
which explanations are acceptable, there is no way to control the number of
alternative ways to complete an inference chain.

In some applications, there is a means of controlling the possible inference
paths.   For example, in a circuit, the structural connectivity indicates the
possible causal connections. This structure has been exploited in a program that
learns by failing to explain (Hall, 1986). The general idea is that if one knows
the function of an entire circuit, and knows how the circuit is realized by a
number of connected components, and knows the functionality of all but one of
the components, it is possible to infer what the functionality of the remaining
component must be.

In OCCAM, there is a mechanism that provides a structure for explanations.
Recall that generalization rules propose abstract explanations that are verified
and refined by domain knowledge (see Section 5.2). The abstract explanation
provides a structure that can focus the learning of an inference rule to complete
an explanation. For example, consider the example illustrated in Figure 8-5.

OCCAM has a generalization rule that proposes an abstract explanation that the state that results from the initial act enables the subsequent action that results in the outcome. OCCAM has enough domain knowledge to verify two of the three causal links proposed in the abstract explanation (see Figure 8-6).

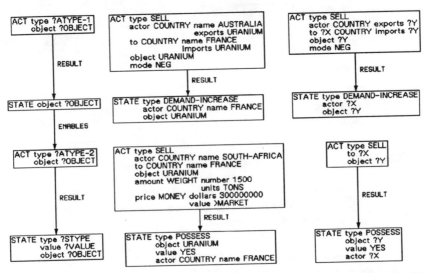

Figure 8-6:   An abstract explanation proposed by a generalization rule is illustrated in the first column. The middle column illustrates the incomplete causal chain. The explanation cannot be completed because an inference rule is missing that indicates that an increased demand for a product by one country can enable another country to sell the product at a price greater than the market price. The last column illustrates two inference rules that produced the incomplete causal chain.

When there is missing knowledge, it should be possible to utilize the abstract explanation to propose a causal link in the detailed explanation and to utilize SBL techniques to acquire an inference rule to be used in future explanations. For example, from Economic-Sanction-1, one would learn that France's increased demand for uranium enabled South Africa to sell the uranium at a premium. From Economic-Sanction-2 (repeated below), one would learn that the Soviet Union's increased demand for grain enabled Argentina to sell the grain at a premium.

Economic-Sanction-2

In 1980, the US refused to sell grain to the Soviet Union unless the Soviet Union withdrew troops from Afghanistan. The Soviet Union paid a higher price to buy grain from Argentina and did not withdraw from Afghanistan.

By finding the common features of the proposed causal link in these two examples, an inference rule could be created that indicates that an increased demand for a commodity by a country that exports arms enables a country in the Southern Hemisphere to sell them the commodity at a premium. Further examples should eventually eliminate the irrelevant coincidental features from this inference rule.

8.2. Summary

In this book, I have shown how a system can start with very little knowledge and become expert in a domain. I have analyzed both empirical and explanation-based learning techniques and shown how their strengths and weaknesses are complementary. I have proposed a learning theory that utilizes empirical techniques to acquire a base-level understanding of the simple regularities in a domain and uses explanation-based learning to create schemata which record the useful implications and interactions of the base-level knowledge.

The theory gives an account of how children might learn about the physical and social world. Through childhood experiences, such as playing with toys or interacting with family and friends, children must acquire many facts and principles. The knowledge acquired through these initial experience influences later learning. This initial knowledge constrains future learning so that it is easier to acquire new knowledge that is consistent with the existing knowledge. Expertise in an area is achieved by creating a memory of abstract experiences that do not contain the irrelevant details of specific experiences. The basic knowledge of a domain is used to distinguish the relevant from the irrelevant details. It is difficult, but not impossible, to learn when new experiences conflict with the existing knowledge. When this occurs, existing knowledge must be revised and factors that were initially believed to be irrelevant must be reconsidered.

I have implemented OCCAM, a computer model, to test the theory of learning developed in this book. OCCAM progresses from a system with very little world knowledge to a system with detailed knowledge of kidnapping and economic sanctions. At first, learning requires many examples as OCCAM acquires its initial knowledge of coercion. Once OCCAM has acquired relevant background knowledge, it requires fewer examples to learn about kidnapping and economic sanctions because it can rely on the background knowledge to identify relevant features.

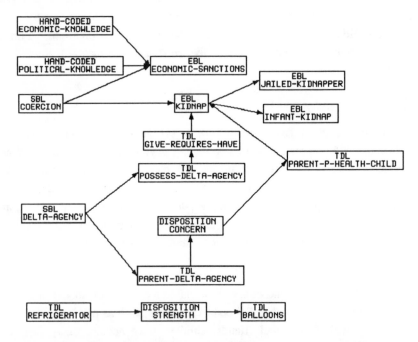

Figure 8-7: The dependencies among the schemata learned by OCCAM.

Figure 8-7 illustrates the dependencies among some of the schemata learned by OCCAM. This figure demonstrates that OCCAM is an integrated system that can make use of the knowledge it acquires to facilitate future learning. For example, by performing similarity-based learning, OCCAM learns about coercion. The coercion knowledge is specialized into kidnapping knowledge via explanation-based learning. The knowledge needed to explain kidnapping was acquired through theory-driven learning. OCCAM learns a schema, which I call `give-requires-have`. This schema states that to give someone an object, an actor must first possess the object. This schema was acquired to account for an exception to **delta-agency**. **delta-agency** is a schema formed by SBL to represent one plan to achieve a goal: ask another person for assistance. OCCAM learns **give-requires-have** when **delta-agency** fails because the actor asks for an object that the potential assistant did not have. **give-requires-have** explains why it is important to demand a ransom from a wealthy person: wealthy people have money and one must have money to be able to pay a ransom.

OCCAM learns another schema that indicates why someone would want to pay a ransom. This schema, which I call **parent-p-health-child**, indicates that parents have a goal of protecting the health of their children. **parent-p-health-child** is acquired via theory-driven learning when OCCAM detects a regularity in examples of people helping a child who is hurt. OCCAM notices that the child's parents are likely to help. When OCCAM makes a distinction between two groups of people, it can be aided by dispositional attributes that encode knowledge of previous distinctions. OCCAM learns a disposition that might be called "caring" or "concern". This disposition was learned to account for the fact that **delta-agency** is more likely to be a successful plan if an actor asks a parent or relative for assistance.

Dispositions can facilitate learning about physical causes as well as social causes. OCCAM learns a disposition called "strength" to account for a distinction between adults and infants: when adults pull on a refrigerator door, it opens. However, infants cannot open a refrigerator. It takes many examples to acquire the "strength" disposition. However, once OCCAM knows that adults are stronger than children, it takes few examples to recognize this distinction in other domains. For example, OCCAM easily learns that adults can inflate balloons but young children cannot.

Learning is more rapid and more accurate when OCCAM has a correct domain theory. In the domain of economic sanctions, OCCAM's domain theory consists of the knowledge of coercion, which it acquired by similarity-based learning, as well as economic and political rules, which were hand-coded. This initial knowledge alone is not sufficient for OCCAM to function as an economic sanction expert. Instead, this knowledge is organized through problem-solving experience so that useful interactions between the initial knowledge can be easily recognized. Several specializations of coercion that represent common patterns of economic sanction incidents are constructed. Once this memory of abstract sanction incidents is acquired, OCCAM can answer questions about hypothetical sanction incidents.

8.3. Conclusions

In this book, I have argued for a theory of explanation that is composed of two different explanatory processes. The first preferred process for producing explanations is a recognize and instantiate strategy. This strategy explains a new event by recognizing the event as an instance of a known schema (i.e., a general class of events) and instantiating a causal chain associated with the schema. The recognition process is guided by a hierarchical organization of schemata in memory. The second process for producing explanations is a constructive strategy that builds new explanations by chaining together separate general facts. This general knowledge of the world can also be represented as schemata in memory. However, the search to construct an explanation is more expensive than the search to recognize an explanation because many combinations of schemata must be attempted to construct a causal chain.

There are two different ways in which learning can improve the explanation process. First, learning can increase the number of situations that one can explain by a recognition process. Explanation-based learning performs exactly this task by exploiting the interactions among existing knowledge and creating a schema that recognizes the class of situations in which these interactions occur. Second, learning can increase the number of situations that one can explain by a construction process. Empirical techniques can detect regularities in data and hypothesize that these regularities will hold in future cases. New schemata created by empirical techniques increase the ability of a learner to construct new explanations as well as the ability to recognize new explanations. An important point of this book is that once new knowledge is acquired by empirical methods, new explanations can be constructed using this knowledge. When new explanations are constructed, they can be generalized by explanation-based techniques, so that the situations in which these explanations apply can be recognized. Empirical learning techniques provide the necessary background knowledge for explanation-based learning. EBL alone is not sufficient for increasing the number of situations that one can explain by constructing explanations.

8.3.1. Integrating empirical and explanation-based learning

For many tasks in OCCAM, there are two separate strategies that could be used. A knowledge-intensive method is attempted first. The knowledge-intensive method is powerful but limited in its applicability. If the knowledge-intensive strategy fails, then a weak method is available that can also perform the task if one is willing to sacrifice time, space, or accuracy. The specific components of OCCAM that utilize these dual methods are:

- Aggregation-- The knowledge-intensive method for grouping events into clusters falls out of the way that OCCAM generalizes with explanation-based learning. If there is no schema that recognizes the explanation for an event, then OCCAM constructs a new explanation (provided there is sufficient background knowledge). A new schema is created by retaining only those features which were needed to produce the explanation. Future events that share these features will be indexed under this schema. The effect of the knowledge-intensive aggregation process is that a schema groups together those events that share the same explanation structure. The weak method that OCCAM uses to aggregate events is to group together those events which have the most features in common (see Section 3.2.2 for the details). This weak method can run into problems if events that share many surface similarities do not share the same explanation structure. In this case, the clusters formed will not group together those events which share the same explanation structure. Generalizations formed from such clusters may not perform well at prediction or explanation tasks (see Section 6.2).

- Generalization-- Explanation-based learning is the knowledge-intensive generalization method in OCCAM. If an event can be explained by constructing a causal chain linking several separate schemata together, EBL can construct a description of the class of events to which that explanation applies. This knowledge-intensive generalization method constructs a generalized event description by retaining only those features of a single example that were needed to form the causal chain. The weak method that OCCAM uses for generalization is an empirical technique that constructs a generalized event description by retaining only those features which are shared by all examples of a group of events. The generalizations produced by empirical techniques may be irrelevant, coincidental regularities. This problem is particularly severe if only a small number of examples is available. In contrast, EBL can identify relevant features and true regularities since this information is derived analytically.

- Exceptions-- There are two methods that can deal with exceptions (i.e., when a schema makes an incorrect prediction). The knowledge-intensive method is to try to explain why the schema makes an incorrect prediction. One such reason is that the schema was formed by EBL but the knowledge used to create the explanation has been discredited (see Section 7.5). Other explanations might be constructed using general world knowledge. For example, in Section 4.7 I discuss an example in which OCCAM encounters an exception to a generalization that indicates that a parent will give a child what the child asks for. Because OCCAM can explain why the parent does not give a requested object (the parent does not have the requested object), it does not reduce confidence in its schema. OCCAM has a weak method for dealing with exceptions to schemata that cannot be explained: with each exception, it reduces confidence in the schema until the schema is finally deleted or revised to accommodate the exception. If these explanations are available for exceptions they should not reduce confidence in established principles. Rather, there is much that can be learned from exceptions.

- Selecting hypotheses-- When learning a new causal relationship, OCCAM has two methods for selecting among hypotheses that are consistent with the data. The knowledge-intensive method is to make use of dispositions, specific world knowledge about the capabilities of actors, and the potentials of objects. Hypotheses that propose differences which are supported by existing dispositions are preferred. The weak method in OCCAM for selecting among consistent hypotheses is random guessing. Those guesses which happen to work out well serve as the foundation for creating dispositions and making new distinctions.

8.3.2. Causal theories

A common theme in the approach to learning in this book is that knowledge-intensive strategies are to be preferred over weak strategies. A corollary might be: a little knowledge is better than no knowledge. The theory-driven component of OCCAM follows this philosophy. Explanation-based learning makes use of detailed specific world knowledge. Theory-driven learning makes use of an approximate, general theory of causal relationships that is not sufficient to make predictions. However, given an example, the general causal knowledge can produce potential explanations that can be supported or discredited by further experiences. In Section 4.6, I demonstrated empirically that theory-driven learning is an improvement over the weaker forms of empirical learning. The experiment that I ran (see Section 4.2.1), demonstrated that it is also easier for people to learn when the experiences conform to a common pattern of causal relationships. Since TDL is more powerful than SBL, TDL is preferred over SBL in OCCAM. However, EBL is preferred to TDL because EBL makes use of specific world knowledge as opposed to an approximate, general theory.

8.3.3. Memory organization

OCCAM provides a solution to some of the issues of indexing explanatory schemata in memory. In particular, schemata are indexed by those surface features that were used to create its explanation. This strategy allows explanatory schemata to be retrieved by following indices corresponding to the surface features of a new event. Once an explanatory schemata is retrieved, the causal chain associated with the schema can be instantiated to explain a new event. Of course, OCCAM does not solve all the issues concerned with memory-based inference. In particular, OCCAM (and EBL) do not address the issue of locating and modifying explanations that seem to "almost" apply to a new case.

The memory organization in OCCAM has also proved useful for indexing rules in memory. Rules are indexed under the most specific schema in memory that accounts for the antecedent of a rule. This organization permits rules to be retrieved and applied in order of decreasing specificity to the situation.

8.4. Final Comments

In this book, I have argued that both empirical and explanation-based learning techniques are necessary components of a system that learns causal relationships. The role of empirical techniques is to acquire background knowledge such as simple causal rules by noticing regularities in observed data. The role of explanation-based techniques is to recognize new interactions among existing knowledge and determine the class of situations in which the interactions occur. The most important results of this research are the analysis of the situations in which each learning strategy is appropriate and the integration of the learning strategies in a single system that takes advantage of the complementary nature of empirical and explanation-based learning. Recent work on the analysis of the limitations of inductive learning algorithms (Valiant, 1984) is in sharp contrast to the versatility demonstrated by human learners. Approaches that integrate empirical and explanation-based learning are central to accounting for the generality of human learning.

References

Alix, E. (1978). *Ransom kidnapping in the United States, 1874-1974: The creation of a capital crime.* Southern Illinios University Press.

Allport, G. (1954). *The nature of prejudice.* New York: Addison-Wesley.

Alterman, R. (1985). Adaptive planning: Refitting old plans to new situations. *Proceedings of the Seventh Annual Conference of the Cognitive Science Society.* Irvine, CA: Lawrence Erlbaum Associates.

Anderson, J.R. (1983). Knowledge compilation: The general learning mechanism. *Proceedings of the Second International Machine Learning Workshop.* Monticello, Ill.

Anderson, J.R. (1987). Causal analysis and inductive learning. *Proceedings of the Fourth International Machine Learning Workshop.* Irvine, CA: Morgan Kaufmann.

Anderson, C.A., Lepper, M.R., & Ross, L. (1980). The perseverance of social theories: The role of explanation in the persistence of discredited information. *Journal of Personality and Social Psychology, 39,* 1037-1049.

Ausubel, D.M. & Schiff, H. M. (1954). The effect of incidental and experimentally induced experience on the learning of relevant and irrelevant causal relationships by children. *Journal of Genetic Psychology, 84,* 109-123.

Barrett, S. & Murphy, G. (1986). *Feature correlations in children's concepts* (Tech. Rep.). Providence, RI: Brown University.

268

Bartlett, F. C. (1932). *Remembering: A study in experimental and social psychology.* New York: Cambridge University Press.

Berenstain, S. & Berenstain, J. (1985). *The Berenstain Bears forget their manners.* New York: Random House.

Berwick, R. (1986). Learning from positive only examples: The subset principle and three case studies. In Michalski, R., Carbonell, J., & Mitchell, T. (Ed.), *Machine learning: An artificial intelligence approach, Volume II.* Los Altos, CA: Morgan Kaufmann.

Birnbaum, L. & Selfridge, M. (1981). Conceptual analysis of natural language. In Schank, R., & Riesbeck, C. (Ed.), *Inside computer understanding: Five programs plus miniatures.* Hillsdale, NJ: Lawrence Erlbaum Associates.

Bower, G. & Trabasso, T. (1968). *Attention in learning: Theory and research.* New York: Wiley.

Brown, M.L. (1985). *Economic sanctions: A cost-benefit approach.* Doctoral dissertation, Harvard University.

Bruner, J.S., Goodnow, J.J., & Austin, G.A. (1956). *A study of thinking.* New York: Wiley.

Buchanan, B. & Mitchell, T. (1978). Model-directed learning of production rules. In Waterman, D. & Hayes-Roth, F. (Ed.), *Pattern-directed inference systems.* New York: Academic Press.

Bullock, M. (1979). *Aspects of the young child's theory of causality.* Doctoral dissertation, University of Pennsylvania.

Bullock, M., Gelman, R. & Baillargeon, R. (1982). The development of causal reasoning. In Friedman, W. (Ed.), *The developmental psychology of time.* New York: Academic Press.

Carey, S. (1984). *Conceptual change in childhood.* Cambridge: MIT Press.

Chapman, L.J., & Chapman, J.P. (1967). Genesis of popular but erroneous diagnostic observations. *Journal of Abnormal Psychology, 72*, 193-204.

Chapman, L.J., & Chapman, J.P. (1969). Illusory correlation as an obstacle to the use of valid psychodiagnostic signs. *Journal of Abnormal Psychology, 74*, 271-280.

Charniak, E. & McDermott, D. (1985). *Introduction to artificial intelligence.* Reading, MA: Addison-Wesley.

Charniak, E., Riesbeck, C. & McDermott, D. (1980). *Artificial intelligence programming.* Hillsdale, NJ: Lawrence Erlbaum Associates.

De Kleer, S. (1984). Choices without backtracking. *Proceedings of the National Conference on Artificial Intelligence.* Austin, TX: Morgan Kaufmann.

Dean, G. (1986). Does astrology need to be true? Part 1: A look at the real thing. *The Skeptical Inquirer, 11*(2), 166-185.

DeJong, G. (1977). *Skimming newspaper stories by computer.* Doctoral dissertation, Yale University.

DeJong, G. (1986). An approach to learning from observation. In Michalski, R., Carbonell, J., & Mitchell, T. (Ed.), *Machine learning: An artificial intelligence approach, Volume II.* Los Altos, CA: Morgan Kaufmann.

DeJong, G. & Mooney, R. (1986). Explanation-based learning: An alternate view. *Machine Learning, 1*(2), 145-176.

Dietterich, T. (1986). Learning at the knowledge level. *Machine Learning, 1*(3), 287-315.

Dolan, C. & Dyer, M. (1985). Learning planning heuristics through observation. *Proceedings of the Ninth International Joint Conference on Artificial Intelligence.* Los Angeles, CA: Morgan Kaufmann.

Doyle, J. (1979). A truth maintenance system. *Artificial Intelligence, 12*(3), 231-272.

Dyer, M. (1983). *In depth understanding*. Cambridge: MIT Press.

Fikes, R., Hart, R., & Nilsson, N. (1972). Learning and executing generalized robot plans. *Artificial Intelligence, 3*, 251-288.

Fisher, D. (1987). Knowledge acquisition via incremental conceptual clustering. *Machine Learning, 2*(2), 139-172.

Fisher, D. & Langley, P. (1985). Approaches to conceptual clustering. *Proceedings of the Ninth International Joint Conference on Artificial Intelligence.* Los Angeles, CA: Morgan Kaufmann.

Flann, N. & Dietterich T. (1986). Selecting appropriate representations for learning from examples. *Proceedings of the National Conference on Artificial Intelligence.* Philadelphia, PA: Morgan Kaufmann.

Freedman, R. O. (1970). *Economic warfare in the Communist Bloc: A study of Soviet economic pressure against Yugoslavia, Albania, and Communist China.* New York: Praeger.

Fu, L. & Buchanan, B. (1985). Learning intermediate concepts in constructing a hierarchical knowledge base. *Proceedings of the Ninth International Joint Conference on Artificial Intelligence.* Los Angeles, CA: Morgan Kaufmann.

Getner, D. (1983). Structure-mapping: A theoretical framework for analogy. *Cognitive Science,* Vol. 7(2).

Goodman, N. (1983). *Fact, fiction and forecast, fourth edition.* Cambridge: Harvard University Press.

Hall, R. (1986). Learning by failing to explain. *Proceedings of the National Conference on Artificial Intelligence.* Philadelphia, PA: Morgan

Kaufmann.

Hammond, K. (1984). *Indexing and causality: The organization of plans and strategies in memory*. Doctoral dissertation, Yale University.

Hammond, K. (1987). Learning and reusing explanations. *Proceedings of the Fourth International Machine Learning Workshop*. Irvine, CA: Morgan Kaufmann.

Hanson, A. & Riseman, E. (Ed.). (1978). *Computer vision systems*. New York: Academic Press.

Hawkins, G. (1965). *Stonehenge decoded*. London: Doubleday.

Hepworth, M. (1975). *Blackmail*. London: Routledge & Kegan Paul.

Hirsh, H. (1987). Explanation-based learning in a logic programming environment. *Proceedings of the Tenth International Joint Conference on Artificial Intelligence*. Milan, Italy: Morgan Kaufmann.

Hoenkamp, E. (1987). An analysis of psychological experiments on non-monotonic reasoning. *Proceedings of the Tenth International Joint Conference on Artificial Intelligence*. Milan, Italy: Morgan Kaufmann.

Hoffman, M. (Ed.). (1986). *The 1987 world almanac and book of facts*. New York: Pharos Books.

Holyoak, K. (1985). The pragmatics of analogical transfer. *The Psychology of Learning and Motivation, 19*, 59-87.

Hosansky, A. (1987). How not to gain weight during the holidays. *Family Circle*, pp. 44-45.

Hoyle, F. (1972). *From Stonehenge to modern cosmology*. San Francisco: W.H. Freeman.

Hufbauer, G.C., & Schott, J.J. (1985). *Economic sanctions reconsidered: History and current policy*. Washington, DC: Institute For International

Economics.

Jones E., Rock L., Shaver K., Goethals, G. & Ward, L. (1968). Pattern of performance and ability attribution: An unexpected primacy effect. *Journal of Personality and Social Psychology, 10*, 317-340.

Josephson, J., Chandraskaran, B., Smith, J., & Tanner, M. (1987). A mechanism for forming composite explanatory hypotheses. *IEEE Transactions on Systems, Man, and Cybernetics, 17*(3), 445-454.

Kass, A. (1986). Modifying explanations to understand stories. *Proceedings of the Eighth Annual Conference of the Cognitive Science Society.* Amherst, MA: Lawrence Erlbaum Associates.

Kedar-Cabelli, S. (1985). Purpose-directed analogy. *Proceedings of the Seventh Annual Conference of the Cognitive Science Society.* Irvine, CA: Lawrence Erlbaum Associates.

Kedar-Cabelli, S. & McCarty, L. (1987). Explanation-based generalization as resolution theorem proving. *Proceedings of the Fourth International Machine Learning Workshop.* Irvine, CA: Morgan Kaufmann.

Keller, R. (1987a). Concept learning in context. *Proceedings of the Fourth International Machine Learning Workshop.* Irvine, CA.

Keller, R. (1987b). Defining operationality for explanation-based learning. *Proceedings of the National Conference on Artificial Intelligence.* Seattle, WA: Morgan Kaufmann.

Kolodner, J. (1984). *Retrieval and organizational strategies in conceptual memory: A computer model.* Hillsdale, NJ: Lawrence Erlbaum Associates.

Kolodner, J. (1987). Extending problem solver capabilities through case-based inference. *Proceedings of the Fourth International Machine Learning*

Workshop. Irvine, CA: Morgan Kaufmann.

Kowalski, R. (1979). *Logic for problem solving.* Amsterdam: North Holland.

Laird, J., Rosenbloom, P., & Newell, A. (1984). Towards chunking as a general learning mechanism. *Proceedings of the National Conference on Artificial Intelligence.* Austin, TX: Morgan Kaufmann.

Laird, J., Rosenbloom, P., & Newell, A. (1986). Chunking in SOAR: The anatomy of a general learning mechanism. *Machine Learning, 1*(1), 11-46.

Langley, P., Bradshaw, G., & Simon, H. (1983). Rediscovering chemistry with the BACON system. In Michalski, R., Carbonell, J., & Mitchell, T. (Ed.), *Machine learning: An artificial intelligence approach.* Palo Alto, CA: Tioga.

Langley, P., Zytkow, J., Simon, H., & Bradshaw, G. (1986). The search for regularity: Four aspects of scientific discovery. In Michalski, R., Carbonell, J., & Mitchell, T. (Ed.), *Machine learning: An artificial intelligence approach, Volume II.* Los Altos, CA: Morgan Kaufmann.

Lau, R.R. (1984). Dynamics of the attribution process. *Journal of Personality and Social Psychology, 46,* 1017-1028.

Leake, D. & Owens, C. (1986). Organizing memory for explanations. *Proceedings of the Eighth Annual Conference of the Cognitive Science Society.* Lawrence Erlbaum Associates.

Lebowitz, M. (1980). *Generalization and memory in an integrated understanding system.* Doctoral dissertation, Yale University.

Lebowitz, M. (1982). Correcting erroneous generalizations. *Cognition and Brain Theory, 5*(4), 367-381.

Lebowitz, M. (1984). *Interest and predictability: Deciding what to learn, when to learn* (Tech. Rep.). New York: Columbia University.

Lebowitz, M. (1986a). Concept learning in an rich input domain: Generalization-based memory. In Michalski, R., Carbonell, J., & Mitchell, T. (Ed.), *Machine learning: An artificial intelligence approach, Volume II*. Los Altos, CA: Morgan Kaufmann.

Lebowitz, M. (1986b). Not the path to perdition: The utility of similarity-based learning. *Proceedings of the National Conference on Artificial Intelligence*. Philadelphia, PA: Morgan Kaufmann.

Lebowitz, M.(1986c). Integrated learning: Controlling explanation. *Cognitive Science, 10*, 219-240.

Lebowitz, M. (1987). Experiments with incremental concept formation: UNIMEM. *Machine Learning, 2*(2), 103-138.

Lehnert, W. (1978). *The process of question answering*. Hillsdale, NJ: Lawrence Erlbaum Associates.

Lehnert, W. (1982). Plot units: A narrative summarization strategy. In Lehnert, W. & Ringle, M. (Ed.), *Strategies for natural language understanding*. Hillsdale, NJ: Lawrence Erlbaum Associates.

Leslie, A., & Keeble, S. (1987). Do six-month-old infants perceive causality? *Cognition, 25*, 265-288.

Levine, M. (1966). Hypothesis behavior by humans during discrimination learning. *Journal of Experimental Psychology, 71*, 331-338.

Levine, M. (1967). The size of the hypothesis set during discrimination learning. *Psychology Review, 74*, 428-430.

McDermott, D. (1983). *DUCK: A Lisp-based deductive system* (Tech. Rep.). Smart Systems Technology.

McDermott, D. (1986). *A critique of pure reason* (Tech. Rep.). New Haven,

CT: Yale University.

McDermott, J., & Forgy, C. (1978). Production system conflict resolution strategies. In Waterman, D. & Hayes-Roth, F. (Ed.), *Pattern-directed inference systems*. New York: Academic Press.

Michalski, R. (1977). A system of programs for computer aided induction: A summary. *Proceedings of the Fifth International Joint Conference on Artificial Intelligence*. Cambridge, MA: Morgan Kaufmann.

Michotte, A. (1963). *The perception of causality*. New York: Basic Books, Inc.

Minsky, M. (1986). *The society of the mind*. New York: Simon and Schuster.

Mitchell, T. (1982). Generalization as search. *Artificial Intelligence, 18*(2), 203-236.

Mitchell, T., Keller, R. & Kedar-Cabelli, S. (1986). Explanation-based learning: A unifying view. *Machine Learning, 1*(1), 47-80.

Mitchell, T., Mahadevan, S., & Steinberg, L. (1986). LEAP: A learning apprentice for VLSI design. *International Meeting on Advances in Learning*. Les Arc, France.

Mooney, R. & Bennett, S. (1986). A domain independent explanation-based generalizer. *Proceedings of the National Conference on Artificial Intelligence*. Philadelphia, PA: Morgan Kaufmann.

Mooney, R. & DeJong, G. (1985). Learning schemata for natural language processing. *Proceedings of the Ninth International Joint Conference on Artificial Intelligence*. Los Angeles, CA: Morgan Kaufmann.

Moorehead, C. (1980). *Hostages to fortune: A study of kidnapping in the world today*. New York: Atheneum.

Mostow, J. (1987). Searching for operational concept descriptions in BAR,

MetaLex, and EBG. *Proceedings of the Fourth International Machine Learning Workshop*. Irvine, CA: Morgan Kaufmann.

Murphy, C. (1987). The longest day. *The Atlantic*.

Murphy, G. & Medin, D. (1985). The role of theories in conceptual coherence. *Psychology Review, 92*(3), 289-316.

Murphy, G. & Wisniewski, E. (1986). *Feature correlations in conceptual representations* (Tech. Rep.). Providence, RI: Brown University.

Neisser, U. (1976). *Cognition and reality*. San Francisco: W.H. Freeman.

Newell, A. (1981). The knowledge level. *AI Magazine, 2*, 1-20.

Nisbett, R. & Ross, L. (1978). *Human inference: Strategies and shortcomings of social judgments*. Engelwood Cliffs, NJ: Prentice-Hall, Inc.

Pazzani, M. (1985). Explanation and generalization-based memory. *Proceedings of the Seventh Annual Conference of the Cognitive Science Society*. Irvine, CA: Lawrence Erlbaum Associates.

Peirce, C. (1932). *The collected papers of Charles Sanders Peirce, Volume 2*. Cambridge: Harvard.

Piaget, J. (1930). *The child's conception of physical causality*. London: Kegan Paul.

Rajamoney, S. & DeJong, G. (1987). The classification, detection and handling of imperfect theory problems. *Proceedings of the Tenth International Joint Conference on Artificial Intelligence*. Milan, Italy: Morgan Kaufmann.

Renwick, R. (1981). *Economic sanctions*. Cambridge, MA: Center for International Affairs, Harvard University.

Robinson J.A. (1965). A machine oriented logic based on the resolution principle. *Journal of the Association of Computing Machinery, 12*, 23-41.

Rocsh, E., C., Gray, W., Johnson, D. & Boyes-Braem, P. (1976). Basic objects in natural categories. *Cognitive Psychology, 8*, 382-439.

Rosch, E. (1978). Principles of categorization. In Rosch, E. & Lloyd, B. (Ed.), *Cognition and categorization*. Hillsdale, NJ: Lawrence Erlbaum Associates.

Rosenbloom, P. & Laird, J. (1986). Mapping explanation-based generalization onto SOAR. *Proceedings of the National Conference on Artificial Intelligence*. Philadelphia, PA: Morgan Kaufmann.

Rumelhart, D., Hinton, G., & Williams, R. (1986). Learning internal representations by error propagation. In Rumelhart, D. & McClelland, J. (Ed.), *Parallel distributed processing: Explorations in the microstructure of cognition. Volume 1: Foundations*. Cambridge: MIT Press.

Sacerdoti E. (1974). Planning in a hierarchy of abstraction spaces. *Artificial Intelligence, 5*, 115-135.

Salzberg, S. (1985). Heuristics for inductive learning. *Proceedings of the Ninth International Joint Conference on Artificial Intelligence*. Los Angeles, CA: Morgan Kaufmann.

Schank, R. (1982). *Dynamic memory: A theory of reminding and learning in computers and people*. Cambridge: Cambridge University Press.

Schank, R.C. (1986). *Explanation patterns: Understanding mechanically and creatively*. Hillsdale, NJ: Lawrence Erlbaum Associates.

Schank, R.C. & Abelson, R.P. (1977). *Scripts, plans, goals, and understanding*. Hillsdale, NJ: Lawrence Erlbaum Associates.

Schank, R., Collins, G. & Hunter, L. (1986). Transcending inductive category formation in learning. *Behavioral and Brain Sciences, 9*, 639-686.

Schlimmer, J. & Granger, R. (1986). Simultaneous configural classical conditioning. *Proceedings of the Eight Annual Conference of the Cognitive Science Society.* Amherst, MA: Lawrence Erlbaum Associates.

Shell, E. (1987). The risks of risk studies. *The Atlantic.*

Shultz, T. (1982). Rules of causal attribution. *Monographs of the Society for Research in Child Development,* Vol. 47.

Shultz, T. & Mendelson, R. (1975). The use of covariation as a principle of causal analysis. *Child Development, 46,* 394-399.

Shultz, T., Fisher, G., Pratt, C., & Rulf, S. (1986). Selection of causal rules. *Child Development, 57,* 143-152.

Skorstad, J., Falkenhainer, B., & Getner, D. (1987). Analogical processing: A simulation and empirical corroboration. *Proceedings of the National Conference on Artificial Intelligence.* Seattle, WA: Morgan Kaufmann.

Smith E.E., & Medin, D. (1981). *Categories and concepts.* Cambridge, MA: Harvard University Press.

Trabasso, T. (1963). Stimulus emphasis and all-or-none learning on concept identification. *Journal of Experimental Psychology, 65,* 83-88.

Valiant, L. (1984). A theory of the learnable. *Communications of the Association of Computing Machinery, 27*(11), 1134-1142.

VanLehn K. (1983). *Felicity conditions for human skill acquisition: Validating an AI-based theory.* Doctoral dissertation, MIT.

Vere, S. (1975). Induction of Concepts in the Predicate Calculus. *Proceedings of the Fourth International Joint Conference on Artificial Intelligence.* Tbilisi, USSR: Morgan Kaufmann.

Waldinger, R. (1977). Achieving several goals simultaneously. *Machine Intelligence,* Vol. 8.

Weiner, B. (1986). *An attributional theory of achievement, motivation and emotion.* New York: Springer-Verlag.

Weiner, B., Frieze, I., Kukla, A., Reed, L., Rest, S. & Rosenbaum, R. (1971). Perceiving the causes of success and failure. In Jones, E., Kanouse, D., Kelley, H., Nisbett, R., Valins, S. & Weiner, B. (Ed.), *Attribution: Perceiving the causes of behavior.* Hillsdale, NJ: Lawrence Erlbaum Associates.

Weiner, B., Russel, D., & Lerman, D. (1978). Affective consequences of causal ascriptions. In Harvey, J.H., Ickes, J.W., & Kidd, R.F. (Ed.), *New directions in attribution research.* Hillsdale, NJ: Lawrence Erlbaum Associates.

Wilensky, R. (1978). *Understanding goal based stories.* Doctoral dissertation, Yale University.

Wilensky, R. (1982). Points: A theory of the structure of stories in memory. In Lehnert, W. & Ringle, M. (Ed.), *Strategies for natural language understanding.* Hillsdale, NJ: Lawrence Erlbaum Associates.

Winston, P.H. (1975). Learning structural descriptions from examples. In Winston, P.H. (Ed.), *The Psychology of Computer Vision.* New York: McGraw-Hill.

Winston, P. (1977). *Artificial intelligence.* Reading, MA: Addison-Wesley.

Appendix A
Data Listing

This appendix contains the Common Lisp source code for the examples processed by OCCAM-LITE, a simplified version of OCCAM[68]. There are a number of differences between OCCAM and OCCAM-LITE:

- OCCAM-LITE is smaller. OCCAM-LITE contains 19 files, 309 definitions (of functions, rules, parameters etc.), 2866 lines of code, and when compiled occupies 114,688 words of memory on a Symbolics 3640. Its longest example (the trace in Appendix B) consumes 360,448 words of memory and takes 133 CPU seconds. OCCAM contains 25 files, 1209 definitions, 10,877 lines of code, and when compiled occupies 720,896 words of memory on a Symbolics 3640. Its largest example, (learning **delta-agency**, **coerce**, **kidnap**, seven sanction schemata and answering two questions) consumes 1,622,316 words of memory and takes 327 CPU seconds.

- OCCAM-LITE does not contain a natural language parser or generator.

- The representation of **coerce** in OCCAM-LITE is considerably simpler than the representation learned and used by OCCAM.

- A role filler in OCCAM can be a CD object or a set of CD objects. In OCCAM-LITE, a role filler can only be a single CD object. This considerably simplifies many utility functions such as copying, matching, and instantiating CD structures which all require a special case for sets of objects.

- When evaluating the accuracy of a schema formed by theory-driven

---

[68]OCCAM-LITE contains 75% less code than our regular OCCAM.

learning or similarity-based learning, OCCAM can tolerate some noise or indeterminacy. OCCAM-LITE deletes a schema when it encounters one exception.

- When OCCAM encounters enough exceptions to a schema formed by similarity-based learning, it revises the schema to accommodate the exceptions by removing only those parts of the schema that are inaccurate. OCCAM-LITE simply deletes the schema and a new schema is formed by similarity-based learning. OCCAM-LITE's approach is simpler to implement but more time consuming. However, the effect of the two processes is the same.

- OCCAM-LITE does not learn or make use of dispositions.

- OCCAM-LITE does not use historical generalization rules. However, a similar effect is achieved by making the pattern matcher following temporal or intentional links when matching the antecedent of a generalization rule.

- OCCAM-LITE does not deal with the situation in which the rules used to justify a schema formed by EBL are shown to be erroneous. Inference rules in OCCAM can have an arbitrary set of preconditions associated with them. In OCCAM-LITE, rules do not have this set of preconditions. The only preconditions expressible (and, therefore, learnable) are restrictions on the features of the antecedent and consequent.

- In OCCAM, during theory-driven learning, a generalized event is constructed by dropping all of the features of objects matched by variables in the pattern. The intent is to generalize the object to the most specific class, but this requires that the most specific class be the "head" of a CD structure. OCCAM-LITE improves upon this by having a special class of features to represent a type hierarchy (e.g., type and sub-type). These type features are no longer dropped automatically and as a consequence, OCCAM-LITE does not require the most specific class to be the head of a CD structure[69].

---

[69]This change was motivated by a discussion with Keith Holyoak.

The following data-files used by OCCAM-LITE are included:

- play-doh: contains definitions of the five goal configurations. These serve as input to OCCAM-LITE.

- genrules: definitions of the generalization rules used by OCCAM-LITE.

- glass: definitions of the three CD structures concerning the effects of dropping cups. These serve as training instances for the theory-driven learning component of OCCAM-LITE.

- rules: contains the definitions of some simple economic rules.

- coerce: contains the definition of a simple coercion schema.

- sanctions: contains the definition of one sanction incident that serves as input for the EBL module of OCCAM-LITE.

A.1. File: play-doh.lisp

This file defines five CD events `zoo-1`, `refrigerator-1`, `play-doh-1`, `pizza-1` and `cookie-1`. These same examples were used to illustrate SBL in Chapter 3.

```
;;; -*- Mode: LISP; Syntax: common-lisp; Package: cl-user; Base: 10 -*-
;;;lynn wants  play-doh
(def-cd play-doh-1
        (goal actor (human name (lynn) age (kid) hair (blond)
                           eyes (blue) unique-id lynn)
              goal (state type (poss-by) unique-id poss-by.5
                          actor (human name (lynn) age (kid)
                                       hair (blond) eyes (blue)
                                       unique-id lynn)
                    value (yes)
                    object (p-obj type (toy)
                                  stype (play-doh)
                                  unique-id play-doh.1))
        unique-id play-doh.1))
```

```
;;;lynn plans to asks mike
(def-cd play-doh-p-1
  (plan actor (human name (lynn) age (kid) hair (blond)
                     eyes (blue) unique-id lynn)
       plan (act type (mtrans) unique-id mtrans.5
                 actor (human name (lynn) age (kid)
                             hair (blond) eyes (blue)
                             unique-id lynn)
                to (human name (mike)
                          relation (ipt type(family-rel)
                                        stype (father)
                                        of (human unique-id lynn))
                          age (grown-up)
                          hair (brown)
                          eyes (green)
                          unique-id mike)
                object (act type (atrans)
                         actor (human name (mike)
                                     relation (ipt type(family-rel)
                                                   stype (father)
                                                   of (human
                                                       unique-id lynn))
                                     age (grown-up)
                                     hair (brown)
                                     eyes (green)
                                     unique-id mike)
                         object (p-obj type (toy)
                                      stype (play-doh)
                                      unique-id play-doh.1)
                         to (human name (lynn)
                                   age (kid)
                                   hair (blond)
                                   eyes (blue)
                                   unique-id lynn)))
       unique-id play-doh-p.1))
```

```
;;;lynn asks mike
(def-cd play-doh-a-1
    (act type (mtrans)
          unique-id mtrans.5
          actor (human name (lynn) age (kid) hair (blond)
                        eyes (blue) unique-id lynn)
          to (human name (mike)
                     relation (ipt type(family-rel)
                                   stype (father)
                                   of (human unique-id lynn))
                     age (grown-up)
                     hair (brown)
                     eyes (green)
                     unique-id mike)
          object (act type (atrans)
                      actor (human name (mike)
                                   relation (ipt type(family-rel)
                                                 stype (father)
                                                 of (human unique-id lynn))
                                   age (grown-up)
                                   hair (brown)
                                   eyes (green)
                                   unique-id mike)
                      object (p-obj type (toy)
                                    stype (play-doh) u
                                    unique-id play-doh.1)
                      to (human name (lynn) age (kid)
                               hair (blond) eyes (blue)
                               unique-id lynn))))


;;;mike wants to give lynn  play-doh
(def-cd play-doh-ga-1
          (goal actor (human name (mike)
                             relation (ipt type(family-rel)
                                           stype (father)
                                           of (human unique-id lynn))
                             age (grown-up)
                             hair (brown)
                             eyes (green)
                             unique-id mike)
                goal (act type (atrans)  unique-id atrans.5
                          actor (human name (mike)
                                       relation (ipt type(family-rel)
                                                     stype (father)
                                                     of (human unique-id lynn))
                                       age (grown-up)
                                       hair (brown)
                                       eyes (green)
                                       unique-id mike)
                          object (p-obj type (toy)
                                        stype (play-doh)
                                        unique-id play-doh.1)
                          to (human name (lynn) age (kid) hair (blond)
                                   eyes (blue) unique-id lynn))
                unique-id play-doh-ga.1))
```

```
;;;;mike gives lynn  play-doh
(def-cd play-doh-a-2
        (act type (atrans)  unique-id atrans.5
             actor (human name (mike)
                          relation (ipt type(family-rel)
                                        stype (father)
                                        of (human unique-id lynn))
                          age (grown-up)
                          hair (brown)
                          eyes (green)
                          unique-id mike)
             object (p-obj type (toy)
                     stype (play-doh)
                     unique-id play-doh.1)
             to (human name (lynn)
                 age (kid)
                 hair (blond)
                 eyes (blue)
                 unique-id lynn)))

;;;lynn gets the play-doh
(def-cd play-doh-r-1
        (goal-outcome type (success)
                      actor (human name (lynn) age (kid)
                                   hair (blond) eyes (blue)
                                   unique-id lynn)
                      goal (state type (poss-by) unique-id poss-by.5
                                  actor (human name (lynn) age (kid)
                                               hair (blond) eyes (blue)
                                               unique-id lynn)
                                  value (yes)
                                  object (p-obj type (toy) stype (play-doh)
                                               unique-id play-doh.1))
                      unique-id play-doh-r.1))


(def-role play-doh-1 plan play-doh-p-1)
(def-ilink play-doh-1 intended-by play-doh-p-1)
(def-ilink play-doh-p-1 intends play-doh-1)
(def-ilink play-doh-p-1 realized-by play-doh-a-1)
(def-ilink play-doh-a-1 realizes play-doh-p-1)
(def-ilink play-doh-a-1 motivates play-doh-ga-1)
(def-ilink play-doh-ga-1 motivated-by play-doh-a-1)
(def-ilink play-doh-a-2 achieves play-doh-1)
(def-ilink play-doh-1 achieved-by play-doh-a-2)
(def-ilink play-doh-a-2 achieves play-doh-ga-1)
(def-ilink play-doh-ga-1 achieved-by play-doh-a-2)
(def-ilink play-doh-1 outcome play-doh-r-1)
(def-ilink play-doh-r-1 outcome-of play-doh-1)
(def-role play-doh-1 outcome play-doh-r-1)
```

```
;karen wants to go to the zoo
(def-cd zoo-1
        (goal actor (human name (karen) age (kid) hair (blond)
                           eyes (blue) unique-id karen)
              goal (state type (location)
                          actor (human name (karen) age (kid) hair (blond)
                                       eyes (blue) unique-id karen)
                          value (yes)
                          object (p-obj type (location)
                                        stype (zoo) unique-id zoo.1))
              unique-id zoo.1))


;;;karen plans to asks mike
(def-cd zoo-p-1
   (plan actor (human name (karen) age (kid) hair (blond)
                      eyes (blue) unique-id karen)
         plan (act type (mtrans) unique-id mtrans.7
                   actor (human name (karen) age (kid) hair (blond)
                                eyes (blue) unique-id karen)
                   to (human name (mike)
                             relation (ipt type(family-rel)
                                           stype (father)
                                           of (human unique-id karen))
                             age (grown-up) hair (brown)
                             eyes (green) unique-id mike)
                   object (act type (ptrans)
                               actor (human name (mike)
                                            relation (ipt type(family-rel)
                                                          stype (father)
                                                          of (human
                                                              unique-id karen))
                                            age (grown-up) hair (brown)
                                            eyes (green) unique-id mike)
                               object (human name (karen)
                                             age (kid)
                                             hair (blond)
                                             eyes (blue)
                                             unique-id karen)
                               to (p-obj type (location)
                                         stype (zoo)
                                         unique-id zoo.1)))
         unique-id zoo-p.1))
```

```
;;;karen asks mike
(def-cd zoo-a-1
    (act type (mtrans) unique-id mtrans.7
         actor (human name (karen) age (kid) hair (blond)
                      eyes (blue) unique-id karen)
         to (human name (mike)
                   relation (ipt type(family-rel)
                                 stype (father)
                                 of (human unique-id karen))
                   age (grown-up) hair (brown)
                   eyes (green) unique-id mike)
         object (act type (ptrans)
                     actor (human name (mike)
                                  relation (ipt type(family-rel)
                                                stype (father)
                                                of (human unique-id karen))
                                  age (grown-up) hair (brown)
                                  eyes (green) unique-id mike)
                     object (human name (karen) age (kid) hair (blond)
                                   eyes (blue) unique-id karen)
                     to (p-obj type (location) stype (zoo)
                               unique-id zoo.1))))


;;;mike wants to take karen to the zoo
(def-cd zoo-ga-1
    (goal actor (human name (mike)
                       relation (ipt type(family-rel)
                                     stype (father)
                                     of (human unique-id karen))
                       age (grown-up) hair (brown)
                       eyes (green) unique-id mike)
          goal (act type (ptrans)
                    actor (human name (mike)
                                 relation (ipt type(family-rel)
                                               stype (father)
                                               of (human unique-id karen))
                                 age (grown-up) hair (brown)
                                 eyes (green) unique-id mike)
                    object (human name (karen) age (kid) hair (blond)
                                  eyes (blue) unique-id karen)
                    to (p-obj type (location)
                              stype (zoo) unique-id zoo.1))
          unique-id zoo-ga.1))


;;;;mike takes karen to the zoo
(def-cd zoo-a-2
     (act type (ptrans)
          actor (human name (mike)
                       relation (ipt type(family-rel)
                                     stype (father)
                                     of (human unique-id karen))
                       age (grown-up) hair (brown)
                       eyes (green) unique-id mike)
          object (human name (karen) age (kid) hair (blond)
                        eyes (blue) unique-id karen)
          to (p-obj type (location) stype (zoo) unique-id zoo.1)
          unique-id zoo-a.2))
```

```
;;;karen goes to the zoo
(def-cd zoo-r-1
    (goal-outcome type (success)
                  actor (human name (karen) age (kid) hair (blond)
                                eyes (blue) unique-id karen)
                  goal (state type (location)
                              actor (human name (karen)
                                           age (kid) hair (blond)
                                           eyes (blue) unique-id karen)
                              value (yes)
                              object (p-obj type (location) stype (zoo)
                                            unique-id zoo.1))
                  unique-id zoo-r.1))

(def-role zoo-1 plan zoo-p-1)
(def-ilink zoo-1 intended-by zoo-p-1)
(def-ilink zoo-p-1 intends zoo-1)
(def-ilink zoo-p-1 realized-by zoo-a-1)
(def-ilink zoo-a-1 realizes zoo-p-1)
(def-ilink zoo-a-1 motivates zoo-ga-1)
(def-ilink zoo-ga-1 motivated-by zoo-a-1)
(def-ilink zoo-a-2 achieves zoo-1)
(def-ilink zoo-1 achieved-by zoo-a-2)
(def-ilink zoo-a-2 achieves zoo-ga-1)
(def-ilink zoo-ga-1 achieved-by zoo-a-2)
(def-ilink zoo-1 outcome zoo-r-1)
(def-ilink zoo-r-1 outcome-of zoo-1)
(def-role zoo-1 outcome zoo-r-1)

;;karen wants to open the refrigerator
(def-cd refrigerator-1
    (goal actor (human name (karen) age (kid) hair (blond)
                        eyes (blue) unique-id karen)
          goal (state object (p-obj type (refrigerator)
                                     color (white)
                                     unique-id ref.001)
                      type (open)
                      value (yes))
          plan (act type (propel)
                    actor (human  unique-id karen)
                    object  (component type (door)
                                       of (p-obj unique-id ref.001))

                   )
          outcome  (goal-outcome type (failure)
                                 actor (human  unique-id karen)
                                 goal (state object (p-obj unique-id ref.001)
                                            type (open)
                                            value (yes)))

          unique-id refrigerator.1))
```

```
;;;karen wants pizza
(def-cd pizza-1
        (goal actor (human name (karen) age (kid) hair (blond)
                           eyes (blue) unique-id karen)
               goal (state type (poss-by) unique-id poss-by.002
                           actor (human name (karen) age (kid) hair (blond)
                                        eyes (blue) unique-id karen)
                           value (yes)
                           object (p-obj type (food) stype (pizza)
                                         unique-id pizza.001))
               unique-id pizza.1))

;;;karen plans to asks mike
(def-cd pizza-p-1
     (plan actor (human name (karen) age (kid) hair (blond)
                        eyes (blue) unique-id karen)
           plan (act type (mtrans) unique-id mtrans.002
                     actor (human name (karen) age (kid) hair (blond)
                                  eyes (blue) unique-id karen)
                     to (human name (mike)
                               relation (ipt type(family-rel)
                                             stype (father)
                                             of (human unique-id karen))
                               age (grown-up) hair (brown)
                               eyes (green) unique-id mike)
                     object (act type (atrans)
                                 actor (human name (mike)
                                              relation
                                                (ipt type(family-rel)
                                                     stype (father)
                                                     of (human
                                                           unique-id karen))
                                              age (grown-up) hair (brown)
                                              eyes (green) unique-id mike)
                                 object (p-obj type (food) stype (pizza)
                                               unique-id pizza.001)
                                 to (human name (karen)
                                           age (kid) hair (blond)
                                           eyes (blue) unique-id karen)))
           unique-id pizza-p.1))
```

```
;;;karen asks mike
(def-cd pizza-a-1
  (act type (mtrans) unique-id mtrans.002
      actor (human name (karen) age (kid) hair (blond)
                      eyes (blue) unique-id karen)
      to (human name (mike)
                  relation (ipt type(family-rel)
                                stype (father)
                                of (human unique-id karen))
                  age (grown-up) hair (brown)
                  eyes (green) unique-id mike)
      object (act type (atrans)
                  actor (human name (mike)
                              relation (ipt type(family-rel)
                                            stype (father)
                                            of (human unique-id karen))
                              age (grown-up)
                              hair (brown)
                              eyes (green) unique-id mike)
                  object (p-obj type (food) stype (pizza)
                              unique-id pizza.001)
                  to (human name (karen) age (kid) hair (blond)
                          eyes (blue) unique-id karen)))))


;;;mike wants to give karen pizza
(def-cd pizza-ga-1
    (goal actor (human name (mike)
                        relation (ipt type(family-rel)
                                      stype (father)
                                      of (human unique-id karen))
                    age (grown-up)
                    hair (brown)
                    eyes (green) unique-id mike)
        goal (act type (atrans) unique-id atrans.002
                  actor (human name (mike)
                              relation (ipt type(family-rel)
                                            stype (father)
                                            of (human unique-id karen))
                              age (grown-up)
                              hair (brown)
                              eyes (green) unique-id mike)
                  object (p-obj type (food) stype (pizza)
                              unique-id pizza.001)
                  to (human name (karen) age (kid) hair (blond)
                          eyes (blue) unique-id karen))
        unique-id pizza-ga.1))
```

```
;;;;mike gives karen pizza
(def-cd pizza-a-2
       (act type (atrans)
              unique-id atrans.002
              actor (human name (mike)
                              relation (ipt type(family-rel)
                                            stype (father)
                                            of (human unique-id karen))
                              age (grown-up)
                              hair (brown)
                              eyes (green) unique-id mike)
              object (p-obj type (food) stype (pizza)
                            unique-id pizza.001)
              to (human name (karen) age (kid) hair (blond)
                        eyes (blue) unique-id karen)
       ))


;;;karen gets the pizza
(def-cd pizza-r-1
       (goal-outcome type (success)
                     actor (human name (karen) age (kid) hair (blond)
                                  eyes (blue) unique-id karen)
                     goal (state type (poss-by)  unique-id poss-by.002
                                 actor (human name (karen)
                                              age (kid) hair (blond)
                                              eyes (blue) unique-id karen)
                                 value (yes)
                                 object (p-obj type (food) stype (pizza)
                                              unique-id pizza.001))
                     unique-id pizza-r.1))


(def-role pizza-1 plan pizza-p-1)
(def-ilink pizza-1 intended-by pizza-p-1)
(def-ilink pizza-p-1 intends pizza-1)
(def-ilink pizza-p-1 realized-by pizza-a-1)
(def-ilink pizza-a-1 realizes pizza-p-1)
(def-ilink pizza-a-1 motivates pizza-ga-1)
(def-ilink pizza-ga-1 motivated-by pizza-a-1)
(def-ilink pizza-a-2 achieves pizza-1)
(def-ilink pizza-1 achieved-by pizza-a-2)
(def-ilink pizza-a-2 achieves pizza-ga-1)
(def-ilink pizza-ga-1 achieved-by pizza-a-2)
(def-ilink pizza-1 outcome pizza-r-1)
(def-ilink pizza-r-1 outcome-of pizza-1)
(def-role pizza-1 outcome pizza-r-1)


;;;karen wants a cookie
(def-cd cookie-1
       (goal actor (human name (karen) age (kid) hair (blond)
                          eyes (blue) unique-id karen)
             goal (state type (poss-by) unique-id poss-by.102
                         actor (human name (karen) age (kid) hair (blond)
                                      eyes (blue) unique-id karen)
                         value (yes)
                         object (p-obj type (food) stype (cookie)
                                      unique-id cookie.001))
             unique-id cookie.1))
```

```
;;;karen plans to asks lynn
(def-cd cookie-p-1
    (plan actor (human name (karen) age (kid) hair (blond)
                       eyes (blue) unique-id karen)
          plan (act type (mtrans) unique-id mtrans.102
                     actor (human name (karen) age (kid) hair (blond)
                                  eyes (blue) unique-id karen)
                     to (human name (lynn)
                              relation (ipt type(family-rel)
                                             stype (sister)
                                             of (human unique-id karen))
                              age (kid) hair (blond)
                              eyes (blue) unique-id lynn)
                     object (act type (atrans)
                                  actor (human name (lynn)
                                               relation
                                                 (ipt type(family-rel)
                                                      stype (sister)
                                                      of (human
                                                             unique-id karen))
                                               age (kid) hair (blond)
                                               eyes (blue) unique-id lynn)
                                  object (p-obj type (food) stype (cookie)
                                                unique-id cookie.001)
                                  to (human name (karen) age (kid) hair (blond)
                                           eyes (blue) unique-id karen)))
          unique-id cookie-p.1))


;;;karen asks lynn
(def-cd cookie-a-1
    (act type (mtrans) unique-id mtrans.102
         actor (human name (karen) age (kid) hair (blond)
                      eyes (blue) unique-id karen)
         to (human name (lynn)
                   relation (ipt type(family-rel)
                                  stype (sister)
                                  of (human unique-id karen))
                   age (kid) hair (blond)
                   eyes (blue) unique-id lynn)
         object (act type (atrans)
                     actor (human name (lynn)
                                  relation (ipt type(family-rel)
                                                 stype (sister)
                                                 of (human unique-id karen))
                                  age (kid)
                                  hair (blond)
                                  eyes (blue) unique-id lynn)
                     object (p-obj type (food) stype (cookie)
                                   unique-id cookie.001)
                     to (human name (karen) age (kid) hair (blond)
                              eyes (blue) unique-id karen))))
```

```
;;;lynn wants to give karen a cookie
(def-cd cookie-ga-1
     (goal actor (human name (lynn)

                          relation (ipt type(family-rel)
                                        stype (sister)
                                        of (human unique-id karen))
                          age (kid)
                          hair (blond)
                          eyes (blue) unique-id lynn)
          goal (act type (atrans) unique-id atrans.102
                    actor (human name (lynn)

                                     relation (ipt type(family-rel)
                                                   stype (sister)
                                                   of (human unique-id karen))
                                     age (kid)
                                     hair (blond)
                                     eyes (blue) unique-id lynn)
                          object (p-obj type (food) stype (cookie)
                                  unique-id cookie.001)
                          to (human name (karen) age (kid) hair (blond)
                                    eyes (blue) unique-id karen))
                 unique-id cookie-ga.1))


;;;;lynn gives karen a cookie
(def-cd cookie-a-2
        (act type (atrans)
             unique-id atrans.102
             actor (human name (lynn)
                          relation (ipt type(family-rel)
                                        stype (sister)
                                        of (human unique-id karen))
                          age (kid)
                          hair (blond)
                          eyes (blue) unique-id lynn)
             object (p-obj type (food) stype (cookie)
                     unique-id cookie.001)
             to (human name (karen) age (kid) hair (blond)
                       eyes (blue) unique-id karen)
        ))


;;;karen gets the cookie
(def-cd cookie-r-1
        (goal-outcome type (success)
                      actor (human name (karen)
                             age (kid) hair (blond)
                             eyes (blue) unique-id karen)
                      goal (state type (poss-by)  unique-id poss-by.102
                                  actor (human name (karen)
                                         age (kid) hair (blond)
                                         eyes (blue) unique-id karen)
                                  value (yes)
                                  object (p-obj type (food) stype (cookie)
                                          unique-id cookie.001))
                      unique-id cookie-r.1))
```

```
(def-role cookie-1 plan cookie-p-1)
(def-ilink cookie-1 intended-by cookie-p-1)
(def-ilink cookie-p-1 intends cookie-1)
(def-ilink cookie-p-1 realized-by cookie-a-1)
(def-ilink cookie-a-1 realizes cookie-p-1)
(def-ilink cookie-a-1 motivates cookie-ga-1)
(def-ilink cookie-ga-1 motivated-by cookie-a-1)
(def-ilink cookie-a-2 achieves cookie-1)
(def-ilink cookie-1 achieved-by cookie-a-2)
(def-ilink cookie-a-2 achieves cookie-ga-1)
(def-ilink cookie-ga-1 achieved-by cookie-a-2)
(def-ilink cookie-1 outcome cookie-r-1)
(def-ilink cookie-r-1 outcome-of cookie-1)
(def-role cookie-1 outcome cookie-r-1)
```

A.2. File: genrules.lisp

This file contains the definitions of three generalization rules. These rules
can be used by the theory-driven learning program to postulate a new
explanation or by the explanation-based learning program to propose an
explanation to be verified by specific world knowledge represented as inference
rules indexed in memory.

```
;;; -*- Mode: LISP; Syntax: common-lisp; Package: cl-user; Base: 10 -*-
;;;If an action on an object always precedes a state change
;;;for the object, then the action results in the state change.
(def-gen-rule gen-result
  (act type (*var* act-type)
       object (*var* object))
  after
  (state type (*var* state-type)
         value (*var* value)
         object (*var* object))
  (((*var* *from*) result (*var* *to*))
   ((*var* *from*) after (*var* *to*))))


;;;If similar actions performed on some objects have different results,
;;;and the objects have different features, the differing features of
;;;the object are responsible for the different result.
(def-gen-rule gen-result-object-difference
  (act type (*var* act-type)
       object (*var* object))
  after
  (state type (*var* state-type)
         value (*var* value)
         object (*var* object))
  (((*var* *from*) result (*var* *to*))
   ((*var* *from*) after (*var* *to*)))
  object)
```

```
;;;If an initial action (?act-1) on an object is always present
;;;when a subsequent action (?act-2) precedes a state change (?state-2)
;;;for the object, then  ?act-1 results in a state (?state-1) that
;;;enables ?act-2 to result in the state change (?state-2).
;;;--note that the antecedent has a "before" role.
;;;this simulates the effect of a historical generalization rule
;;;because the pattern matcher can follow temporal or intentional links
(def-gen-rule prev-action
  (act type (*var* atype-2)
       object  (*var* obj)
       before (*var* act-1 (act type (*var* atype-1)
                                 object (*var* obj))))
  after
  (state type (*var* ptype)
         value (*var* value)
         object (*var* obj))
  (
   ((*var* *from*) result (*var* *to*))
   ((*var* act-1) result (*var* state-1 (state object (*var* obj))))
   ((*var* state-1) enables (*var* *from*))
   ((*var* *from*) after (*var* *to*))
   ((*var* act-1) after (*var* *from*))

  )
  )
```

A.3. File: glass.lisp

This file contains three examples of a cup falling. These are used as input to the TDL module.

```
;;; -*- Mode: LISP; Syntax: common-lisp; Package: cl-user; Base: 10 -*-
;;lynn dropped a clear glass cup,
(def-cd glass-1-a
        (act type (propel)
             actor (human name (lynn) age (kid)
                          hair (blond) eyes (blue) unique-id lynn)
             object (p-obj type (cup) color (clear)
                           composition (glass)
                           UNIQUE-ID glass.1)
             to (p-obj type (floor) location (kitchen))))
;;the cup breaks
(def-cd glass-1-r
        (state type (broken)
               object (p-obj type (cup) color (clear)
                             composition (glass)
                             UNIQUE-ID glass.1)
               value (yes)))
(def-ilink glass-1-a after glass-1-r)
(def-ilink glass-1-r before glass-1-a)
```

```
;lynn drops a red plastic glass-- nothing happened
(def-cd glass-2-a
        (act type (propel)
             actor (human name (lynn) age (kid)
                          hair (blond) eyes (blue) unique-id lynn)
             object (p-obj type (cup) color (red)
                          composition (plastic)
                          UNIQUE-ID glass.2)
             to (p-obj type (floor) location (kitchen))))

;lynn drops a red glass cup
(def-cd glass-3-a
        (act type (propel)
             actor (human name (lynn) age (kid)
                          hair (blond) eyes (blue) unique-id lynn)
             object (p-obj type (cup) color (red)
                          composition (glass)
                          UNIQUE-ID glass.3)
             to (p-obj type (floor) location (kitchen))))
;;the cup breaks
(def-cd glass-3-r
        (state type (broken)
             object (p-obj type (cup) color (red)
                          composition (glass)
                          UNIQUE-ID glass.3)
                 value (yes)))
(def-ilink glass-3-a after glass-3-r)
(def-ilink glass-3-r before glass-3-a)


(defvar *all-tdls* (list glass-1-a glass-2-a glass-3-a))
```

A.4. File: rules.lisp

```
;;; -*- Mode: LISP; Syntax: common-lisp; Package: cl-user; Base: 10 -*-
;;;sell results in possessing
(def-rule sell-->possess
          (ACT type (SELL)
               TO (*var* x)
               OBJECT (*var* y)
               mode (yes))
  result
  (STATE TYPE (POSSESS)
         OBJECT (*var* y )
         VALUE (YES)
         ACTOR (*var* x))
  )
```

```
;;;refusing to sell results in an increased demand
(def-rule refuse-to-sell-->demand-increase
            (ACT type (SELL)
                 actor (polity exports (*var* y)
                        )
                 TO (*var* x (polity imports (*var* y)))
                 OBJECT (*var* y (commodity))
                 mode (neg))
  result
   (STATE TYPE (demand-increase)
          actor (*var* x)
          VALUE (YES)
          OBJECT (*var* y)))

;;;An increased demand allows a provide to sell at a greater than market rate
(def-rule demand-increase-->price-increase
            (STATE TYPE (demand-increase)
                   VALUE (YES)
                   actor (*var* x (polity economic-health (strong)))
                   OBJECT (*var* y))
  enables
   (ACT type (SELL)
        actor (polity exports (*var* y)
                       business-relationship (*var* x))
        TO (*var* x)
        OBJECT (*var* y)
        price (money value (>market))
        mode (yes)))
```

A.5. File: coerce.lisp

This file contains the definition of a simple coercion schema. This schema is specialized to create an economic sanction schema.

```
;;; -*- Mode: LISP; Syntax: common-lisp; Package: cl-user; Base: 10 -*-
(def-cd the-goal (goal actor (*var* actor)
                       goal (*var* demand)))
(def-cd the-plan (plan actor (*var* actor)))
(def-cd the-threat ((*var* threat)))
(def-cd the-result ((*var* result)))
(def-cd the-response ((*var* response)))
(def-schema coerce (coerce)
  (coerce
    actor (*var* actor)
    object (*var* object)
    target (*var* target)
    demand (*var* demand)
    threat (*var* threat)
    response (*var* response)
    result (*var* result))
  (list the-goal the-plan the-threat the-response the-result)
  )
```

```
(setf (schema-outcome-slot (get 'coerce 'schema)) 'result)
(def-ilink the-plan intends the-goal)
(def-ilink the-goal intended-by the-plan)
(def-ilink the-threat  realizes the-plan)
(def-ilink the-plan realized-by the-threat)
(def-ilink the-threat after the-response)
(def-ilink the-response before the-threat)
(def-ilink the-response after the-result)
(def-ilink the-result before the-response)
```

A.6. File: sanctions.lisp

This file contains the CD representation of Economic-Sanction-1 which is repeated below. This example is generalized by the EBL program.

Economic-Sanction-1

In 1983, Australia refused to sell uranium to France, unless France ceased nuclear testing in the South Pacific. France paid a higher price to buy uranium from South Africa and continued nuclear testing.

```lisp
;;; -*- Mode: LISP; Syntax: common-lisp; Package: cl-user; Base: 10 -*-
(def-cd sanction-83-1
  (coerce actor (polity type (country) name (australia)
                        language (english)
                        location (southern-hemisphere)
                        government (democracy)
                        economic-health (strong)
                        continent (australia)
                        exports (*role* object)
                        imports (oil))
          object (commodity type (uranium))
          target (polity type (country) name (FRANCE)
                         language (FRENCH)
                         government (democracy)
                         economic-health (strong)
                         continent (europe)
                         location (northern-hemisphere)
                         imports (*role* object)
                         exports (commodity type (wine)))
          demand (act type (explode)
                      actor (*role* target)
                      object (weapons type (nuclear))
                      location (southern-hemisphere)
                      mode (neg))
          threat (act type (sell)
                      actor (*role* actor)
                      object (*role* object)
                      to (*role* target)
                      mode (neg))
          response (act type (sell)
                        actor (polity type (country) name (south-africa)
                                      language (english)
                                      location (southern-hemisphere)
                                      business-relationship (*role* target)
                                      continent (africa)
                                      exports (*role* object)
                                      imports (oil))
                        object (*role* object)
                        price (money dollars (3000000) value (>market))
                        to (*role* target))
          result (state type (possess)
                        actor (*role* target)
                        value (yes)
                        object (*role* object)))))
```

Appendix B
Program Traces

This appendix contains annotated traces of OCCAM-LITE. These traces illustrate the similarity-based, theory-driven and explanation-based learning components. The traces are edited slightly to conserve space. The only changes from the actual traces are the deletion of features from objects when the object is printed more than once.

B.1. Similarity-Based Learning Trace

The similarity-based learning module is presented with the Conceptual Dependency representation of five goals and their resolution. The program creates and refines a **delta-agency** schema from four of these examples. To run OCCAM-LITE on these examples the following command is typed:

```
(mapc #'occam-lite *all-sbls*)
```

The program processes the examples one at a time. First, **zoo-1** is added to memory. **zoo-1** describes a situation in which Karen wants to go to the zoo, so she asks her father, Mike, and he takes her.

```
------------------------------------------------------------------
Looking for most specific schema for <ZOO-1 GOAL>
(GOAL ACTOR (HUMAN NAME (KAREN)
                  AGE (KID)
                  HAIR (BLOND)
                  EYES (BLUE)
                  UNIQUE-ID KAREN)
       GOAL (STATE TYPE (LOCATION)
                  ACTOR (HUMAN NAME (KAREN)
                               ... ...)
                  VALUE (YES)
                  OBJECT (P-OBJ TYPE (LOCATION)
                               STYPE (ZOO)
                               UNIQUE-ID ZOO.1))
       UNIQUE-ID ZOO.1
       PLAN (PLAN ACTOR (HUMAN NAME (KAREN)
                               ... ...)
                  PLAN (ACT TYPE (MTRANS)
                             UNIQUE-ID MTRANS.7
                             ACTOR (HUMAN NAME (KAREN)
                                          ... ...)
                             TO (HUMAN NAME (MIKE)
                                       RELATION
                                          (IPT TYPE (FAMILY-REL)
                                               STYPE (FATHER)
                                               OF (HUMAN UNIQUE-ID KAREN))
                                       AGE (GROWN-UP)
                                       HAIR (BROWN)
                                       EYES (GREEN)
                                       UNIQUE-ID MIKE)
                             OBJECT (ACT TYPE (PTRANS)
                                          ACTOR (HUMAN NAME (MIKE)
                                                       ... ...)
                                          OBJECT (HUMAN NAME (KAREN)
                                                       ... ...)
                                          TO (P-OBJ TYPE (LOCATION)
                                                     STYPE (ZOO)
                                                     UNIQUE-ID ZOO.1)))
                  UNIQUE-ID ZOO-P.1)
       OUTCOME (GOAL-OUTCOME TYPE (SUCCESS)
                  ACTOR (HUMAN NAME (KAREN)
                               ... ...)
                  GOAL (STATE TYPE (LOCATION)
                             ACTOR (HUMAN NAME (KAREN)
                                          ... ...)
                             VALUE (YES)
                             OBJECT (P-OBJ TYPE (LOCATION)
                                          STYPE (ZOO)
                                          UNIQUE-ID ZOO.1))
                  UNIQUE-ID ZOO-R.1))
Found most specific schema for event: <ZOO-1 GOAL>
Event is accounted for by:
(GOAL)
Attempting explanation-based learning for new event.
Attempting theory driven learning for new event.
Attempting similarity-based learning for new event.
Indexing event <ZOO-1 GOAL> under schema <GOAL <CD-4422 GOAL>>.
```

Explanation-based learning does not apply because there are no rules that would explain why Mike took Karen to the zoo. Theory-driven learning does not apply because this event does not correspond to any known causal pattern. Similarity-based learning does not apply because there are not any similar examples in memory indexed under the goal schema. The event is simply indexed under the goal schema.

The next example is `refrigerator-1`, which describes a situation in which Karen wants to open the refrigerator, so she pulls on the door but it doesn't open.

```
--------------------------------------------------------------------
Looking for most specific schema for <REFRIGERATOR-1 GOAL>
(GOAL ACTOR (HUMAN NAME (KAREN)
                        ... ...)
        GOAL (STATE OBJECT (P-OBJ TYPE (REFRIGERATOR)
                                  COLOR (WHITE)
                                  UNIQUE-ID REF.001)
                    TYPE (OPEN)
                    VALUE (YES))
        PLAN (ACT TYPE (PROPEL)
                 ACTOR (HUMAN UNIQUE-ID KAREN)
                 OBJECT (COMPONENT TYPE (DOOR)
                                   OF (P-OBJ UNIQUE-ID REF.001)))
        OUTCOME (GOAL-OUTCOME TYPE (FAILURE)
                              ACTOR (HUMAN UNIQUE-ID KAREN)
                              GOAL (STATE OBJECT (P-OBJ UNIQUE-ID REF.001)
                                                 TYPE (OPEN)
                                                 VALUE (YES)))
        UNIQUE-ID REFRIGERATOR.1)
Found most specific schema for event: <REFRIGERATOR-1 GOAL>
Event is accounted for by:
(GOAL)
Attempting explanation-based learning for new event.
Attempting theory driven learning for new event.
Attempting similarity-based learning for new event.
Indexing event <REFRIGERATOR-1 GOAL> under schema <GOAL <CD-4422 GOAL>>.
```

This event is also indexed in memory under the goal schema. Similarity-based learning is not appropriate because there are too few events in memory under the goal schema.

The next event is `play-doh-1` in which Lynn wants some Play-doh, so she asks her father Mike to get her some and he does.

```
-----------------------------------------------------------------
Looking for most specific schema for <PLAY-DOH-1 GOAL>
(GOAL ACTOR (HUMAN NAME (LYNN)
                   AGE (KID)
                   HAIR (BLOND)
                   EYES (BLUE)
                   UNIQUE-ID LYNN)
      GOAL (STATE TYPE (POSS-BY)
                   UNIQUE-ID POSS-BY.5
                   ACTOR (HUMAN NAME (LYNN)
                               ... ...)
                   VALUE (YES)
                   OBJECT (P-OBJ TYPE (TOY)
                                 STYPE (PLAY-DOH)
                                 UNIQUE-ID PLAY-DOH.1))
      UNIQUE-ID PLAY-DOH.1
      PLAN (PLAN ACTOR (HUMAN NAME (LYNN)
                   ... ...)
            PLAN (ACT TYPE (MTRANS)
                      UNIQUE-ID MTRANS.5
                      ACTOR (HUMAN NAME (LYNN)
                                  ... ...)
                      TO (HUMAN NAME (MIKE)
                              ... ...)
                      OBJECT (ACT TYPE (ATRANS)
                                  ACTOR (HUMAN NAME (MIKE)
                                              ... ...)
                                  OBJECT (P-OBJ TYPE (TOY)
                                               ... ...)
                                  TO (HUMAN NAME (LYNN)
                                          ... ...)))
                  UNIQUE-ID PLAY-DOH-P.1)
      OUTCOME (GOAL-OUTCOME TYPE (SUCCESS)
                      ACTOR (HUMAN NAME (LYNN)
                                  ... ...)
                      GOAL (STATE TYPE (POSS-BY)
                                  ... ...)
                      UNIQUE-ID PLAY-DOH-R.1))
Found most specific schema for event: <PLAY-DOH-1 GOAL>
Event is accounted for by:
(GOAL)
Attempting explanation-based learning for new event.
Attempting theory driven learning for new event.
Attempting similarity-based learning for new event.
Indexing event <PLAY-DOH-1 GOAL> under schema <GOAL <CD-4422 GOAL>>.
```

This event is also indexed in memory under the goal schema. Similarity-based learning is not appropriate. There are now enough events indexed under the goal schema for similarity-based learning to apply, but these particular events do not share a sufficient number of features to form a new schema.

A fourth event is now added to memory. `pizza-1` describes a situation in which Karen wants some pizza, so she asks Mike for some and he gives it to her.

```
-----------------------------------------------------------------
Looking for most specific schema for <PIZZA-1 GOAL>
(GOAL ACTOR (HUMAN NAME (KAREN)
                        ... ...)
      GOAL (STATE TYPE (POSS-BY)
                        UNIQUE-ID POSS-BY.002
                        ACTOR (HUMAN NAME (KAREN)
                                        ... ...)
                        VALUE (YES)
                        OBJECT (P-OBJ TYPE (FOOD)
                                       STYPE (PIZZA)
                                       UNIQUE-ID PIZZA.001))
      UNIQUE-ID PIZZA.1
      PLAN (PLAN ACTOR (HUMAN NAME (KAREN)
                              ... ...)
                 PLAN (ACT TYPE (MTRANS)
                            UNIQUE-ID MTRANS.002
                            ACTOR (HUMAN NAME (KAREN)
                                          ... ...)
                            TO (HUMAN NAME (MIKE)
                                    ... ...)
                            OBJECT (ACT TYPE (ATRANS)
                                        ACTOR (HUMAN NAME (MIKE)
                                                      ... ...)
                                        OBJECT (P-OBJ TYPE (FOOD)
                                                       ... ...)
                                        TO (HUMAN NAME (KAREN)
                                                ... ...)))
                 UNIQUE-ID PIZZA-P.1)
      OUTCOME (GOAL-OUTCOME TYPE (SUCCESS)
                            ACTOR (HUMAN NAME (KAREN)
                                          ... ...)
                            GOAL (STATE TYPE (POSS-BY)
                                        ... ...)
                            UNIQUE-ID PIZZA-R.1))
Found most specific schema for event: <PIZZA-1 GOAL>
Event is accounted for by:
(GOAL)
Attempting explanation-based learning for new event.
Attempting theory driven learning for new event.
Attempting similarity-based learning for new event.
Retrieved cluster of similar events.
(<PIZZA-1 GOAL> <ZOO-1 GOAL> <PLAY-DOH-1 GOAL>)
```

There are now enough similarities between a large enough group of events for a new schema to be created. The similarities between pizza-1, zoo-1 and play-doh-1 are found and a new schema is formed which specializes the goal schema.

```
Indexing event <PIZZA-1 GOAL> under schema <SCHEMA-6072 <CD-5875 GOAL>>.
Indexing event <ZOO-1 GOAL> under schema <SCHEMA-6072 <CD-5875 GOAL>>.
Indexing event <PLAY-DOH-1 GOAL> under schema <SCHEMA-6072 <CD-5875 GOAL>>.
```

schema-6072 is the new specialization of the goal schema. Its generalized event is given below:

```
Creating new specialization:
(GOAL ACTOR (HUMAN AGE (KID)
                  HAIR (BLOND)
                  EYES (BLUE))
      GOAL (STATE ACTOR (HUMAN AGE (KID)
                              ... ...)
                  VALUE (YES)
                  OBJECT (P-OBJ))
      PLAN (PLAN ACTOR (HUMAN AGE (KID)
                              ... ...)
              PLAN (ACT TYPE (MTRANS)
                      ACTOR (HUMAN AGE (KID)
                                  ... ...)
                      TO (HUMAN NAME (MIKE)
                              RELATION (IPT TYPE (FAMILY-REL)
                                            STYPE (FATHER)
                                            OF (HUMAN))
                          AGE (GROWN-UP)
                          HAIR (BROWN)
                          EYES (GREEN))
                      OBJECT (ACT ACTOR (HUMAN NAME (MIKE)
                                          ... ...))))
      OUTCOME (GOAL-OUTCOME TYPE (SUCCESS)
                  ACTOR (HUMAN AGE (KID)
                              ... ...)
                  GOAL (STATE ACTOR (HUMAN AGE (KID)
                                      ... ...)
                          VALUE (YES)
                          OBJECT (P-OBJ))))
```

This generalization indicates that when a child with blue eyes and blond hair wants something and asks her father Mike who has brown hair and green eyes, the child's goal will succeed. Obviously, this generalization is not correct, but it is a reasonable summary of the examples encountered so far.

Because this generalization describes a complex situation that contains many intentional links, a macro schema will also be formed:

```
Creating a macro schema
Creating new schema called DELTA-AGENCY.
```

The name for a macro-schema and the roles can be specified by the user. The program will next create the roles of delta-agency by finding those components that occur more than ones in the generalized goal configuration.

```
Creating new role called THE-PLAN.
(PLAN ACTOR (HUMAN AGE (KID)
                   HAIR (BLOND)
                   EYES (BLUE))
     PLAN (ACT TYPE (MTRANS)
               ACTOR (HUMAN AGE (KID)
                       ... ...)
               TO (HUMAN NAME (MIKE)
                       RELATION (IPT TYPE (FAMILY-REL)
                                 STYPE (FATHER)
                                 OF (HUMAN))
                       AGE (GROWN-UP)
                       HAIR (BROWN)
                       EYES (GREEN))
               OBJECT (ACT ACTOR (HUMAN NAME (MIKE
                                  ... ...))))
Creating new role called ASK.
(ACT TYPE (MTRANS)
     ACTOR (HUMAN AGE (KID)
             ... ...)
     TO (HUMAN NAME (MIKE)
             ... ...)
     OBJECT (ACT ACTOR (HUMAN NAME (MIKE)
                        ... ...)))
Creating new role called SUB-GOAL.
(GOAL ACTOR (HUMAN NAME (MIKE)
             ... ...)
     GOAL (ACT ACTOR (HUMAN NAME (MIKE)
                      ... ...)))
Creating new role called SUB-ACT.
(ACT ACTOR (HUMAN NAME (MIKE)
            ... ...))
Creating new role called OUTCOME.
(GOAL-OUTCOME TYPE (SUCCESS)
               ACTOR (HUMAN AGE (KID)
                       ... ...)
               GOAL (STATE ACTOR (HUMAN AGE (KID)
                           ... ...)
                           VALUE (YES)
                           OBJECT (P-OBJ)))
Creating new role called GOAL.
(GOAL ACTOR (HUMAN AGE (KID)
             ... ...)
     GOAL (STATE ACTOR (HUMAN AGE (KID)
                 ... ...)
                 VALUE (YES)
                 OBJECT (P-OBJ))
     PLAN (PLAN ACTOR (HUMAN AGE (KID)
                 ... ...)
                 PLAN (ACT TYPE (MTRANS)
                       ... ...))
     OUTCOME (GOAL-OUTCOME TYPE (SUCCESS)
                 ... ...))
Creating new role called HELPER.
(HUMAN NAME (MIKE)
     RELATION (IPT TYPE (FAMILY-REL)
                   STYPE (FATHER)
                   OF (HUMAN))
     AGE (GROWN-UP)
     HAIR (BROWN)
     EYES (GREEN))
```

```
Creating new role called THE-ACTOR.
(HUMAN)
Creating new role called THE-OBJ.
(P-OBJ)
```

Once the macro-schema is created, the events are re-represented and indexed under the macro-schema. A representational transfer is created to change between the two representations.

```
Indexing event <CD-30 DELTA-AGENCY> under schema
 <SCHEMA-77 <CD-6191 DELTA-AGENCY>>.
Indexing event <CD-38 DELTA-AGENCY> under schema
 <SCHEMA-77 <CD-6191 DELTA-AGENCY>>.
Indexing event <CD-76 DELTA-AGENCY> under schema
 <SCHEMA-77 <CD-6191 DELTA-AGENCY>>.
Creating representational transfer.
(*VAR* GOAL(GOAL ACTOR (*VAR* THE-ACTOR)
                 GOAL (STATE ACTOR (*VAR* THE-ACTOR)
                             OBJECT (*VAR* THE-OBJ))
                 PLAN (*VAR* THE-PLAN (PLAN ACTOR (*VAR* THE-ACTOR)
                                            PLAN (*VAR* ASK
                                                      (ACT TO(*VAR* HELPER)
                                                         ... ...))))
                 OUTCOME (*VAR* OUTCOME (GOAL-OUTCOME ... ...)))))
```

The above pattern can be matched against an example represented in terms of CD goals and plans. It recognizes instances of **delta-agency** and binds several variables. The **delta-agency** representation can be formed by instantiating the following pattern.

```
(DELTA-AGENCY GOAL (*VAR* GOAL)
              OUTCOME (*VAR* OUTCOME)
              SUB-ACT (ACT ACTOR (*VAR* HELPER))
              SUB-GOAL (GOAL ACTOR (*VAR* HELPER)
                             GOAL (ACT ACTOR (*VAR* HELPER)))
              ASK (*VAR* ASK)
              THE-PLAN (*VAR* THE-PLAN)
              HELPER (*VAR* HELPER)
              THE-ACTOR (*VAR* THE-ACTOR)
              THE-OBJ (*VAR* THE-OBJ))
```

The generalized event for the macro schema is created next.

```
Creating macro schema.
(DELTA-AGENCY GOAL (GOAL ACTOR (*ROLE* THE-ACTOR)
                        GOAL (STATE ACTOR (*ROLE* THE-ACTOR)
                                    VALUE (YES)
                                    OBJECT (*ROLE* THE-OBJ))
                  PLAN (*ROLE* THE-PLAN)
                  OUTCOME (*ROLE* OUTCOME))
          OUTCOME (GOAL-OUTCOME TYPE (SUCCESS)
                              ACTOR (*ROLE* THE-ACTOR)
                              GOAL (STATE ACTOR (*ROLE* THE-ACTOR)
                                          VALUE (YES)
                                          OBJECT (*ROLE* THE-OBJ)))
          SUB-ACT (ACT ACTOR (*ROLE* HELPER))
          SUB-GOAL (GOAL ACTOR (*ROLE* HELPER)
                        GOAL (ACT ACTOR (*ROLE* HELPER)))
          ASK (ACT TYPE (MTRANS)
                  ACTOR (*ROLE* THE-ACTOR)
                  TO (*ROLE* HELPER)
                  OBJECT (ACT ACTOR (*ROLE* HELPER)))
          THE-PLAN (PLAN ACTOR (*ROLE* THE-ACTOR)
                        PLAN (*ROLE* ASK))
          HELPER (HUMAN NAME (MIKE)
                        RELATION (IPT TYPE (FAMILY-REL)
                                      STYPE (FATHER)
                                      OF (*ROLE* THE-ACTOR))
                        AGE (GROWN-UP)
                        HAIR (BROWN)
                        EYES (GREEN))
          THE-ACTOR (HUMAN)
          THE-OBJ (P-OBJ))
```

B.1.1. Revising a schema

Given the above four examples, OCCAM-LITE creates a `delta-agency` schema. This schema is the most specific description of the examples that form the `delta-agency` cluster. Some of the roles of the schema are much too specific and further examples will cause them to be generalized further.

The program is next presented with `cookie-1` in which Karen wants a cookie, so she asks her sister Lynn to get her one and her goal succeeds. This example conforms to most of the `delta-agency` schema, except the `helper` is predicted to be the father of the actor.

```
------------------------------------------------------------------
Looking for most specific schema for <COOKIE-1 GOAL>
(GOAL ACTOR (HUMAN NAME (KAREN)
                    ... ...)
        GOAL (STATE TYPE (POSS-BY)
                    UNIQUE-ID POSS-BY.102
                    ACTOR (HUMAN NAME (KAREN)
                                ... ...)
                    VALUE (YES)
                    OBJECT (P-OBJ TYPE (FOOD)
                                    STYPE (COOKIE)
                                    UNIQUE-ID COOKIE.001))
        UNIQUE-ID COOKIE.1
        PLAN (PLAN ACTOR (HUMAN NAME (KAREN)
                            ... ...)
                    PLAN (ACT TYPE (MTRANS)
                            UNIQUE-ID MTRANS.102
                            ACTOR (HUMAN NAME (KAREN)
                                        ... ...)
                            TO (HUMAN NAME (LYNN)
                                    RELATION
                                        (IPT TYPE (FAMILY-REL)
                                            STYPE (SISTER)
                                            OF (HUMAN UNIQUE-ID KAREN))
                                    AGE (KID)
                                    HAIR (BLOND)
                                    EYES (BLUE)
                                    UNIQUE-ID LYNN)
                            OBJECT (ACT TYPE (ATRANS)
                                    ACTOR (HUMAN NAME (LYNN)
                                                ... ...)
                                    OBJECT (P-OBJ TYPE (FOOD)
                                                ... ...)
                                    TO (HUMAN NAME (KAREN)
                                                ... ...)))
                    UNIQUE-ID COOKIE-P.1)
        OUTCOME (GOAL-OUTCOME TYPE (SUCCESS)
                    ACTOR (HUMAN NAME (KAREN)
                                ... ...)
                    GOAL (STATE TYPE (POSS-BY)
                                ... ...)
                    UNIQUE-ID COOKIE-R.1))
```

This example conflicts with the **delta-agency** schema and the schema is deleted. This is one difference between OCCAM and OCCAM-LITE. OCCAM would revise the schema instead of deleting it.

```
Deleting schema, incorrect prediction.
(GOAL PLAN
        (PLAN PLAN (ACT TO (HUMAN NAME (MIKE)
                        RELATION (IPT STYPE (FATHER))
                        AGE (GROWN-UP)
                        HAIR (BROWN)
                        EYES (GREEN))
                    OBJECT (ACT ACTOR (HUMAN NAME (MIKE)
                                        RELATION (IPT STYPE (FATHER))
                                        AGE (GROWN-UP)
                                        HAIR (BROWN)
                                        EYES (GREEN))))))
```

When the **delta-agency** schema is deleted, its events are re-indexed under the next most general schema. In this example, **play-doh-1, zoo-1** are indexed **pizza-1** under the goal schema. The goal schema is the most specific schema for the new event.

```
Indexing event <PLAY-DOH-1 GOAL> under schema <GOAL <CD-4422 GOAL>>.
Indexing event <ZOO-1 GOAL> under schema <GOAL <CD-4422 GOAL>>.
Indexing event <PIZZA-1 GOAL> under schema <GOAL <CD-4422 GOAL>>.
Found most specific schema for event: <COOKIE-1 GOAL>
Event is accounted for by:
(GOAL)
Attempting explanation-based learning for new event.
Attempting theory driven learning for new event.
Attempting similarity-based learning for new event.
Retrieved cluster of similar events.
(<COOKIE-1 GOAL> <PLAY-DOH-1 GOAL> <ZOO-1 GOAL> <PIZZA-1 GOAL>)
```

At this point, the program repeats the process of constructing a new schema and macro-schema using a cluster of four events instead of three. Rather than repeating all the details, only the result is shown. The only difference between this version and the previous **delta-agency** schema is the **helper** role. The helper can now be any family member rather than an adult father named Mike with brown hair and green eyes.

```
Creating macro schema.
(DELTA-AGENCY GOAL (GOAL ACTOR (*ROLE* THE-ACTOR)
                         GOAL (STATE ACTOR (*ROLE* THE-ACTOR)
                                     VALUE (YES)
                                     OBJECT (*ROLE* THE-OBJ))
                         PLAN (*ROLE* THE-PLAN)
                         OUTCOME (*ROLE* OUTCOME))
                  OUTCOME (GOAL-OUTCOME TYPE (SUCCESS)
                                        ACTOR (*ROLE* THE-ACTOR)
                                        GOAL (STATE ACTOR (*ROLE* THE-ACTOR)
                                                    VALUE (YES)
                                                    OBJECT (*ROLE* THE-OBJ)))
                  SUB-ACT (ACT ACTOR (*ROLE* HELPER))
                  SUB-GOAL (GOAL ACTOR (*ROLE* HELPER)
                                 GOAL (ACT ACTOR (*ROLE* HELPER)))
                  ASK (ACT TYPE (MTRANS)
                           ACTOR (*ROLE* THE-ACTOR)
                           TO (*ROLE* HELPER)
                           OBJECT (ACT ACTOR (*ROLE* HELPER)))
                  THE-PLAN (PLAN ACTOR (*ROLE* THE-ACTOR)
                                 PLAN (*ROLE* ASK))
                  HELPER (HUMAN RELATION (IPT TYPE (FAMILY-REL)
                                              OF (*ROLE* THE-ACTOR)))
                  THE-ACTOR (HUMAN)
                  THE-OBJ (P-OBJ))
```

B.2. Theory-Driven Learning Trace

In this section, OCCAM-LITE is presented with three examples of cups being dropped. To run this demonstration, the following command is typed:

```
(mapc #'occam-lite *all-tdls*)
```

The first example is **glass-1-a** in which a clear glass cup is dropped and the cup breaks. The representation of **glass-1-a** is connected by a temporal link (i.e., **before**) to **glass-1-r**, which describes the glass breaking (see the file glass.lisp on page 295).

```
Looking for most specific schema for <GLASS-1-A ACT>
(ACT TYPE (PROPEL)
     ACTOR (HUMAN NAME (LYNN)
                  AGE (KID)
                  HAIR (BLOND)
                  EYES (BLUE)
                  UNIQUE-ID LYNN)
     OBJECT (P-OBJ TYPE (CUP)
                   COLOR (CLEAR)
                   COMPOSITION (GLASS)
                   UNIQUE-ID GLASS.1)
     TO (P-OBJ TYPE (FLOOR)
               LOCATION (KITCHEN)))
Found most specific schema for event: <GLASS-1-A ACT>
Event is accounted for by:
(ACT TYPE (PROPEL))
Attempting explanation-based learning for new event.
Attempting theory driven learning for new event.
Situation matches exceptionless gen rule.
(ACT TYPE (*VAR* ACT-TYPE)
     OBJECT (*VAR* OBJECT))
(STATE TYPE (*VAR* STATE-TYPE)
       VALUE (*VAR* VALUE)
       OBJECT (*VAR* OBJECT))
```

This example matches the situation in which an action on an object precedes a state change for the object. The mechanism of this generalization rule is instantiated. The generalization rule, **gen-result** is the first generalization rule in the file genrules.lisp on page 294. A new schema is created that states that when a force is applied to a cup, the cup will break.

```
Instantiating mechanism.
(ACT TYPE (PROPEL)
     OBJECT (P-OBJ TYPE (CUP)))
RESULT
(STATE TYPE (BROKEN)
      VALUE (YES)
       OBJECT (P-OBJ TYPE (CUP)))
Instantiating mechanism.
(ACT TYPE (PROPEL)
     OBJECT (P-OBJ TYPE (CUP)))
AFTER
(STATE TYPE (BROKEN)
      VALUE (YES)
       OBJECT (P-OBJ TYPE (CUP)))
Indexing event <GLASS-1-A ACT> under schema <SCHEMA-7367 <CD-7365 ACT>>.
```

A rule representation is also created and stored with the schema. This rule could be used as part of an explanation chain (e.g., to explain how someone who walked on the floor after a cup was dropped was lacerated).

```
Creating new RESULT rule
(ACT TYPE (PROPEL)
     OBJECT (*VAR* OBJECT (P-OBJ TYPE (CUP))))
(STATE TYPE (BROKEN)
      VALUE (YES)
       OBJECT (*VAR* OBJECT))
```

The schema formed from the previous example is abandoned when the next example is presented. The next example is of a red plastic cup that does not break.

```
------------------------------------------------------------------

Looking for most specific schema for <GLASS-2-A ACT>
(ACT TYPE (PROPEL)
     ACTOR (HUMAN NAME (LYNN)
                  AGE (KID)
                  HAIR (BLOND)
                  EYES (BLUE)
                  UNIQUE-ID LYNN)
     OBJECT (P-OBJ TYPE (CUP)
                  COLOR (RED)
                  COMPOSITION (PLASTIC)
                  UNIQUE-ID GLASS.2)
     TO (P-OBJ TYPE (FLOOR)
              LOCATION (KITCHEN)))
Deleting schema, incorrect prediction.
(STATE TYPE (BROKEN)
      VALUE (YES)
       OBJECT (P-OBJ TYPE (CUP)))
Indexing event <GLASS-1-A ACT> under schema <PROPEL-SCHEMA <CD-4439 ACT>>.
```

The schema is deleted and the previous example is stored under a `propel` schema.

```
Found most specific schema for event: <GLASS-2-A ACT>
Event is accounted for by:
(ACT TYPE (PROPEL))
Attempting explanation-based learning for new event.
Attempting theory driven learning for new event.
Attempting similarity-based learning for new event.
Indexing event <GLASS-2-A ACT> under schema <PROPEL-SCHEMA <CD-4439 ACT>>.
```

OCCAM-LITE cannot apply theory-driven learning because the current example has no following state change to match a generalization rule. OCCAM-LITE must wait until another positive example is seen to apply a dispositional generalization rule. The next example, `glass-3`, describes a red, glass cup that is dropped and breaks. This situation will match the dispositional generalization rule `gen-result-object-difference`.

```
Looking for most specific schema for <GLASS-3-A ACT>
(ACT TYPE (PROPEL)
      ACTOR (HUMAN NAME (LYNN)
                  AGE (KID)
                  HAIR (BLOND)
                  EYES (BLUE)
                  UNIQUE-ID LYNN)
      OBJECT (P-OBJ TYPE (CUP)
                  COLOR (RED)
                  COMPOSITION (GLASS)
                  UNIQUE-ID GLASS.3)
      TO (P-OBJ TYPE (FLOOR)
              LOCATION (KITCHEN)))
Found most specific schema for event: <GLASS-3-A ACT>
Event is accounted for by:
(ACT TYPE (PROPEL))
Attempting explanation-based learning for new event.
Attempting theory driven learning for new event.
Situation matches dispositional gen rule.
(ACT TYPE (*VAR* ACT-TYPE)
      OBJECT (*VAR* OBJECT))
(STATE TYPE (*VAR* STATE-TYPE)
        VALUE (*VAR* VALUE)
        OBJECT (*VAR* OBJECT))
Attributing difference to OBJECT.
(P-OBJ COMPOSITION (GLASS))
```

This generalization rule states that when actions are performed on some objects with different results, and the objects have different features, the differing features of the object are responsible for the different result.

```
Instantiating mechanism.
(ACT TYPE (PROPEL)
      OBJECT (P-OBJ TYPE (CUP)))
RESULT
(STATE TYPE (BROKEN)
        VALUE (YES)
        OBJECT (P-OBJ TYPE (CUP)))
```

```
Instantiating mechanism.
(ACT TYPE (PROPEL)
     OBJECT (P-OBJ TYPE (CUP)))
AFTER
(STATE TYPE (BROKEN)
     VALUE (YES)
     OBJECT (P-OBJ TYPE (CUP)))
Indexing event <GLASS-3-A ACT> under schema <SCHEMA-7460 <CD-7457 ACT>>.
Indexing event <GLASS-1-A ACT> under schema <SCHEMA-7460 <CD-7457 ACT>>.
Creating new RESULT rule
(ACT TYPE (PROPEL)
     OBJECT (*VAR* OBJECT (P-OBJ COMPOSITION (GLASS)
                                  TYPE (CUP))))

(STATE TYPE (BROKEN)
     VALUE (YES)
     OBJECT (*VAR* OBJECT))
```

The new schema indicates that when a force is applied to a glass cup, the result will be a broken cup.

B.3. Explanation-Based Learning Trace

The trace illustrates the explanation-based learning component. The example input is the CD representation of Economic-Sanction-1:

Economic-Sanction-1

In 1983, Australia refused to sell uranium to France, unless France ceased nuclear testing in the South Pacific. France paid a higher price to buy uranium from South Africa and continued nuclear testing.

To run the example, the following is typed:

```
(occam-lite sanction-83-1)
```

The CD representation of this example is from the file sanctions.lisp on page 298.

```
-----------------------------------------------------------------
Looking for most specific schema for <SANCTION-83-1 COERCE>
(COERCE ACTOR (POLITY TYPE (COUNTRY)
                      NAME (AUSTRALIA)
                      LANGUAGE (ENGLISH)
                      LOCATION (SOUTHERN-HEMISPHERE)
                      GOVERNMENT (DEMOCRACY)
                      ECONOMIC-HEALTH (STRONG)
                      CONTINENT (AUSTRALIA)
                      EXPORTS (*ROLE* OBJECT)
                      IMPORTS (OIL))
        OBJECT (COMMODITY TYPE (URANIUM))
        TARGET (POLITY TYPE (COUNTRY)
                      NAME (FRANCE)
                      LANGUAGE (FRENCH)
                      GOVERNMENT (DEMOCRACY)
                      ECONOMIC-HEALTH (STRONG)
                      CONTINENT (EUROPE)
                      LOCATION (NORTHERN-HEMISPHERE)
                      IMPORTS (*ROLE* OBJECT)
                      EXPORTS (COMMODITY TYPE (WINE)))
        DEMAND (ACT TYPE (EXPLODE)
                   ACTOR (*ROLE* TARGET)
                   OBJECT (WEAPONS TYPE (NUCLEAR))
                   LOCATION (SOUTHERN-HEMISPHERE)
                   MODE (NEG))
        THREAT (ACT TYPE (SELL)
                   ACTOR (*ROLE* ACTOR)
                   OBJECT (*ROLE* OBJECT)
                   TO (*ROLE* TARGET)
                   MODE (NEG))
        RESPONSE (ACT TYPE (SELL)
                     ACTOR (POLITY TYPE (COUNTRY)
                                   NAME (SOUTH-AFRICA)
                                   LANGUAGE (ENGLISH)
                                   LOCATION (SOUTHERN-HEMISPHERE)
                                   BUSINESS-RELATIONSHIP (*ROLE* TARGET)
                                   GOVERNMENT (APARTHEID)
                                   CONTINENT (AFRICA)
                                   EXPORTS (*ROLE* OBJECT)
                                   IMPORTS (OIL))
                     OBJECT (*ROLE* OBJECT)
                     PRICE (MONEY DOLLARS (3000000)
                                  VALUE (>MARKET))
                     TO (*ROLE* TARGET))
        RESULT (STATE TYPE (POSSESS)
                   ACTOR (*ROLE* TARGET)
                   VALUE (YES)
                   OBJECT (*ROLE* OBJECT)))
Found most specific schema for event: <SANCTION-83-1 COERCE>
Event is accounted for by:
(COERCE)
Attempting explanation-based learning for new events.
```

The example is accounted for by the coerce schema. The example is decomposed by matching against the coercion schema and instantiating its sequence of event. The simple CD representation of the coercion events indicates that after the threat is made, the target performs a response that results in an outcome. This does not adequately explain the event because it does not indicate why the particular response was chosen and what the particular outcome will be. The instantiated sequence of events is displayed in Figure 5-3 on page 156. This sequence of events is matched against the generalization rules to produce an abstract explanation. The third generalization rule in the file genrules.lisp (see **prev-action** on page 294) matches this situation. The mechanism of this generalization rule suggest as abstract explanation (see Figure 5-6 on page 160): refusing to sell the uranium results in some intermediate state that enables South africa to sell France the uranium at a higher than market rate. The economic rules (illustrated in the file rules.lisp on page 296) are used to verify and refine this explanation:

```
Attempting to infer RESULT.
(ACT TYPE (SELL)
     ACTOR (POLITY TYPE (COUNTRY)
                   NAME (SOUTH-AFRICA)
                   LANGUAGE (ENGLISH)
                   LOCATION (SOUTHERN-HEMISPHERE)
                   BUSINESS-RELATIONSHIP (POLITY NAME (FRANCE)
                                                ... ...)
                   CONTINENT (AFRICA)
                   EXPORTS (COMMODITY TYPE (URANIUM))
                   IMPORTS (OIL))
     OBJECT (COMMODITY TYPE (URANIUM))
     PRICE (MONEY DOLLARS (3000000)
                  VALUE (>MARKET))
     TO (POLITY NAME (FRANCE)
               ... ...))
(STATE TYPE (POSSESS)
       ACTOR (POLITY NAME (FRANCE)
                     LANGUAGE (FRENCH)
                     GOVERNMENT (DEMOCRACY)
                     ECONOMIC-HEALTH (STRONG)
                     CONTINENT (EUROPE)
                     LOCATION (NORTHERN-HEMISPHERE)
                     IMPORTS (COMMODITY TYPE (URANIUM))
                     EXPORTS (COMMODITY TYPE (WINE)))
       VALUE (YES)
       OBJECT (COMMODITY TYPE (URANIUM)))
Established by inference rule.
(ACT TYPE (SELL)
     TO (*VAR* X)
     OBJECT (*VAR* Y)
     MODE (YES))
(STATE TYPE (POSSESS)
       OBJECT (*VAR* Y)
       VALUE (YES)
       ACTOR (*VAR* X))
```

This inference rule indicates that France possessing the uranium is a result of South Africa selling the uranium to France.

```
Attempting to infer RESULT.
(ACT TYPE (SELL)
     ACTOR (POLITY TYPE (COUNTRY)
                     NAME (AUSTRALIA)
                     LANGUAGE (ENGLISH)
                     LOCATION (SOUTHERN-HEMISPHERE)
                     GOVERNMENT (DEMOCRACY)
                     ECONOMIC-HEALTH (STRONG)
                     CONTINENT (AUSTRALIA)
                     EXPORTS (COMMODITY TYPE (URANIUM))
                     IMPORTS (OIL))
     OBJECT (COMMODITY TYPE (URANIUM))
     TO (POLITY NAME (FRANCE)
                ... ...)
     MODE (NEG))
(*VAR* STATE-1 (STATE OBJECT (*VAR* OBJ)))
Established by inference rule.
(ACT TYPE (SELL)
     ACTOR (POLITY EXPORTS (*VAR* Y))
     TO (*VAR* X (POLITY IMPORTS (*VAR* Y)))
     OBJECT (*VAR* Y (COMMODITY))
     MODE (NEG))
(STATE TYPE (DEMAND-INCREASE)
     ACTOR (*VAR* X)
     VALUE (YES)
     OBJECT (*VAR* Y))
```

Refusing to sell the uranium results in an increased demand for the uranium.

```
Attempting to infer ENABLES.
(STATE TYPE (DEMAND-INCREASE)
     ACTOR (POLITY NAME (FRANCE)
                 ... ...)
     VALUE (YES)
     OBJECT (COMMODITY TYPE (URANIUM)))
(ACT TYPE (SELL)
     ACTOR (POLITY NAME (SOUTH-AFRICA)
                 ... ...)
     OBJECT (COMMODITY TYPE (URANIUM))
     PRICE (MONEY DOLLARS (3000000)
                 VALUE (>MARKET))
     TO (POLITY NAME (FRANCE)
                 ... ...))
Established by inference rule.
(STATE TYPE (DEMAND-INCREASE)
     VALUE (YES)
     ACTOR (*VAR* X (POLITY ECONOMIC-HEALTH (STRONG)))
     OBJECT (*VAR* Y))
(ACT TYPE (SELL)
     ACTOR (POLITY EXPORTS (*VAR* Y)
                   BUSINESS-RELATIONSHIP (*VAR* X))
     TO (*VAR* X)
     OBJECT (*VAR* Y)
     PRICE (MONEY VALUE (>MARKET))
     MODE (YES))
```

This rule completes the causal chain. The increased demand for the uranium enables South Africa to sell the uranium at a higher than market rate. Next,

OCCAM-LITE must verify that the temporal links specified by the generalization rule are also present:

```
Attempting to infer AFTER.
(ACT TYPE (SELL)
     ACTOR (POLITY NAME (SOUTH-AFRICA)
                   ... ...)
     OBJECT (COMMODITY TYPE (URANIUM))
     PRICE (MONEY DOLLARS (3000000)
                    VALUE (>MARKET))
     TO (POLITY NAME (FRANCE)
              ... ...))
(STATE TYPE (POSSESS)
      ACTOR (POLITY NAME (FRANCE)
                  ... ...)
      VALUE (YES)
      OBJECT (COMMODITY TYPE (URANIUM)))
Established by following link.
Attempting to infer AFTER.
(ACT TYPE (SELL)
     ACTOR (POLITY NAME (AUSTRALIA)
                   ... ...)
     OBJECT (COMMODITY TYPE (URANIUM))
     TO (POLITY NAME (FRANCE)
              ... ...)
     MODE (NEG))
(ACT TYPE (SELL)
     ACTOR (POLITY NAME (SOUTH-AFRICA)
                   ... ...)
     OBJECT (COMMODITY TYPE (URANIUM))
     PRICE (MONEY DOLLARS (3000000)
                     VALUE (>MARKET))
     TO (POLITY NAME (FRANCE)
              ... ...))
Established by following link.
```

Now the example can be generalized by retaining only those features marked during matching the rules in the explanation chain.

```
Indexing event <SANCTION-83-1 COERCE> under schema
 <SCHEMA-7775 <CD-7774 COERCE>>.
Creating generalization with EBL
(COERCE ACTOR (POLITY EXPORTS (*ROLE* OBJECT))
          OBJECT (COMMODITY)
          TARGET (POLITY ECONOMIC-HEALTH (STRONG)
                         IMPORTS (*ROLE* OBJECT))
          THREAT (ACT TYPE (SELL)
                       ACTOR (*ROLE* ACTOR)
                       OBJECT (*ROLE* OBJECT)
                       TO (*ROLE* TARGET)
                       MODE (NEG))
          RESPONSE (ACT TYPE (SELL)
                         ACTOR (POLITY BUSINESS-RELATIONSHIP (*ROLE* TARGET)
                                       EXPORTS (*ROLE* OBJECT))
                         OBJECT (*ROLE* OBJECT)
                         PRICE (MONEY VALUE (>MARKET))
                         TO (*ROLE* TARGET))
          RESULT (STATE TYPE (POSSESS)
                       ACTOR (*ROLE* TARGET)
                       VALUE (YES)
                       OBJECT (*ROLE* OBJECT)))
```

This generalization indicates that if a country that exports a commodity tries to coerce a wealthy country which imports the commodity by refusing to sell them the commodity, then a response might be to buy the commodity at a higher price from another country.

Finally, the sequence of events is created. This saves the relationships found in the explanation, so that the next time a similar event is seen, the explanation can be found by recognition and instantiation rather than by chaining.

```
Formed event <CD-7708 (*VAR* RESULT)> with links
<<CD-7708 (*VAR* RESULT)> RESULTED-FROM <CD-7721 (*VAR* RESPONSE)>>
<<CD-7708 (*VAR* RESULT)> BEFORE <CD-7721 (*VAR* RESPONSE)>>
(*VAR* RESULT)

Formed event <CD-7721 (*VAR* RESPONSE)> with links
<<CD-7721 (*VAR* RESPONSE)> ENABLED-BY <CD-7757 STATE>>
<<CD-7721 (*VAR* RESPONSE)> RESULT <CD-7708 (*VAR* RESULT)>>
<<CD-7721 (*VAR* RESPONSE)> AFTER <CD-7708 (*VAR* RESULT)>>
<<CD-7721 (*VAR* RESPONSE)> BEFORE <CD-7724 (*VAR* THREAT)>>
(*VAR* RESPONSE)
Formed event <CD-7757 STATE> with links
<<CD-7757 STATE> ENABLES <CD-7721 (*VAR* RESPONSE)>>
<<CD-7757 STATE> RESULTED-FROM <CD-7724 (*VAR* THREAT)>>
(STATE TYPE (DEMAND-INCREASE)
       ACTOR (*VAR* TARGET)
       VALUE (YES)
       OBJECT (*VAR* OBJECT))
```

```
Formed event <CD-7724 (*VAR* THREAT)> with links
<<CD-7724 (*VAR* THREAT)> RESULT <CD-7757 STATE>>
<<CD-7724 (*VAR* THREAT)> AFTER <CD-7721 (*VAR* RESPONSE)>>
<<CD-7724 (*VAR* THREAT)> REALIZES <CD-7754 PLAN>>
(*VAR* THREAT)

Formed event <CD-7754 PLAN> with links
<<CD-7754 PLAN> REALIZED-BY <CD-7724 (*VAR* THREAT)>>
<<CD-7754 PLAN> INTENDS <CD-7753 GOAL>>
(PLAN ACTOR (*VAR* ACTOR))

Formed event <CD-7753 GOAL> with links
<<CD-7753 GOAL> INTENDED-BY <CD-7754 PLAN>>
(GOAL ACTOR (*VAR* ACTOR)
     GOAL (*VAR* DEMAND))
```

Notice that in the explanation saved with the sanction schema, an intermediate state, the increased demand for the object by the target, is saved. In addition, the fact that this state enables the response to occur is also represented.

Appendix C
Prolog Occam

This appendix contains the source code listing of a simple version of OCCAM implemented in Prolog. There are many differences between this version and OCCAM or even OCCAM-LITE. However, the top-level control is similar:

1. When a new example is encountered, try to recognize an explanation. In OCCAM, this consists of finding the most specific schema in memory that accounts for the new event. In OCCAM_PROLOG, this consists of finding a causal rule that in one step connects a cause and effect.

2. If the above step fails, try to construct an explanation by chaining together existing knowledge. Generalize the explanation and create a new schema (or rule) that recognizes when the explanation applies. OCCAM_PROLOG uses a generalization algorithm that was derived from PROLOG-EBG (Kedar-Cabelli & McCarty, 1987).

3. If explanation-based learning fails, then empirical techniques are tried. PROLOG_OCCAM uses a variation of Bruner's wholist method (Bruner et al., 1956) that incrementally generalizes a rule by removing those features that differ between the present definition and a incorrectly classified positive example. PROLOG_OCCAM's empirical generalization step also requires that those sub-components that were identical in the training example are identical in the rule definition.

The differences between OCCAM and PROLOG_OCCAM include:

- PROLOG_OCCAM does not create a hierarchy to represent its causal knowledge. It relies on Prolog's indexing scheme and unification to select the appropriate rule. This results in a linear search through all causal rules to make an inference.

- PROLOG_OCCAM does not use the taxonomy of causal and intentional links. Instead, it uses only one link, `cause`.

- PROLOG_OCCAM has an extremely simple clustering algorithm. It groups together all events that have the same type of outcome and assumes that there is only one conjunctive class of actions for each type of outcome. The type of an outcome is explicitly present in the input.

- The empirical component of PROLOG_OCCAM does not deal with negative examples.

- PROLOG_OCCAM does not create macro-schemata.

- PROLOG_OCCAM does not deal with noise in the data or relationships that are "usually" true.

- Rules and training examples have the same fixed syntax. In OCCAM, the order of the roles in a CD structure is not fixed (i.e., it uses a role and role filler representation). In PROLOG_OCCAM, the position of a role is important. This allows PROLOG_OCCAM to take advantage of Prolog's efficient unification algorithm.

- OCCAM has an interpreter for theory-driven learning. The generalization rules serves as data for this interpreter. In PROLOG-OCCAM, there are only two patterns for inducing causal relationships. These patterns are built in to the learning algorithm.

In spite of its limitations, PROLOG_OCCAM serves to illustrate the the central point of this dissertation: knowledge-intensive learning techniques when applicable are preferable to data-intensive techniques. Data-intensive learning techniques can provide the necessary background knowledge that increases the ability of knowledge-intensive techniques to exploit interactions between existing knowledge structures.

Prolog tends to be more concise than lisp. However, the major reason that PROLOG_OCCAM is so much shorter than OCCAM_LITE is that has fewer capabilities. In addition, only those capabilities that are simple to implement in Prolog were implemented. These capabilities take advantage of Prolog's built-in procedures for backward chaining, depth-first search with chronological backtracking, pattern-matching and database indexing. In the lisp version, I had to implement routines to perform these tasks. In many cases, the capability that I implemented are superior to Prolog's built-in routines because my lisp implementation was designed for my specific goals. For example, OCCAM indexes its rules in a hierarchy of schemata. In effect, there is a discrimination net for finding the most specific rule. Searching a discrimination net is typically logarithmic in the number of rules. With the representation I have chosen for rules, most prologs will perform a linear search to find a causal rule. Of course, one could implement a hierarchical memory of schemata in prolog. The most important contributions of this dissertation are the description of a learning process. This process does not depend upon a particular language or computer.

C.1. Code Listing of PROLOG_OCCAM

PROLOG_OCCAM runs under Quintus Prolog Release 2.0. With the exception of **format** and **listing** which are used to print trace output, PROLOG_OCCAM makes use of constructs that are found in almost all implementations of Prolog. It has also been run under SICStus Prolog. The top-level predicate is PROLOG_OCCAM.

```
%%% the cause predicate "cause(X,Y)" indicates that X causes Y
%%% cause is declared dynamic because prolog_occam dynamically
%%% creates new "cause" structures. Some Prolog's do not require
%%% or understand this declaration.
:-dynamic cause/2.
```

```
%%% prolog_occam has the same general top-level control as occam
%%% 1. It attempts to explain why Y occurred after X by
%%% seeing if there it is already known that X cause Y
%%% 2. It tries EBL (via chain_explanation) by seeing if
%%% X causes Y can be derived by chaining together existing causal knowledge.
%%% 3. Empirical methods are tried.
%%% prolog_occam contains two simple patterns for inducing new causal rules.


prolog_occam(after(X,Y),cause(X,Y)):-
        cause(X,Y),!.
        %% already explained in one step
prolog_occam(after(X,Y),cause(NewX,NewY)):-
        chain_explanation(cause(X,Y),cause(NewX,NewY)),!,
        assert(cause(NewX,NewY)).
        %%explanation is chained and generalized
%%The next two clause implement a causal pattern that states
%%that if an action on an object precede a state change for the object
%%then the action causes the state change.
%%Note that the variable "O" appears in both the cause and the effect
prolog_occam(after(act(At,A,O,D),state(T,O)),V):-
        cause(act(OldAt,OldA,OldO,OldD),state(T,OldO)),!,
        %%existing causal rule is retrieved.
        retract(cause(act(OldAt,OldA,OldO,OldD),state(T,OldO))),
        %%the rule must be too specific, so it is deleted and generalized
        find_common(cause(act(At,A,O,D),state(T,O)),
                    cause(act(OldAt,OldA,OldO,OldD),state(T,OldO)),
                    V, [], _),
        %%a new rule is created by retaining common features between
        %%the old rule and the new example.
        assert(V).
prolog_occam(after(act(At,A,O,D),state(T,O)),V):-
        !,
        %%this is the first instance of this state
        %%so a new rule is created for just this case
        find_common(cause(act(At,A,O,D),state(T,O)),
                    cause(act(At,A,O,D),state(T,O)),
                    V, [], _),
        %% here find common is called to change ids to variables
        assert(V).
%%The last two clauses implement a second causal pattern
%%if an state-change precedes an affect, then the state change
%%caused the affect.
prolog_occam(after(state(T,O),affect(X,Y)),V):-
        cause(state(T,OldO),affect(OldX,OldY)),!,
        retract(cause(state(T,OldO),affect(OldX,OldY))),
        find_common(cause(state(T,O),affect(X,Y)),
                    cause(state(T,OldO),affect(OldX,OldY)),
                    V, [], _),
        assert(V).
prolog_occam(after(state(T,O),affect(X,Y)),V):-
        !,
        find_common(cause(state(T,O),affect(X,Y)),
                    cause(state(T,O),affect(X,Y)),
                    V, [], _),
        assert(V).
```

```
%%find_common(CD1,CD2,GenCD,InBindings,Outbindings)
%%find_common substitutes variables for all features that differ
%%between two structures.  In addition, it ensures that all "ids"
%%that are the same are replaced by the same variable.
find_common(X,Y,X,B,B):-atom(X),X==Y,!.
        %X and Y are identical, so X is retained
find_common(id(X),id(Y),id(Z),I,I):-
        find_var(X,Y,Z,I),!.
        %The variable for X and Y is found in I and used
find_common(id(X),id(Y),id(Z),I,[v(X,Y,Z) | I]):-!.
        %since the variable was not found,
        %a new one is created and added to I
find_common(X,Y,Z,I,O):-
        nonvar(X),nonvar(Y),
        functor(X,F,A),
        functor(Y,F,A),
        %X and Y are two structures with identical predicates and arity
        %so find_common is recursively called on the arguments
        !,
        functor(Z,F,A),
        find_common(A,X,Y,Z,I,O).
find_common(_,_,_,I,I).
        %when all else fails,
        %the feature is dropped by substituting a variable

%%find_common(ArgumentNO,CD1,CD2,GenCD,InBindings,Outbindings)- iterates down
%%argument structure, calling find_common on arguments.
find_common(0,_,_,_,I,I)  :- !.
find_common(N,X,Y,Z,I,O)  :-
        arg(N,X,Xn),
        arg(N,Y,Yn),
        arg(N,Z,Zn),
        N1 is N - 1,
        find_common(Xn,Yn,Zn,I,IO),
        find_common(N1,X,Y,Z,IO,O).

%%find_var(Id1,Id2,IdVar,Varlist)- looks up a variable for
%%the pair Id1, Id2 in Varlist.
find_var(_,_,_,[]):-!,fail.
find_var(A,B,V,[v(A1,B1,V)|_]):-A1==A,B1==B,!.
find_var(A,B,V,[_|R]):-find_var(A,B,V,R).

%%Chain_explanation(cause(Cause,Effect),GeneralCause)- determines if a causal
%%chain between Cause and Effect can be constructed.  If it can,
%%the most general conditions under which that chain can be constructed
%%are recorded in General cause.
chain_explanation(cause(Cause,Effect),cause(GenCause,GenEffect)) :-
        cause(GenCause,GenEffect),
        copy(cause(GenCause,GenEffect),cause(Cause,Effect)).
%%The second clause constructs chains by transitively finding a cause.
chain_explanation(cause(Start,End),cause(GenStart,GenEnd)):-
        cause(Start,Mid),
        chain_explanation(cause(Start,Mid),cause(GenStart,GenMid)),
        chain_explanation(cause(Mid,End),cause(GenMid,GenEnd)).

%%copy creates a new version of O, by using a Prolog trick
%%of asserting and retracting O.  This gets "new" instances
%%of the variables in O.
copy(O,N) :- assert('$marker'(O)),retract('$marker'(NO)),NO=N.
```

```
%%%test runs prolog_occam on several examples.
test:-
        cd(g1,G1),
        cd(g2,G2),
        cd(g3,G3),
        cd(b1,B1),
        cd(b2,B2),
        cd(e1,E1),
        retractall(cause(_,_)),
        %reinitialize the database
        prolog_occam(G1,_),
        format('~n Running prolog_occam on g1',[]),
        listing(cause),
        prolog_occam(G2,_),
        format('~n Running prolog_occam on g2',[]),
        listing(cause),
        prolog_occam(G3,_),
        format('~n Running prolog_occam on g3',[]),
        listing(cause),
        %the above three examples are about objects breaking
        prolog_occam(B1,_),prolog_occam(B2,_),
        format('~n Running prolog_occam on b1 and b2',[]),
        listing(cause),
        %these two examples are about people getting angry when objects break
        prolog_occam(E1,_),
        format('~n Running prolog_occam on e1',[]),
        listing(cause).
        %The final example is of a person getting angry when a glass object
        %is struck.
```

C.2. Data for PROLOG_OCCAM

This section presents the training examples used to test OCCAM_PROLOG. There are three sets of training examples.

- g1, g2 and g3: examples of glass objects breaking.

- b1 and b2: examples of people getting angry when objects they own are broken.

- e1: an example of a person getting angry when a cat knocks over her vase.

```
%%%g1- Mike drops a clear glass cup and it breaks.
cd(g1,
  after(act(propel, actor(human, name(mike),
                                 age(adult),
                                 hair(brown),
                                 id(hum_001)),
                    object(cup, color(clear),
                                composition(glass),
                                owner(human, name(mike),
                                             age(adult),
                                             hair(brown),
                                             id(hum_001)),
                                id(glass_001)),
                    to(floor)),
       state(broken, object(cup, color(clear),
                                  composition(glass),
                                  owner(human, name(mike),
                                               age(adult),
                                               hair(brown),
                                               id(hum_001)),
                                  id(glass_001))))).

%%g2- Jill knocks over a red, glass vase and it breaks.
cd(g2,
  after(act(propel, actor(cat, name(jill),
                               age(kitten),
                               hair(tan),
                               id(cat_002)),
                    object(vase, color(red),
                                 composition(glass),
                                 owner(human, name(chris),
                                              age(adult),
                                              hair(brown),
                                              id(hum_002)),
                                 id(glass_002)),
                    to(table)),
       state(broken, object(vase, color(red),
                                  composition(glass),
                                  owner(human, name(chris),
                                               age(adult),
                                               hair(brown),
                                               id(hum_002)),
                                  id(glass_002))))).
```

```
%%g3- Mike drops  the cat's bowl and it breaks.
cd(g3,
  after(act(propel, actor(human, name(mike),
                                 age(adult),
                                 hair(brown),
                                 id(hum_001)),
                    object(bowl, color(clear),
                                 composition(glass),
                                 owner(cat, name(jill),
                                            age(kitten),
                                            hair(tan),
                                            id(cat_002)),
                                 id(glass_003)),
                    to(floor)),
        state(broken, object(bowl, color(clear),
                                   composition(glass),
                                   owner(cat, name(jill),
                                              age(kitten),
                                              hair(tan),
                                              id(cat_002)),
                                   id(glass_003))))).


%b1-  Chris gets angry after her watch breaks
cd(b1,
   after(state(broken, object(watch, color(white),
                                     composition(plastic),
                                     owner(human, name(chris),
                                                  age(adult),
                                                  hair(brown),
                                                  id(hum_002)),
                                     id(watch_001))),
         affect(angry, actor(human, name(chris),
                                    age(adult),
                                    hair(brown),
                                    id(hum_002))))).

%b2- Lynn gets angry after her pencil breaks.
cd(b2,
   after(state(broken, object(pencil, color(yellow),
                                      composition(wood),
                                      owner(human, name(lynn),
                                                   age(kid),
                                                   hair(blond),
                                                   id(hum_003)),
                                      id(pencil_001))),
         affect(angry, actor(human, name(lynn),
                                    age(kid),
                                    hair(blond),
                                    id(hum_003))))).
```

```
%%e1- Chris gets angry after Jill knocks her vase over.
cd(e1,
   after(act(propel, actor(cat, name(jill),
                               age(kitten),
                               hair(tan),
                               id(cat_002)),
                     object(vase, color(red),
                                  composition(glass),
                                  owner(human, name(chris),
                                               age(adult),
                                               hair(brown),
                                               id(hum_002)),
                                  id(glass_002)),
                     to(table))),
         affect(angry, actor(human, name(chris),
                                    age(adult),
                                    hair(brown),
                                    id(hum_002)))))).
```

C.3. A Trace of PROLOG_OCCAM

This section presents an annotated trace of PROLOG_OCCAM. To run PROLOG_OCCAM on this data, the command **test** is typed to Prolog. The output from Prolog is edited slightly to make it easier to read. The only changes are the formatting of the rules learned by PROLOG_OCCAM by adding spaces to align columns. First, PROLOG_OCCAM is presented with examples of glass objects breaking. The first example, **g1** is the CD representation of "Mike drops a clear glass cup and it breaks.".

```
Running prolog_occam on g1

cause(act(propel, actor(human, name(mike), age(adult),
                               hair(brown), id(A)),
                  object(cup, color(clear), composition(glass),
                              owner(human, name(mike), age(adult),
                                           hair(brown), id(A)),
                         id(B)),
                  to(floor)),
          state(broken, object(cup, color(clear), composition(glass),
                               owner(human, name(mike), age(adult),
                                            hair(brown), id(A)),
                         id(B)))).
```

From this example, PROLOG_OCCAM creates a rule that indicates that when an adult named Mike with brown hair drops a clear glass cup that he owns, it will cause the cup to break. This rule is created by the empirical component, because there is no existing causal knowledge that would explain **g1**. Note that the actor and the owner of the cup must be identical[70]. This is indicated by the

---

[70]In Prolog, variables are capitalized.

fact that their id role must unify (i.e., they must have the same id.). The next
example, g2 describes Jill knocking over and breaking a red, glass vase. This
forces PROLOG_OCCAM to generalize the previous rule.

```
Running prolog_occam on g2

cause(act(propel,actor(A,name(B),age(C),hair(D),id(E)),
                 object(F,color(G),composition(glass),
                        owner(human,name(H),age(adult),
                                   hair(brown),id(I)),
                        id(J)),
             to(K)),
      state(broken,object(L,color(M),composition(glass),
                          owner(human,name(N),age(adult),
                                   hair(brown),id(I)),
                          id(J)))).
```

The rule now indicates that when a glass object owned by an adult with
brown hair is struck, then the object will break. A variable can serve two
purposes in Prolog. First, a singleton variable (i.e., one that appears only once
in a Prolog clause.) indicates that the rule applies no matter what constant will
replace the variable in an example. This implements the "dropping condition"
operator for generalization. In the above rule, the singleton variables are A, B,
C, D, E, F, G, H, K, M and N. Second, a variable that is repeated more than once
indicates that in an example the same object must occur in the corresponding
position for each instance of the variable. In the above rule, I and J occur more
than once. These variables are inserted by find_common because in g1 and
g2, the same object is both the object that is struck and the object that breaks.

A third example, forces PROLOG_OCCAM to remove the constraint that the
object which breaks be owned by an adult with brown hair. This example is g3
which describes Mike dropping and breaking the cat's bowl.

```
Running prolog_occam on g3

cause(act(propel,actor(A,name(B),age(C),hair(D),id(E)),
                 object(F,color(G),composition(glass),
                        owner(H,name(I),age(J),hair(K),id(L)),
                        id(M)),
             to(N)),
      state(broken,object(O,color(P),composition(glass),
                          owner(Q,name(R),age(S),hair(T),id(L)),
                          id(M)))).
```

The final version of the rule is also created by empirical means. The rule
now indicates that applying a force to a glass object causes the object to break.

PROLOG_OCCAM is next presented with two examples of a person getting angry after an object owned by the person breaks. Using the empirical learning component, it creates a new causal rule:

```
Running prolog_occam on b1 and b2

cause(state(broken,object(A,color(B),composition(C),
                          owner(human,name(D),age(E),hair(F),id(G)),
                          id(H))),
      affect(angry,actor(human,name(I),age(J),hair(K),id(G)))).
```

This rule indicates that when an object breaks, it causes the owner of the object to become angry. Note that the **id** of the owner and actor must be the same.

Now that `prolog_occam` has sufficient background knowledge, it can utilize its knowledge-intensive learning method to exploit the interaction between its existing causal rules. `prolog_occam` is presented with an example that can be explained by chaining together the two previous rules. This example, **e1**, describes an event in which Chris gets angry when the cat knocks over her vase.

```
Running prolog_occam on e1

cause(act(propel,actor(A,name(B),age(C),hair(D),id(E)),
              object(F,color(G),composition(glass),
                          owner(H,name(I),age(J),hair(K),id(L)),
                          id(M)),
              to(N)),
      affect(angry,actor(human,name(O),age(P),hair(Q),id(L)))).
```

Since this new causal rule is created by explanation-based learning, it only requires one example to analytically derive the conditions under which the causal relationship will hold. The rule states that when a force is applied to a glass object, then the owner of the object will get angry. The constraint that the object be made of glass is retained because this is a precondition of the rule that indicates that the object will break. The condition that the person who gets angry be the owner of the object is required by the rule that indicates that the owner of an object that breaks will get angry.

PROLOG_OCCAM is quite simple and has many limitations. However, I hope it will be taken in the spirit in which it was intended: as a simple illustration of the benefits of utilizing empirical techniques to acquire the background knowledge for explanation-based learning. Even in this simple example, the benefits are apparent, because PROLOG_OCCAM requires three examples to learn empirically that that glass objects break when struck, two examples to learn empirically that people get angry when their possessions are broken, but only one example to learn analytically that people get angry when a possession made of glass is struck.

Appendix D
OCCAM's Generalization Rules

This appendix contains the listing of all of OCCAM's generalization rules. They are divided into two categories. The first section lists the rules used to infer physical causes and the second section describes those which are used to infer goals in social situations. The syntax of these rules is slightly different than that presented in the text and in OCCAM-LITE. The format of these generalization rules is:

```
(def-gen-rule <name>            ;;the name of the rule
              <class>           ;;a token indicating the class
                                ;;the class is used for dispositional rules
              <focus>           ;;the ilink to be learned
              <lhs>             ;;the antecedent pattern
              <link>            ;;the link between antecedent and consequent
              <rhs>             ;;the consequent pattern
              <exceptions>      ;;indicates dispositional or historical rule
              <mechanism>       ;;the causal mechanism to be postulated
         )
```

The causal generalization rules are much more complete than the social rules (in the sense of covering what people seem to know about general theories of causality).

D.1. Physical Causality

```
;if an action on an object precedes a
;state change for the object,
;then the action results in the state change.
(def-gen-rule
  gen-result
  :state-action
  result
  (*var* state-1 (state type (*var* ptype)
                        value (*var* value)
                        object (*var* object)))
  before
  (*var* act-1 (act type (*var* atype)
                     object (*var* object)))
  ()
  (((*var* act-1) result (*var* state-1))
   ((*var* act-1) after (*var* state-1)))
  )
```

```
;if an action on a destination precedes a state change for the destination,
;then the action results in the state change.
(def-gen-rule
  gen-result-dest
  :state-action
  result
  (*var* state-1 (state type (*var* ptype)
                              value (*var* value)
                              object (*var* to)))

  before
  (*var* act-1 (act type (*var* atype)
                     object (*var* object)
                     to (*var* to)))

  ()
  (((*var* act-1) result (*var* state-1))
   ((*var* act-1) after (*var* state-1)))
  )

;if an action on a component of an object
;precedes a state change for the object,
;then the action results in the state change.
(def-gen-rule
  gen-result-component
  :state-action
  result
  (*var* state-1 (state type (*var* ptype)
                              value (*var* value)
                              object (*var* object)))

  before
  (*var* act-1 (act type (*var* atype)
                     object (component type (*var* ct)
                                       of (*var* object))))

  ()
  (((*var* act-1) result (*var* state-1))
   ((*var* act-1) after (*var* state-1)))
  )

;;object dispositional version of gen-result
(def-gen-rule
  gen-result-different-object-features
  :state-action-exception-object
  result
  (*var* state-1 (state type (*var* ptype)
                              value (*var* value)
                              object (*var* object)))

  before
  (*var* act-1 (act type (*var* atype)
                     object (*var* object)))

  (:slot object)
  (((*var* act-1) result (*var* state-1))
   ((*var* act-1) after (*var* state-1)))
  )
```

```
;;object dispositional version of gen-result-component
(def-gen-rule
  gen-result-different-object-features-component
  :state-action-exception-object
  result
  (*var* state-1 (state type (*var* ptype)
                               value (*var* value)
                               object (*var* object)))
  before
  (*var* act-1 (act type (*var* atype)
                     object   (component type (*var* ct)
                                          of (*var* object))))
  (:slot object of)
  (((*var* act-1) result (*var* state-1))
   ((*var* act-1) after (*var* state-1)))
  )

;;destination dispositional version of gen-result-dest
(def-gen-rule
  gen-result-different-dest-features
  :state-action-exception-to
  result
  (*var* state-1 (state type (*var* ptype)
                               value (*var* value)
                               object (*var* to)))
  before
  (*var* act-1 (act type (*var* atype)
                     object (*var* object)
                     to   (*var* to)))
  (:slot to)
  (((*var* act-1) result (*var* state-1))
   ((*var* act-1) after (*var* state-1)))
  )

;;actor dispositional version of gen-result-no-exception
(def-gen-rule
  gen-result-object-different-features-actor
  :state-action-exception-actor
  result
  (*var* state-1 (state type (*var* ptype)
                               value (*var* value)
                               object (*var* object)))
  before
  (*var* act-1 (act type (*var* atype)
                     actor (*var* actor)
                     object (*var* object)))
  (:slot actor)
  (((*var* act-1) result (*var* state-1))
   ((*var* act-1) after (*var* state-1)))
  )
```

```
;;actor dispositional version of    gen-result-component
(def-gen-rule
  gen-result-object-different-features-actor-component
  :state-action-exception-actor
  result
  (*var* state-1 (state type (*var* ptype)
                             value (*var* value)
                             object (*var* object)))
  before
  (*var* act-1 (act type (*var* atype)
                    actor(*var* actor)
                    object  (component type (*var* ct)
                                       of (*var* object)))))
  (:slot actor)
  (((*var* act-1) result (*var* state-1))
   ((*var* act-1) after (*var* state-1)))
  )

;;actor dispositional version of gen-result-dest
(def-gen-rule
  gen-result-dest-different-features-actor
  :state-action-exception-actor
  result
  (*var* state-1 (state type (*var* ptype)
                             value (*var* value)
                             object (*var* to)))
  before
  (*var* act-1 (act type (*var* atype)
                    actor(*var* actor)
                    object (*var* object)
                    to   (*var* to)))
  (:slot actor)
  (((*var* act-1) result (*var* state-1))
   ((*var* act-1) after (*var* state-1)))
  )
```

```
;if an initial action on a dest is always present when a subsequent
;action precedes a state change  for the dest, then
;the initial action results in a state which enables
;the subsequent action to result in the state change.
(def-gen-rule prev-action-dest
                :state-action-state-action
                result (*var* state-2
                               (state type (*var* ptype)
                                      value (*var* value)
                                      object (*var* to)))
                before
                (*var* act-2 (act type (*var* atype)
                               object (*var* object)
                               to   (*var* to)))
                (:link before (*var* act-1 (act type (*var* atype-1)
                                            from  (*var* to)
                                            object (*var* object))))

                (
                 ((*var* act-2) result (*var* state-2))
                  ((*var* act-1) result (*var* state-1
                                              (state object (*var* to))))
                 ((*var* state-1) enables (*var* act-2))
                 ((*var* act-2) after (*var* state-2))
                 ((*var* act-1) after (*var* act-2))

                 )
                )
;if an initial action on an object is always present when a subsequent
;action precedes a state change  for the object, then
;the initial action results in a state which enables
;the subsequent action to result in the state change.
(def-gen-rule prev-action
                :state-action-state-action
                result (*var* state-2
                               (state type (*var* ptype)
                                      value (*var* value)
                                      object (*var* object)))
                before
                (*var* act-2 (act type (*var* atype)
                               object (*var* object)))

                (:link before (*var* act-1 (act type (*var* atype-1)
                                                object (*var* object))))

                (
                 ((*var* act-2) result (*var* state-2))
                  ((*var* act-1) result (*var* state-1
                                              (state object (*var* object))))
                 ((*var* state-1) enables (*var* act-2))
                 ((*var* act-2) after (*var* state-2))
                 ((*var* act-1) after (*var* act-2))
                 )
                )
```

D.2. Social Causality

```
;if a goal to perform an action is blocked by a state
;then the opposite state is an enabling condition for the action
(def-gen-rule goal-thwart
              :goal-thwart
  blocked-by
  (*var* state-1 (state type (*var* ptype)
                         value (no)
                         actor (*var* actor)
                         object (*var* object)))
  blocks
  (goal actor (*var* actor)
        goal (*var* act-1 (act type (*var* atype)
                               actor (*var* actor)
                               object (*var* object))))
  ()
  (
   ((*var* act-1 (act type (*var* atype)
                      actor (*var* actor)
                      object (*var* object)))
    enabled-by
    (state type (*var* ptype)
                 value (yes)
                 actor (*var* actor)
                 object (*var* object)))
  ))
```

```
;goal failure caused by difference in helper
(def-gen-rule goal-failure
              :goal-fail-exception
  outcome
  (*var* outcome (goal-outcome type (*var* g)
                               actor (*var* actor)
                               goal (*var* goal-state
                                           (state object (*var* o)
                                                  value (*var* v))))))
  outcome-of
  (*var* goal
         (goal plan
               (*var* plan (plan plan
                                 (*var* act
                                        (act type (*var* mtype)
                                             object (act actor (*var* h))
                                             to (*var* h)
                                             actor (*var* actor)
                                             ))
                                 actor (*var* actor)))
               goal
               (state object (*var* o)
                      value (*var* v)
                      actor (*var* actor))
               actor
               (*var* actor)))
  (:slot plan plan to)
  ( ((*var* outcome) outcome-of (*var* goal))
    ((*var* goal) intended-by (*var* plan))
    ((*var* plan) realized-by (*var* act))
    ((*var* act) motivates (goal goal (act actor (*var* h))
                                 actor (*var* h))
                 (*var* g) (success))
    ((*var* goal) achieved-by (act actor (*var* h))
                 (*var* g) (success))
  )
  )
```

```
;;simple goal-plan analysis
;a goal is achieved by an event1 which comes after event2 then maybe
;event2 motivates the goal
(def-gen-rule goal-outcome
              :goal-outcome
  outcome (*var* outcome
                  (goal-outcome
                   type (*var* g)
                   goal (*var* goal-state
                               (state value (*var* v)
                                      type (*var* stype)
                                      object (*var* actor))))))

  outcome-of
  (*var* goal (goal goal (state value (*var* v) type (*var* stype)
                                object (*var* actor))
                    actor (*var* actor)
                    after (*var* final-act (act type (*var* aact)
                                                actor (*var* aactor)))
                    motivated-by (act))
         )
  ()

  (((act object (*var* actor)
         motivates (goal goal (state value (*var* v) type (*var* stype)
                                     object (*var* actor))
                         actor (*var* actor)))
    motivates
    (goal goal (state value (*var* v) type (*var* stype)
                      object (*var* actor))
          actor (*var* aactor)))
   ((*var* goal) outcome(*var* outcome)))

  )
```

```
;goal failure analogue of goal-outcome
(def-gen-rule goal-outcome-2
                :goal-fail-exception
  outcome (*var* outcome
                  (goal-outcome type (*var* g)
                                goal (*var* goal-state
                                              (state value (*var* v)
                                                     type (*var* stype)
                                                     object (*var* actor)))))

   outcome-of
   (*var* goal (goal goal (state value (*var* v) type (*var* stype)
                                 object (*var* actor))
                     actor (*var* actor)
                     after (*var* final-act (act type (*var* aact)
                                                  actor (*var* aactor)))
                     motivated-by (*var* init-act (act)))
          )
   (:slot after actor)
   (
   ( (act object (*var* actor)
          motivates (goal goal (state value (*var* v) type (*var* stype)
                                      object (*var* actor))
                          actor (*var* actor)))
     motivates (goal goal (state value (*var* v) type (*var* stype)
                                 object (*var* actor))
                     actor (*var* aactor))
     (*var* g)(success))
    ((*var* goal) outcome(*var* outcome)))
   )


;;this rule is used by many successful sanction incidents
;;it traces the goal success to the plan which achieves the goal
(def-gen-rule outcome-10
       :outcome-success
       outcome
       (*var* outcome
              (goal-outcome type (success)
                            outcome-of (*var* goal
                                              (goal goal (*var* goal-state)))
                            goal (*var* g (goal goal (*var* goal-state)
                                                actor (*var* a)))
                            actor (*var* a)))
       before
       (*var* act-1 (act))
       ()
       (
       ((*var* act-1) achieves (*var* goal))
       ((*var* act-1) result (*var* goal-state))
       ((*var* goal) intended-by (*var* plan))
       ((*var* plan) realized-by (*var* act-2))
       ((*var* act-2) motivates (*var* sub-goal))
       ((*var* sub-goal) intended-by (*var* plan2
                                           (plan plan (*var* act-1))))
       ((*var* plan2) realized-by (*var* act-1))
       )
               )
```

```
;;this rule is used by many unsuccessful sanction incidents
;it traces the goal failure to the act that thwarts the goal.
(def-gen-rule
  outcome-11
  :outcome-failure
  outcome
  (*var* outcome
         (goal-outcome type (failure)
                       outcome-of (*var* goal
                                         (goal goal (*var* goal-state)))
                       goal (*var* g (goal goal (*var* goal-state)
                                             actor (*var* a)))
                       actor (*var* a)))
  before
  (*var* act-1 (act))
  ()

  (
   ((*var* act-1) thwarts (*var* goal))
   ((*var* goal) intended-by (*var* plan))
   ((*var* plan) realized-by (*var* act-2))
   ((*var* act-2) motivates (*var* sub-goal))
   ((*var* sub-goal) intended-by (*var* plan2 (plan plan (*var* act-1))))
   ((*var* plan2) realized-by (*var* act-1))
   )
  )


;abstract explanation for goal failure in jailed kidnapper
;blames failure on an act that result enables an act that
;result enables the that that thwarts the goal.
;the sparseness of the social rules is apparent here because
;there should be similar rules with result-enable chain of length 1.
(def-gen-rule unforeseen-goal-failure
              :explain-goal-failure
  thwarts
  (*var* goal (goal))
  thwarted-by
  (*var* act (act))
  ()
  ( ((*var* act) before (*var* act-2))
    ((*var* act-2) result-enables (*var* act-3))
    ((*var* act-3) result-enables (*var* act))
    ((*var* act) thwarts (*var* goal))))


;;if a preparation is performed on an object,
;;look for other schemata which have a goal failure.
;;Postulate the preparation avoids the goal
failure).
(def-gen-rule avoid-goal-failure
              :explain-goal-failure
  the-prep
  (*var* act-1 (act object (*var* object)))
  result-enables
  (*var* act-2 (act))
  (:exists (*var* g) goal-failure object goal)
  (((*var* act-1) avoids-goal-failure (*var* g)))
  )
```

Appendix E
Listing of Economic Sanction Incidents

E.1. Actual Incidents

1921 League of Nations vs. Yugoslavia
threat: Refuse to import to Yugoslavia
demand: Stop invading Albania
outcome: success

1925 League of Nations vs. Greece
threat: Refuse to import to Greece
demand: Stop invading Bulgaria
outcome: success

1935 League of Nations vs. Italy
threat: Refuse to sell weapons
demand: Stop invading Abyssinia
outcome: (failure) Italy conquers Abyssinia.

1948 USSR vs. Yugoslavia
threat: Cut off foreign aid
demand: Stop political independence
outcome: (failure) US give economic aid

1960 US vs. Cuba
threat: Cut off imports and exports
demand: Change government policies
outcome: (failure) Soviets give aid, buy sugar

1961 US vs. Ceylon
threat: Cut off foreign aid (17 million)
demand: Pay for expropriated oil companies
outcome: success

1961 USSR vs. Albania
threat: Refuse to sell grain
demand: Stop economic ties with China
outcome: (failure) China sells Albania Canadian wheat

1962 US vs. Brazil
threat: Cut off foreign aid ($174 million)
demand: Pay for expropriated oil companies
outcome: success

1965 UK vs. Rhodesia
threat: Cutoff oil & food imports, tobacco exports
demand: Allow black majority to rule
outcome: (failure) Diversify agriculture;
         Import oil from South Africa

1968 US vs. Peru
threat: Cut off foreign aid ($30 million),
demand: Pay for expropriated oil, telephone industries
outcome: success

1976 US vs. Ethiopia
threat: Stop aid (57 million)
demand: Stop human rights violations
outcome: (failure) Soviets provide aid

1980 US vs. USSR
threat: Cut off grain sales
demand: Withdraw troops from Afghanistan
outcome: (failure) Buy grain from argentina

1981 US vs. USSR
threat: Not sell equipment for gas pipeline
demand: Lift martial law in poland
           outcome: (failure) France supplies equipment

1982 South Africa vs. Lesotho
threat: Not allow trains in and out of Lesotho
demand: Expel African National Congress Refugees
outcome: success

1983 Australia vs. France
threat: Not sell uranium
demand: Stop nuclear tests
outcome: (failure) France buys from South Africa

E.2. Hypothetical Incidents

H1 US vs. South Korea
threat: Stop sales of computers
demand: Limit car exports
outcome: fail

H2 US vs. Iran
threat: Release $100 million of Iranian assets
demand: Pay $25 million for nationalized oil companies
outcome: succeed

H3 US. vs. Ethiopia
threat: Limit food aid
demand: modernize agricultural production
outcome: failure

H4: US vs. Israel
threat: Refuse to sell missile guidance technology
demand: Withdraw troops from lebanon
outcome: failure

H5: Us vs. Greece
threat: Cutoff off foreign aid
demand: Allow US bases to expand
outcome: failure

E.3. CD Representation

This section contains the complete CD representation of 1962 economic sanction incident between the US and Brazil.

```
(coerce
 the-actor (polity type (country) name (us)
                   economic-health (strong)
                   location (northern-hemisphere)
                   continent (north-america)
                   imports (*set* (*role* threat-obj)
                                  (commodity type (oil))
                                  (commodity type (electronics)))
                   exports (*set* (commodity type (food))
                                  (commodity type (weapons))
                                  (commodity type (electronics))
                                  (commodity type (manufactured-goods)))
                   pol-rels (*set*
                             (cordial with (polity type (country)
                                                   name (uk)))
                             (cordial with (polity type (country)
                                                   name (france)))
                            ))
 the-bene (polity type (country) name (us)
                   economic-health (strong)
                   location (northern-hemisphere)
                   continent (north-america)
                   imports (*set* (*role* threat-obj)
                                  (commodity type (oil))
                                  (commodity type (electronics)))
                   exports (*set* (commodity type (food))
                                  (commodity type (weapons))
                                  (commodity type (electronics))
                                  (commodity type (manufactured-goods)))
                   pol-rels (*set*
                             (cordial with (polity type (country)
                                                   name (uk)))
                             (cordial with (polity type (country)
                                                   name (france))
                                    )))
```

```
the-target (polity type (country) name (brazil)
                location (southern-hemisphere)
                language (portuguese)
                continent (south-america)
                economic-health (strong)
                strategic-importance (med)
                bus-rels (*set* (polity type (country)
                                        name (us))
                                (polity type (country)
                                        name (saudia-arabia))
                                (polity type (country)
                                        name (japan))
                         )
                imports (*set* (commodity type (machinery))
                               (commodity type (manufactured-good))
                               (commodity type (pharmaceuticals)))
                exports (*set* (commodity type (soybeans))
                               (commodity type (coffee)))
                )
threat-obj (commodity type (money)
                     amount (dollars number (174000000)))
the-threat (act type (atrans)
                actor (*role* the-actor)
                object (*role* threat-obj)
                to (*role* the-target)
                mode (no))
the-alt-obj (commodity type (money)
                     amount (dollars number (174000000)))
the-alternative (act type (atrans)
                     actor (*role* the-actor)
                     object (*role* the-alt-obj)
                     to (*role* the-target)
                     mode (yes))
demand-obj (commodity type (money)
                     amount (dollars number (7300000)))
the-demand (act type (atrans)
                actor (*role* the-target)
                from (*role* the-target)
                object (*role* demand-obj)
                to (*role* the-actor)
                action-initiated-by (act type (atrans)
                                         actor (*role* the-target)
                                         to (*role* the-target)
                                         from (*role* the-actor)
                                         object (company type (oil)))
                mode (yes))
  the-ask (act object (cond if (*role* the-demand)
                            then (*role* the-alternative)
                            else (*role* the-threat))
              to (*role* the-target)
              actor (*role* the-actor)
              type (mtrans))
plan (plan plan (*role* the-ask)
           actor (*role* the-actor))
response-obj (commodity type (money)
                     amount (dollars number (7300000)))
the-target-response (act type (atrans)
                         actor (*role* the-target)
                         object (*role* response-obj)
                         to (*role* the-actor)
                         mode (yes))
```

```
goal-state (state type (poss-by)
                   value (yes)
                   actor (*role* the-bene)
                   object (*role* demand-obj))
outcome (goal-outcome type (success)
                       actor (*role* the-actor)
                       goal (goal actor (*role* the-actor)
                                  goal (*role* goal-state)))
goal (goal actor (*role* the-actor)
           goal (*role* goal-state))
the-actor-response (act type (atrans)
                        actor (*role* the-actor)
                        object (*role* the-alt-obj)
                        to (*role* the-target)
                        mode (yes))
)
```

Index

350